Lockerbie and Libya

Lockerbie and Libya

A Study in
International Relations

KHALIL I. MATAR
and ROBERT W. THABIT

McFarland & Company, Inc., Publishers
Jefferson, North Carolina, and London

To the soul of my father, who taught me, if
I did something, to do my best or not at all.

To my loving wife, Zeina, and
our children, Malak and Ibrahim.

—*Khalil*

To the soul of my wife, Afifeh Vivian,
and our dear children, Allen and Mona.

—*Robert*

LIBRARY OF CONGRESS CATALOGUING-IN-PUBLICATION DATA

Matar, Khalil I., 1960–
    Lockerbie and Libya : a study in international relations /
Khalil I. Matar and Robert W. Thabit.
        p.   cm.
    Includes bibliographical references and index.

    ISBN 0-7864-1609-2 (softcover : 50# alkaline paper) ∞

    1. Pan Am Flight 103 Bombing Incident, 1988.   2. Terrorism—
United States—Case studies.   3. Terrorism—Europe—Case
studies.   4. Bombing investigation—Scotland—Lockerbie.
5. Libya—Foreign relations—United States.   6. United States—
Foreign relations—Libya.   I. Thabit, Robert W., 1924–
II. Title.
HV6431.M378   2004
363.12'465'094147—dc22   2003021126

British Library cataloguing data are available

On the cover: the nose section of the Pan Am Flight 103 aircraft,
near Lockerbie (*UK Air Accidents Investigation Branch*).

Manufactured in the United States of America

McFarland & Company, Inc., Publishers
    Box 611, Jefferson, North Carolina 28640
    www.mcfarlandpub.com

Contents

Part IV. The Reactions of the United Kingdom and the United States

Part V. The Role of Prominent Personalities, and the Handover

Part VI. The Scottish Court in the Netherlands

Acknowledgments

After almost twenty years covering the United Nations and the United States as a reporter for different Arab media and dealing with many of my American and European colleagues as well as the great many diplomats and politicians I encountered, I got to a point where simple daily news was something I could not accept without understanding what is behind it: the real reasons behind events, the real intention behind actions and statements, the real story that reporters and the public are not told. I thought the best way to get back my energy in that field was to get deeper into the issues. It seemed to me that writing a book, even in this age of Internet and technology, might be the best way to achieve deep knowledge of whatever issue I chose.

At the time, the issues surrounding the Lockerbie incident were being dragged along the path toward a solution. So I chose these issues as the subject of this book. I was discussing my feelings with a friend, Steve. He was the first to encourage me to find the time and energy. Then I had to find the officials willing to help in the research and exploration of the reality behind the public face—and I knew, through my contacts and sources, that a more extensive story was there. Many American, British and other European diplomats helped but will remain nameless, for most of them continue to occupy official positions. Some retired but preferred to be nameless as well. Many Libyan officials helped me understand how they tackled the issues. Especially I must thank Mohammed

Zwai for his constant receptiveness to my repeated enquiries. My co-author, Bob, made sure the legal aspects he studies and dealt with as an observer were properly discussed. More important, he made sure I stayed on the path when the loneliness of book writing, as well as various daily bread-and-butter necessities, caused me to drift a little.

In the end it is hoped that this book will help the reader understand that history does not come from a void—although those in the process of making history may fail to reflect on what has gone before.

—Khalil Matar
New York
October 1, 2003

Introduction

Before September 11, 2001, terrorist acts resulting in mass deaths were becoming less commonplace. The phenomenon of terrorism, including state terrorism, had been declining. The United Nations has attempted to adopt measures against such acts but so far has not been able to agree on a definition of terrorism. The problem is that one man's terrorist is another man's freedom fighter. A universally acceptable definition of "terrorist" has therefore been elusive.

Nevertheless the bombing of Pan Am 103 over Lockerbie, Scotland, on December 21, 1988, resulted in possibly the highest number of deaths by terrorist act (259 on board and 11 on the ground) until the 2001 attack on the World Trade Center.

Because Pan Am was an American airline, the United States took the matter very seriously both unilaterally and internationally. This book examines the American political and diplomatic thrust, supported by Great Britain and, to a lesser extent, France; Libya's diplomatic response; and how an acceptable solution was agreed on.

Even after the trial of the two Libyans accused of the crime, there were still reverberations and a number of loose ends had to be tied up in order to close the Lockerbie case. By September 12, 2003, that chapter was closed with the official lifting of UN sanctions off Libya after an agreement was reached whereas Libya acknowledges civil responsibility for the actions of one of its citizens and pay $2.7 billion in compensation.

The incidents of September 11 and what followed helped Libya throw off its label of terrorist state and, to some extent, provided the United States with an opportunity to throw off its label of aggressor.

On April 5, 1999, many dignitaries were present on the dusty tarmac of Tripoli International Airport, under the heat of the desert sun. Abdelbaset Al-Megrahi and Al Amin Khalifa Fhima, the two Libyan citizens accused of blowing up Pan Am 103, walked toward a United Nations airplane that was to transfer them to the Netherlands. There they would be handed over to the Dutch authorities, then Scottish authorities, to stand trial in a Scottish court.

That walk, more than ten years after Pan Am 103 went down, set the stage for the gradual ending of one of the most painful periods of Libya's revolutionary years. It also represented one of the rare successes of real international diplomacy, even as it marked one of the most unexpected precedents in international law.

Less than two years later, on January 31, 2001, a panel of three Scottish judges found Al-Megrahi guilty of planning and executing the bombing and sentenced him to life with a minimum of twenty years in prison. Fhima was acquitted of the charges against him and set free. Al-Megrahi appealed the judgment while Fhima headed home to Libya, where his verdict was considered a political move to save face for the United States and Britain. The Libyans based their judgment of the court's decision on many legal opinions that considered the evidence presented in court hardly sufficient to convict, even in a conservative, intelligent court in a third-world country.

A painful story was written during these years of extensive diplomacy, politics and maneuvers that manipulated the fate of two groups of people: The families of the victims were awaiting justice for their lost loved ones, and the Libyan people were awaiting an end to their suffering as a result of accusations leveled by the United States and the United Kingdom against two Libyans. Five million Libyans suffered for more than seven years because the United States and the United Kingdom convinced the United Nations Security Council to adopt international sanctions against Libya. The most notable factor of the complicated process toward a solution was the precedent set: For the first time in history, a court conducted official hearings outside its national border. A Scottish court was set up in the Netherlands solely for this trial, using Scottish law and precedents.

When sanctions were first imposed on Libya, the United States and the United Kingdom differed in their expectations. The United States thought sanctions would lead to the toppling of Colonel Muammar Qadhafi's regime in Libya. The United Kingdom thought it could, among other possibilities, get Libya to stop its support of the Irish Republican

Army, leading to a solution to the Northern Ireland problem. The least expected possibility was the isolation of the Libyan regime in order to stop its support of "terrorism." However, the announced pretext was the accusation of involvement in and responsibility for not only the Lockerbie tragedy but also the downing of UTA Flight 772 over the Niger on September 19, 1989, which led to France's participation in imposing sanctions.

Politically, however, whether the Libyans were proven guilty or innocent, the issue goes far beyond the Lockerbie tragedy. The battle of wills between two opposing systems of government is thought to date back to an earlier conflict between the United States and Libya. Tensions between the two had built up before the final phase of the Lockerbie case played out.

But in 1999, after seven years of limited sanctions, Libya, through that tarmac walk, was setting the stage for the suspension of sanctions by the UN, as well as beginning its return to normal relations with most countries of the international community. Important questions about the legal authority of the UN's most important organ, the Security Council, over such a case remain unanswered.

Against all expectations, the parties, with the help of a new set of unlikely intermediaries, managed to negotiate a solution which ended the standoff. Full cooperation by Libya theoretically led to the official lifting of sanctions by the UN Security Council, while the other parties tried to agree on compensation for the victims' families.

Despite the court's verdict of guilty for one of the accused Libyans and the unsuccessful appeal, and despite any diplomatic solutions necessitated by political considerations, the underlying question of responsibility has still not been unequivocally answered. It may never be answered. The political realities of the United States may not lead to a full closure of its conflict with Libya for a long time, although there will likely be efforts to sweep differences aside. In any case, many parties to this conflict, if not all, will feel victorious.

The Libyan economy and people had tired of sanctions. Having them lifted became the main goal of Libya's leadership after efforts to prove the country's innocence were overtaken by political developments. Libya tried to nullify the Security Council's resolutions at the International Court of Justice, but it did not succeed. It then turned to a series of secret contacts and mediation, also without success. After a long wait, Libya launched a campaign to line up support through regional organizations and personal intermediaries who had been looking for a role in the post-cold war era. This effort proved successful. This support, along with new political leadership in Britain, forced a change of policy in the West, leading to a solution.

After the Labor Party took over the British government for the first time since the early eighties, the United Kingdom realized that a change of policy was necessary. The West's main demand was justice for the victims' families. All efforts were concentrated toward that aim; it was achieved.

The United States' position, however, was ambiguous. Justice for the families was but one of its aims. It was losing the diplomatic and political battle on the international scene. With the British Labor government's encouragement, the United States reluctantly joined the process toward a solution. American officials also began to recognize the change in Libyan policies and conduct. This new U.S. position provided a small positive step toward improved relations. The improvement began with an official meeting, for the first time in about twenty years, and continued through visits of former officials and business executives to Libya while those in office began a slow evolution in their tone when speaking about Libya. A series of official meetings between the two countries took place in different forums, and progress was made, leading finally to direct official meetings aimed at sorting out U.S.-Libyan outstanding issues, hence a process to lift U.S. sanctions and normalizing the relations between the two countries.

Libya and its leadership learned many difficult lessons about the new realities of the post–Cold War era. The world was changing, and they too had to change, although their fundamental principles and beliefs have still not altered substantially. New instruments and directions of policies have developed. But the official end of sanctions, along with normalization of relations with the United States and Great Britain, continues to be the cornerstone of Libya's goals.

What follows is a study in international relations between Libya, the United States, the United Kingdom and the United Nations, demonstrating Libya's increasing maturity in dealing with a complex international situation and its favorable resolution, as well as the vitality of the role of political mediation, most notably by Saudi Arabia's Prince Bandar bin Sultan and South African president Nelson Mandela.

Nothing, however, would have been achieved had one personality decided not to adapt to new realities: Muammar Qadhafi. He learned many lessons the hard way. It is worth noting that he led his country out of isolation—an isolation that could have further drowned Libya's economy and its future—even as he preserved independence. Such a standard is rarely achieved in today's world.

PART I

Early Theories Fail; Sanctions Are Imposed on Libya

1

Accusations and the United Nations

On December 21, 1988, while en route between London and New York, Pan Am Flight 103 exploded over Lockerbie. Two hundred and fifty-nine crew members and passengers as well as eleven of the town's residents lost their lives. It was one of the worst crashes in aviation history.

After months of painstaking collection of debris as evidence, investigators from both the United States and the United Kingdom concluded this was not an accident but a crime. It was labeled an act of terrorism. Criminal investigators began an extensive effort to identify the perpetrators, exploring many leads.

Early theories about the responsibility blamed different groups and states, including a drug-smuggling operation with claims of a connection to the Central Intelligence Agency (CIA). Libya was not initially among the accused, which included Iran, directly or by proxy, Syria and radical Palestinian groups aligned with both countries.

Those who accused Iran claimed the main incentive for this attack dated a few months back, to July 1988, when an American naval vessel, the *USS Vincennes*, downed a civilian Iranian plane on its way from the United Arab Emirates to Tehran, over the Persian Gulf, killing 290 people aboard. The vessel was operating in the Gulf as part of Washington's efforts to protect the flow of oil from a region facing an eight-year war between Iraq and Iran. While the United States apologized to Tehran for the incident, which it called an accident, the Iranians felt that the only reason the Iraqis were advancing on Iran was their receipt of American aid. The American navy was hitting Iranian economic and military targets on a daily basis. The Iranians considered the attack part of an American-Iraqi effort against Iran, especially during the last years of the war. In 1988 Iran's leader, Imam Khomeini, gave in and accepted an end to a war launched by the Iraqis against his regime, a war seen in the West as the best effort to contain Islamic radicalism, Shiite style. Khomeini compared his decision to "taking poison."

Since the fall of the Shah in 1979, Iran had supported many political groups in the Middle East. It established strategic relations with Syria. Some of the groups supported by Tehran were Palestinian organizations based in Syria, among them the Popular Front for the Liberation of Palestine-General Command (PFLP-GC). The PFLP-GC was led by a man called Ahmad Jibril, whom the West considers a very dangerous terrorist. His group has operated inside and outside the Palestinian-occupied territories, with some camps in Lebanon.

Intelligence information connected to the operation some Palestinian members of the PFLP-GC residing in Germany. All evidence was leading in that direction. Politically, however, the Americans were not in a position to confront heavyweights such as Iran and Syria.[1] Neither were they in a position to publicly explore either a theory based on misunderstandings about a CIA operation against drug dealers and terrorists leading indirectly to the loading of explosives onto an airplane in Frankfurt (and later the Pan Am flight) or the possibility of revenge for the *Vincennes* incident.

Further complicating the situation was the fact that while the United Nations Security Council's attention was turning to Libya in response to American and British pressure, American and British newspapers were quoting officials who were directing blame to the original suspects. One of those reports said that investigators could not rule out the participation of Iran and Syria. The Arab street was hearing widespread rumors that the accusations against Libya "were a payoff to Syria, for its participation in Desert Storm against Iraq, and Iran, for standing aside."[2] Though plausible, neither theory could yet be proven.

Washington and London were in a quagmire that lasted three years. Pressure was mounting from the families of the victims to accuse somebody, anybody. The pressure increased when Pan Am declared bankruptcy in the United States, leaving the victims' families with no responsible party to pay substantial compensation.

The Indictments and Libya's Reaction

Toward the summer of 1991, while investigators in the United States and the United Kingdom were exploring the Iran-Syria-Jibril connection for responsibility in the Pan Am flight case, the FBI lab investigating the evidence suddenly "discovered" a link between remnants of timers found on the scene in Lockerbie and similar timers discovered in Africa. From then on, the investigation reverted to the original theory. A case was constructed around the timers and the connection with Megrahi and Fhima. An FBI agent later accused that same FBI laboratory of meddling with evidence in other cases.

On November 14, 1991, almost three years after Lockerbie the incident, the United States District Court for the District of Columbia and the Lord Advocate of Scotland announced their discoveries and indictments.

In Washington, the indictments of two Libyan citizens, Abdelbaset Al-Megrahi and Al Amin Khalifa Fhimah, alleged that the "defendants and co-conspirators, as officers and operatives of the Jamahiriya Security Organization (JSO), utilized the resources and facilities of the nation of Libya, including the JSO, to carry out the scheme to destroy an American aircraft by means of an explosive device and to kill passengers on board the aircraft" in 193 counts.[3]

In London, the authorities announced their accusations of the two Libyans as "being members of the Libyan Intelligence Services, and in particular Megrahi being the Head of Security of Libyan Arab Airlines and thereafter Director of the Centre for Strategic Studies, Tripoli, Libya and Fhima being the Station Manager of Libyan Arab Airlines in Malta, did conspire together and with others to further the purposes of the Libyan Intelligence Services by criminal means, namely the commission of acts of terrorism directed against nationals and the interests of other countries and in particular the destruction of a civil passenger aircraft and murder of its occupants."

The Lord Advocate went on to say, "the terms of the United States indictment and the Scottish petition have been drawn up in full consultation.... The charges are essentially identical and are in respect the same two accused persons."[4]

On the political level, British Foreign Secretary Douglas Hurd made a statement in the House of Commons the same day, saying, "The Lord Advocate said a demand is being made of the Libyan authorities for the surrender of the accused to stand trial. I repeat that demand on behalf of the whole government. I know the House will unreservedly endorse it."

In the same statement Hurd made a more political and noteworthy assertion: "I understand that the investigation has revealed no evidence to support suggestion of involvement by other countries. This matter does not therefore affect our relations with other countries in the region." Libyans and others interpreted these words as a response to and confirmation of previous accusations the United States and the United Kingdom had leveled against Iran, Syria and the PFLP-GC. Hurd seemed to be providing some type of an apology to both countries with assurances that the case against them was closed. Still, many continued to believe non-Libyan hands were involved in this tragedy. Libya insinuated as much on November 20, 1991, in a letter from its foreign minister, Ibrahim Bishari, to the United Nations Secretary General (UNSG):

> Libya has heard, just as the world heard, the statements of some United States and British leaders denying that Libya has any association with the incident and directing their suspicions against other parties. The United States of America has, however, with the power of one capable of doing so, endeavored to refute the accusations made against other parties and to exculpate them. It has accused Libya, which it had previously exonerated, perhaps because of something in Libyan policy that does not please the United States administration, with the premeditated intention of engaging in aggression in order to change the popular democratic regime by force, a popular political regime of which the United States administration does not approve, thereby violating the provisions of the charter of the United Nations prohibiting the threat or use of force and calling for the peaceful solution of problems between States by means of dialogue.

The announcement of the indictments was the first step in a process that had begun a few months earlier. When the investigators discovered the Libyan link, the politicians began work on the course of punishment. They needed to arrange support among the international community, through the United Nations Security Council, in order to get a long-sought international response to Libya's political defiance. With the Soviet Union beginning to fall apart and with China witnessing world events and becoming worried about protecting itself from the storm that was breaking the Socialist bloc, France was the only other permanent member of the Security Council capable of involvement. France had its own problems with Libya dating back to confrontations in Chad, including Libya's alleged terrorist activities against the French in Africa. The United States and the United Kingdom easily managed to get France's support. Its justification was the downing of a UTA flight over the Niger on September 19, 1989. France had accused Libya of destroying that plane, which resulted in three permanent members of the UNSC jointly leading the campaign against Libya.

Preparing for what turned out to be a trilateral effort against Libya, the presidency of the French Republic and the ministry of foreign affairs issued a statement on the twelfth anniversary of that catastrophe, thus formally accusing Libya.[5] The statement read as follows:

> The judicial inquiry with regard to the attack on the UTA DC-10, which resulted in 171 deaths on 19 September 1989 places heavy presumptions of guilt for this odious crime on several Libyan nationals.
>
> Accordingly, following the summoning of the Ambassador of Libya to France by the Minister of State, Minister for Foreign Relations, the French government reiterates its demand that the libyan authorities cooperate immediately, effectively and by all possible means with the French justice in order to help to establish responsibility for this terrorist act.
>
> To that end, France calls upon Libya:
>
> —To produce all the material evidence in its possession and to facilitate access to all documents that might be useful for establishing the truth.
>
> —To facilitate the necessary contacts and meetings, *inter alia*, for the assembly of witnesses.
>
> —To authorize the responsible Libyan officials to respond to any request made by the examining magistrate responsible for judicial information.

Libya immediately began to analyze these accusations. Their interpretation saw the developments as a pretext for a military attack. This belief was further confirmed during the following months when leaders and officials from neighboring and other states would convey to Libya threats of military force by the United States in the event that it failed to accept the Security Council resolutions.

The official reaction of Tripoli came in a communiqué issued by the People's Committee for Foreign Liaison and International Cooperation, that is, the Foreign Ministry. In it, the committee

> categorically denies that Libya had any association with the incident or that there was any knowledge of it on the part of the Libyan authorities, reaffirms its condemnation of terrorism in all its forms, and extends the sympathy of the Libyan people to the families affected by the incident and expresses its solidarity with them.[6]

As for the political aspect of that reaction, the committee said: "When a small, developing country such as Libya finds itself accused by superpowers such as the United States and the United Kingdom, it reserves its full right to legitimate self-defense before a fair and impartial jurisdiction, before the United Nations and before the International Court of Justice and other bodies." It continued: "No contact has been established with the competent judicial authorities in Libya with a view to exploring the truth and verifying these allegations," calling on the United States and the United Kingdom to "seek the judgement of impartial international commissions of inquiry or of the ICJ."

The United States and the United Kingdom never claimed to have contacted the Libyans prior to issuing indictments and accusations. The absence of diplomatic relations was not a logical justification since governments always find ways to communicate with other governments either through "interest sections" that replace embassies in such cases or through intermediaries such as other governments or the United Nations Secretariat or even through direct meetings between ambassadors at the United Nations, as was the case in many instances between the two countries and Iraq. Similarly, the two governments would later find a way to communicate those indictments to Libya. The absence of that direct communication added to the Libyan belief in a conspiracy. The foreign minister sent a letter to the UN Secretary General on November 20 in which he explained:

> Raising issues as a means of propaganda and escalating them in this way without making any official contacts with the Libyan authorities and making insinuations and threats regarding the adoption of economic measures against the Great Jamahiriya before completion of the Legal procedures, confirms our suspicion that these states seek only to intimidate us. It also recalls their interventions in the course of events that we have mentioned.[7]

Sanctions Chosen, Not the ICJ or Montreal Convention

The Libyan reaction was all but ignored in Washington, London, and other capitals as well. The escalation in preparation for the adoption of sanctions against Libya by the UN Security Council went on uninterrupted. The international scene was set for a state of unity with the Americans. On November 27, Washington and London issued a joint statement identifying the major elements that would later constitute demands by the Security Council:

> —Surrender for trial all those charged with the crime and accept complete responsibility for the action of Libyan officials.

—Disclose all it knows of this crime, including the names of all those responsible, and allow full access to all witnesses, documents and other material evidence, including all the remaining timers.
—Pay appropriate compensation.

The two capitals ended their statements by announcing they were "conveying our demands to Libya through the Italians, as our protecting power: We expect Libya to comply promptly and in full."

This statement was a very clear expression of the victor's mentality. Libya was asked to acknowledge complete responsibility before a trial was held, to pay compensation before a judicial process assessed the responsibility, and to respond to allegations not yet heard in any court. Libya, in short, was asked to surrender.

Another statement was issued that same day by the three governments:

> The three States reaffirm their complete condemnation of terrorism in all its forms and denounce any complicity of States in terrorism acts. The three States reaffirm their commitment to put an end to terrorism.
> They consider that the responsibility of States begins whenever they take part directly in terrorist actions, or indirectly through harboring, training, providing facilities, arming, or providing financial support, or any form of protection, and that they are responsible for their actions before the individual States and the United Nations.
> In this connection, following the investigation carried out into the bombings of Pan Am 103 and UTA 772 the three States have presented specific demands to the Libyan authorities related to the judicial procedures that are under way. They require that Libya complies with all these demands, and, in addition, that Libya commit itself concretely and definitively to cease all forms of terrorist action and all assistance to terrorist groups. Libya must promptly, by concrete actions, prove its renunciation of terrorism.

This is the language used by a victor intending to impose its will. The statement provided no room for discussion. It was a clear order, with the clear implication that failure to comply would cause the one ordered to pay dearly.

Libya responded to these statements in a communiqué by the foreign ministry,[8] on November 29. As a victim of terrorism, Libya reaffirmed its public policy that it was against all terrorism and would not permit its territory to be used by terrorists. Libya's judicial authorities declared they would deal with the charges "in a positive and constructive spirit" and use a copy of the minutes of their investigations in order to interrogate the accused. Libya would act in accordance with international legitimacy and the rights of sovereignty to ensure justice for the accused and the victims. Libya said it would welcome a commission of Arab and international jurists to follow the investigation. In a letter to the Secretary General of the UN, Libya offered to enter into a dialogue with the United States, the United Kingdom and France to resolve any political dispute and, if there be one, resort to the International Court of Justice and urge the three countries to submit the official records of their investigations to Libya's judicial authorities.[9]

Further exploring the political venues for a direct dialogue, Libya tried to communicate directly with Washington and London. Libyan foreign minister Ibrahim Bishari sent a letter to his counterparts James Baker and Douglas Hurd in those capitals, offering a dialogue. In that letter, dated 18 January 1992, dismissed in favor of a move to the Security Council, the Libyan foreign minister explained his country's positions regarding the accusations:

> The case was, indeed, submitted to the judicial authorities, and an examining magistrate was appointed (a counsellor of the Supreme Court). He instituted judicial procedures to ascertain the presence of the two suspects, initiated a preliminary inquiry and issued an order for the two suspects to be taken into custody, on a tentative basis. The states mentioned in article 5, paragraph 1, of the Montreal Convention were notified accordingly and were requested to cooperate with the Libyan judicial authorities. The Libyan judicial authorities appointed to conduct the inquiry made the same request in official communications addressed to the following: The Attorney General of the United States of America; the Foreman of the Grand Jury in the District of Columbia, United States of America; the French examining magistrate. As of the present moment, however, there has been no response to any of these requests.

He went on to say:

> Libya urges the United States of America and the United Kingdom to be governed by the voice of reason and law, to give their prompt agreement to arbitration in accordance with article 14, paragraph 1, of the Convention and to sit down with the United States as soon as possible in order to elaborate details in order to assist in the preparation of the dispute for arbitration.

Libya never received any of the information requested or a response.

Washington's claims had to be translated by swiftly employing (some might say exploiting) the events of that year, a period so eloquently and accurately later described by Kofi Annan, the United Nations Secretary General, in a report to the General Assembly[10] as the peak of a "frenzy era."

Hoping to influence the council members to oppose U.S. and British efforts, Libya sent two of its top diplomats to New York to lobby the members of the council against the resolution prior to its adoption. The officials were Jadallah Azzouz El-Talhi, who was to become Minister for Foreign Affairs in a few days, and Ali Treiki, Libya's former ambassador to the UN and its next foreign minister. Ambassador Ali Al-Houdeiri, Libya's representative at the UN, was also involved in Libya's lobbying efforts. The Libyan diplomats insisted that the U.S. and British efforts constituted a political campaign by the United States. They also maintained that Libya had appointed a judge to investigate the allegations but that the Americans and British had refused to cooperate.

Ignoring Libya's views as well as those of many scholars, and laying aside diplomatic urgings, the United States, Great Britain and France continued on a course whose premeditated purpose was increasingly clear. On January 3, 1992, the ambassadors of those three countries visited the new United Nations Secretary General, the Egyptian Boutros Boutros-Ghali. In that meeting, the three ambassadors informed Ghali of their intentions to pave the way for imposing sanctions against Libya. In a matter of days, these countries submitted to the Security Council a draft resolution, exercising all sorts of pressure, and within a month the Security Council held an official meeting to discuss the request of the United States, the United Kingdom and France, finally adopting its UNSC Resolution 731 (1992) on January 21, 1992.[11]

The main points of this resolution were the condemnation of the destruction of the U.S. and French planes, the disapproval of the "fact that the Libyan government has not yet responded effectively" to the requests of the three countries "urging the Libyan government immediately to provide a full and effective response to those requests," and a request that the Secretary General "seek the cooperation of the Libyan government to respond fully and effectively with those requests."

The Libyan delegation succeeded in some of its efforts, leading to what could be described as cosmetic changes in the Western draft. The caucus of nonaligned members of the council insisted on a paragraph demanding the Secretary General play a mediating role. The United States, the United Kingdom and France rejected that role because it might entail a settlement or political pressure on them to provide substantial information regarding their allegations. The compromise was that the text would mention a "request" that the Secretary General "seek the cooperation of the Libyan government" without authority to play a role in any mediation. The condition the three countries set for accepting that inclusion was that the resolution be adopted unanimously. The caucus accepted, as did all members of the council, including China, which had always refused to accept any resolutions that even hinted at any interference in internal affairs of any country.

What was stunning at the UN was the fact that this resolution was adopted with relative ease. The process set a precedent, exposing an example of what the role of the Security Council might be in the newly emerging post–Cold War world. The argument used by the Americans and the British for bringing such a case to the council, as mentioned in the text itself, is that the incidents threatened international peace and security, the preservation of which is referred to in the United Nations Charter as the most important task of the Security Council. Many, including the Libyans, questioned that justification, considering the incidents in question mere legal issues.

Furthermore, all members of the council knew at the time that the United States and the United Kingdom were preparing to impose sanctions against Libya. Although UNSCR 731 was not adopted under Chapter VII of the charter, it contributed to setting the stage for those actions. All that every member wanted was to prevent any U.S. anger against them. Legal and logical considerations were shelved in favor of political self-protection.

UNSG Ghali Tries, but to No Avail

Knowing the whole scenario had been designed long before, the UNSG appeared to cooperate. This Coptic Christian Egyptian had just taken over the top post for international diplomacy at the beginning of that same year, 1992. France was eager to have a Francophile in this position, whereas Britain was pushing for an Anglophile, and the United States, busy with other affairs, requested a delay in choosing the next Secretary General. France did not want to miss such an opportunity. It played a diplomatic trick against the United States and the United Kingdom leading to Boutros Boutros-Ghali's winning this post despite their objections. Ghali was fully aware of the objections of the United States and the United Kingdom. He possessed enough political maturity to realize he could not succeed unless he followed most of America's policies, forgetting what had happened, hoping to get Washington's support for a second term.

The morning after his election, Ghali received a letter from U.S. Secretary of State James Baker in which he was informed he would be in that post for only one term.[12] Still, the Secretary General believed he was one Egyptian the United States should not oppose.

He was among the very few of his people that had helped President Anwar Sadat in his attempts to achieve peace with Israel, when many had deserted him. This made him a hated figure among the Egyptians and Arabs opposed to Sadat, one of whom was Muammar Qadhafi, although the Libyan leader dealt with him reluctantly under the presidency of Hosni Mubarak in Egypt. Furthermore, Ghali was married to a Jewish woman from Egypt and thus was considered to have direct personal contact with the Israelis. He enjoyed reminding people that he "shared the ideas and principles that America stands for. I have paid a political price for this in the past. After the Suez Canal was nationalized by Nasser I was labeled 'pro-American' and not permitted to travel abroad."[13]

The first major issue Ghali had to deal with in his new post was Israel's expulsion of some Palestinians from the occupied territories. The second was resolution 731 and the political and diplomatic efforts that followed. After the Security Council adopted this resolution, he had to implement his part as the council required.

Ghali sent Undersecretary General Vasily Safronchuk; a retired Russian diplomat, to Libya. The choice was significant. For a Russian to go, practically on behalf of the Americans and the British, to a country formerly accused of being an agent of the Soviet Union would send that country a further message: The whole world is against you, even your former allies.

Days after the visit, the Secretary General presented a report to the council in which he provided details of his efforts.[14] Although a rather detailed account, it was not substantive, being a mere restatement of Libya's willingness to proceed and the reluctance of the United States and the United Kingdom to provide details of the charges. Libya did agree to look into the French charges since they "did not infringe upon the sovereignty of Libya" and requested that the Secretary General set up a mechanism in that regard.

Thus, Ghali's report lacked a clear position, if the reader was Western, but contained a negative tone if the reader was not, especially if Libya's views were taken into consideration. Ghali saw the situation differently. He was more concerned with what would affect his acceptability by the Americans.

The Libyan issue was also a major element of a major event that signified Ghali's single term, namely the summit meeting of the Security Council held on January 31, 1992, one month to the day after he took office. That was the only meeting the council held in which heads of state and government participated. It was presided over by British Prime Minister John Major, whose country happened to be presiding over the council that month, and attended by dignitaries such as Presidents George Bush Sr., Boris Yeltsin, François Mitterand, King Hassan of Morocco and the Prime Ministers of China, Japan, India, Belgium and others. For Ghali, that was easily the most fascinating event of his life. There he was, sitting among the most important leaders of the world, receiving their praise and congratulations, a norm for such a meeting that merely reflected traditional diplomatic compliments. With the second term already on his mind, he had his own personal agenda. He wanted to use this summit as a justification for strengthening his position early in his post at the UN.

During this meeting, Ghali paid the most attention to the statement made by President Bush. In his autobiography, Ghali remembers noticing that Bush "made two demands: No normalization with Iraq was possible as long as Saddam Hussein remained in power. And Libya must comply fully with the positions of the United States, Britain and France concerning Pan Am Flight 103 and UTA flight 772, the aircraft destroyed by terrorist bombs." Bush stressed that the Security Council had unanimously called upon Libya to comply with Resolution 731 of 1992. "The American president's demands worried me," Ghali wrote later in his book, "...because Iraq and Libya would expect me, as an Arab, to understand their point of view, while the United States would expect me to follow its lead in pressuring these 'pariah' states. I was determined to follow one rule: to support and seek to fulfil all resolutions of the United Nations."[15]

A superficial reading of this last sentence would find it expressing neutrality. The situation was more complicated, however, and neutrality was never as easy as Ghali imagined. The international stage was clearly set for a world that had the United States as the single superpower. It was a world in frenzy. Overestimating one's abilities and powers would only add to the overwhelming chaos in such a period of history, especially when coming from a person occupying a post such as Ghali's. That is almost exactly what happened to him. He ended up leaving the most prestigious international post in the world deprived of many statements of support, beginning a new era of his life asking, while in that thirty-eighth floor office on First Avenue in Manhattan, what should I have said? But did Boutros-Ghali even know what Boutros-Ghali really wanted?

2

Sanctions and Early Mediations

While Ghali tried to play his self-proclaimed "even-handed diplomacy" on the Libya issue, he was not the only self-appointed intermediary. Many American and British lawyers, businessmen, former officials and possible con men tried to convince the Libyans they could find a solution and bypass the Security Council. They swarmed into Tripoli with offers. Not only was Tripoli fooled by many of them, most of whom were only looking for quick financial rewards, but Washington was not leaving any room for compromise through intermediaries or even through heads of state or officials of other countries, including President Mubarak, King Hassan of Morocco, and other leaders. Some, including these, were message carriers between Libya and the United States. Two of the intermediaries tried to achieve results; they faced many doubts in the early stages but succeeded later. One was President Mandela, who began his efforts prior to becoming president of South Africa. The other was Saudi Prince Bandar bin Sultan.

Despite the wholesale rebuffing of mediation attempts, diplomatic efforts were still exploring any possible opening. The UN was one forum where some of these efforts were played out. They seemed not to have a clear idea what the answers to the political questions were. Some might say the ambassadors communicated only ambiguous answers intentionally. Ghali himself was at times confused, although he was given a clear idea about the political position from the U.S. Secretary of State. During a meeting in Mexico held prior to the Security Council's adoption of resolution 731, Baker had told him that he "had heard that North African countries were inclined toward conciliation with Libya, with me [Ghali] as Secretary-General as mediator. He asked me to avoid the issue. The United States wanted a United Nations resolution passed calling on Libya to turn over the suspects."[1] US Ambassador Thomas Pickering was much clearer in his communication with his colleagues and with Ghali himself regarding the future imposition of sanctions, asking the Secretary General on Sunday, March 1, to convey that such action was coming "very soon if Libya does not comply with resolution 731."

Ghali did not stop with his February 1992 report. He was looking for a way to satisfy repeated requests from President Mubarak, among others. Ghali was quite aware of Libya's lost love for him and its knowledge of his worse feelings toward a government that had labeled him a "traitor" for his enthusiastic support of the late President Sadat for making "peace" with Israel.

On March 3 he presented the council with a follow-up, in which he reported that he had met the ambassadors of the three Western countries on February 17, and they requested that the Secretary General convey six points to the Libyan leader:

1. that they consider Libya's responses a "step forward only if supported by action";

2. that they "support the request of the French government and wish to be informed of the mechanism by which the Libyan authorities will hand over the records and documentation requested";

3. that they "would like to know the time, place and modality of the hand-over by the Libyan authorities of the two persons charged and the information and evidence requested and the precise measures that the Libyan government intends to take in order to end support for terrorism in all its forms";

4. that they "have no objection to the hand-over of the suspects and the information requested taking place through the Secretary General of the UN";

5. that they "believe that their requests are clear and precise and that they do not require further clarification"; and

6. that they "seek to obtain assurances from the Libyan Arab Jamahiriya with regards to its responsibility" toward the question of compensation.[2]

Ghali's report went on to document the Libyan response (as conveyed by Safronchuk, who was sent back to Libya and met Qadhafi on

February 24), which was that "constitutional obstructions" prevented the handover of the suspects. The most important element mentioned by Qadhafi was intended as a further effort to achieve some dialogue with the West. Qadhafi, according to the report, explained that "improvement of bilateral relations between the Libyan Arab Jamahiriya and the United States would make it possible to hand-over the two suspects to the United States authorities." Qadhafi, for the first time, also indicated the possibility of handing the two over for trial in France "once the constitutional problems were solved." Other countries, such as Malta or any Arab country, were possibilities for the locus of the trial as well. He stated that his country was "prepared to cooperate in every way possible to put an end to terrorist activities and sever its relations with all groups and organizations that target innocent civilians," insisting it was "premature" to discuss the issue of compensation, "which can only result from a civil court decision" providing guarantees that it will do so in that event.

In that same report, Ghali included letters from Minister Bishari further elaborating Libya's position. He also mentioned he had met in Geneva with "a special envoy of Colonel Qadhafi, Mr. Yusef Debri, Head of Libyan Intelligence, with whom the entire situation was reviewed." Ghali's conclusion was the following:

> From the foregoing, it will be seen that while resolution 731 (1992) has not yet been complied with, there has been certain evolution in the position of the Libyan authorities since the Secretary-General's earlier report of 11 February 1992. The Security Council may wish to consider this in deciding on its future course of action."

It was clear Ghali was advancing his personal agenda a little further than what he had concluded in his last report. However, it could be said as well that he was not really seasoned, for he hoped that his report and his efforts would affect the American efforts seeking sanctions. The Americans demonstrated they would not stop unless there was a full Libyan surrender. There were other American demands in accordance with a hidden U.S. agenda.

The United States continued its escalation on two levels. One was through requests made to countries such as Thailand and South Korea and the European countries that have economic relations with Libya to minimize them to the lowest possible levels. The other was at the Security Council level, where ideas on sanctions were presented: prohibition of flights from and to Libya; prohibition of any sale to Libya of any weapons; and lowering of the levels of diplomatic representation in Libya and Libyan representation in other countries.

On March 18, the three ambassadors officially presented the council with their draft resolution, aimed at preempting an International Court of Justice decision on Libya's request to nullify resolution 731. They wanted to influence that decision by sending the following message: The Security Council is the political instrument, and it has made its decision; the court is a legal body, and it should justify the political decision, not vice versa. Any decision by the court in Libya's favor would mean losing votes at the Security Council. This conflict of opinions was reflected in the council through the support the sanctions would receive. As it stood then, this support was nothing like the unanimity that resolution 731 achieved. Only ten of the fifteen members of the council supported the new draft, one of whom was China, a permanent member with veto power. In a statement to the press by Ambassador Houdeiri, Libya announced that it considered any such resolution, if adopted by the council, as a "declaration of war against Libya."

While the ambassadors were working at the UN, President Mubarak was meeting Syria's president Hafez Al-Assad in Cairo. After the meeting, the two expressed their "deep concern" at the Western effort that called for "providing the evidence that confirms Libya's involvement." Mubarak said Egyptian and Arab citizens "will not accept such harsh measures against Libya, especially the neighboring countries which are to be affected by any sanctions imposed on Libya," calling on the UN and the Security Council to "take into consideration those feelings of the Arabs and be aware of results affecting the neighbors, prior to adopting a resolution." Assad warned that "any measure against Libya could affect the peace process (in the Middle East), since peace is not in the interest of the Arabs only, it is in the interest of the whole world." Assad added, "the Arabs are one nation that is affected by all that happens in the region. Thus, world states should appreciate our feelings when taking any measures against an Arab brotherly country."[3]

No signal came from Washington expressing any willingness to heed these public Arab calls. Ghali was still trying, and on March 23 a discussion of a possible handing over of the two Libyan suspects took place between Ghali and Houdeiri in New York. The main idea was to hand them over to the Arab League in an effort to avoid the upcoming sanctions. It was, however, a discussion that could go no further, considering America's intentions. Because Washington was interested in sanctions, the Americans pressed ahead at the Security Council and at the ICJ, which began its consideration of Libya's case on March 27, 1992.

That same day, Qadhafi warned that Libya would boycott the countries that became enemies of Libya and would maintain economic relations with friendly countries. "I am saying it clearly, and what I say is a warning: those who support our cause will benefit from our projects, and those who will stand against our political case will get nothing."[4]

The Americans began counting votes. They were concerned only about China's possible use of the veto. That is why they threatened, publicly and privately, that any such use of the veto would affect China's economic relations with the United States, where it is designated as a "most favored nation," a status accorded only to countries with which it has special relations.

China was in a very awkward position. It is a country that sought membership in the Non-Aligned movement. The movement was never able to accept that membership, fearing China's weight would affect its policies. China was seeking to increase its international influence. The movement could have been China's NATO or even Warsaw Pact. That did not happen and China was accorded only observer status. When the cold war was over, China continued its efforts to find status in the new world being formed. Its weak economic condition did not afford it the ability to be fully independent. It was too reliant on the economies of the West, providing the three countries with the most effective blackmail tools possible: money and trade. China had to accept the pressure of the West against its ideological beliefs. The sanctions against Libya were a definite test. Contacts with Beijing succeeded in transforming the Chinese position to a mere abstention.

The situation was getting clearer in Libya. Its officials were following all these developments while noting that all calls for mediation and political-diplomatic solutions were falling on deaf ears in the West. Even in the Arab world no one would defend Libya's position, including its calls for dealing with this case in a legal forum.

The political editor of Libya's news agency,[5] JANA, wrote on March 29: "It seems that Washington, London and Paris were committed to continuing their efforts against Libya even if the suspects were handed over. It is confirmed that even if we assumed that Libya handed over the two suspects to the United States and Britain, these countries are using their pressure on the Security Council to adopt resolutions harmful to Libya, its economy and sovereignty."

Three and a half months had passed since the first accusations against Libya were announced. The United States and the United Kingdom could wait no more. Any nationals of other countries who needed time to leave had done so. Those who still needed time were given another fifteen days as per the text of the resolution, stating it would become effective on April 15, 1992. On March 30, the three countries presented their draft, moderately modified from the original text, and the Security Council was set to vote the following day. Adopting is what the council did on March 31. Far from the unanimity the previous resolution received, this one, known as number 748, was adopted with only ten votes. The other five members abstained, while no one voted against the resolution.[6] The support the United States had initially received was beginning to waver, and sanctions have never easily been imposed by the Security Council since.

In this new resolution, the council prohibited any Libyan flights or any other flights going to or coming from Libya, as well as any dealings with the Libyan air industry. It also prohibited any military dealings with Libya and called on states to "significantly reduce" the number and the level of the staff at Libyan diplomatic missions and "restrict or control the movement" of all such staff who remained. It established a committee composed of all members of the council to examine the "humanitarian" flights, exempted by the resolutions but which still had to be approved by this new committee, which came to be known as the "sanctions committee."

The second operative paragraph of the resolution mentioned, in general terms, the council's demands on Libya. After persistent requests and demands by the nonaligned caucus in the council and others to explain in specific detail what those demands were, the following points were communicated on April 2 by the three Western representatives. The nonaligned caucus members were to present these points to the Libyans:

1. Accept full responsibility for and cooperate in the investigations of the Lockerbie incident, while handing over the two suspects and paying compensation; surrender all remaining equipment similar to that used in destroying that plane (Libya was accused of purchasing it from Switzerland)

2. Cooperate with the French authorities in the matter of the UTA flight

3. Cease all types of training for "terrorists" in Libyan camps; stop supporting and aiding them; cooperate with Western requests regarding those organizations by handing over any information, or even personalities

4. Cease all support and aid to the Irish Republican Army (IRA) and provide the British authorities with all available information regarding that relation

These points gave the whole process a different dimension. They revealed some of the intentions of the three, especially the United States and the United Kingdom. Some considered the third and fourth points the most important and the main motives for the whole issue, although some British officials deny that; one said the issue of the IRA was inserted "hastily to beef up the demands with the insistence of the Caucus for clarifications, and it worked."

Public Reactions to Sanctions

Reactions of anger prevailed around the Arab world. But while that anger was merely verbal in other countries, the Libyans took to the streets with countrywide demonstrations. And since, for that month, the Security Council was presided over by Venezuela, demonstrators attacked and totally destroyed the Venezuelan embassy. The embassy's staff was not harmed and escaped to safe areas with the help of the Libyan authorities.

The council strongly condemned "the violent attacks" in a statement issued after a meeting of the council on April 2. The council demanded that the Libyan government "take all necessary measures to honor its international legal obligations" and further demanded "that the Libyan Arab Jamahiriya pay to the Government of Venezuela immediate and full compensation for the damage caused." Most important, the council's statement insisted that "any suggestion that those acts of violence were not directed against the government of Venezuela but against and in reaction to resolution 748 (1992) is extremely serious and totally unacceptable."

Official Libya tried to calm the popular reactions of anger. Qadhafi personally called on his people to "exercise restraint and protect the security of foreign embassies and their personnel" while the ministry of justice and general security asked the foreign ministry to call on diplomats to move from their official buildings to "where their security can be guaranteed, until the situation calms down." At the same time, the foreign ministry formally apologized to Venezuela in response to the Venezuelan protest on April 5. That apology was communicated to the Security Council in an official document.[7] Venezuela accepted Libya's apology "on the understanding that there will be no repetition of such acts of violence, that there will be full compensation for the material damage and that the diplomatic relations between the two countries will be conducted, both in matters on which they agree and in matters on which they disagree, in accordance with the norms of international law and of civilized coexistence among nations."

The rage in the Libyan streets was translated into a diplomatic statement issued the next day by the foreign ministry as a reaction to the sanctions resolution:

> The countries that voted for the sanctions did not possess the actual quorum, practically and legally, to adopt (the resolution). These countries are within the Western alliance, while the countries that abstained represent more than two-thirds of the human and geographical world, while Russia has not even completed its proper legal representation in

the Council through a resolution by the Security Council and the necessary approval of the members comprising the former Soviet Union.

By now, fears of a military attack were growing for the Libyans since they considered the sanctions resolution as a legitimizing factor for such an action. While Libya justified its acceptance of the resolution, despite its insistence on innocence, as a prevention of the implementation of these threats, Douglas Hurd answered such fears the day after the adoption of the resolution, while the Americans kept silent. He said the Western countries "had no plan currently to attack Libya militarily" if it refused to accept the resolution. He insisted that pressure would be applied only through sanctions. Washington did not even hint at the improbability of a military strike. Libya continued to sense danger.

Further Mediation Fails Once Again

At the UN, Ghali did not see the case as closed yet. In conversation with colleagues, he had often mentioned with a touch of pride, that Egypt's president Mubarak had been telling him, ever since Ghali's election as Secretary General, to try to find a solution to this problem. And try he did. Results were something else. He overestimated his ability to override political and historical considerations as well as reality.

On April 11 and 12, at his request, Ghali met with a high-level Libyan delegation in Geneva. The Libyans presented him with an idea in response to his suggestion of a step-by-step process. "I had in mind the Arab-Israeli peace process, in which the hardest issues, such as Jerusalem, had been left until the very end of the process. Grant what is most tolerable for your Government. ...Above all, avoid delay, which only runs the risk of new sanctions."[8]

The Libyans attending the meeting didn't see him as being clear and direct. Still, they countered with an immediate proposal for him to send a commission of inquiry composed of Chinese and Indian officials to Libya in order to verify that no terrorist camps were there.

When he returned to New York, Ghali presented the idea to the ambassadors of the three countries and got their agreement to send a commission with a condition: that Vladimir Petrovsky, the Soviet Deputy Foreign Minister during the last years of the Soviet Union and the early days of the new arrangement for Russia (who had just taken over the top Russian post at the UN after the retirement of Safronchuk) lead it. Petrovsky left for Libya just before the sanctions the Security Council adopted went into effect.

Here, another element of suspense arose. Days before Petrovsky went to Libya, Ghali claimed in his autobiography, "an American military officer came to show the photographs taken by satellite that showed that where once there had been terrorist training camps, there were now peaceful rural landscapes. So, the United States declared, there was no need for a commission to go to Libya, because it would not find any such camps there."

Libya then viewed the Petrovsky mission differently. This Russian diplomat had a contradictory personality that reflected American humor in private and Soviet strictness in public. He would show only the latter in dealing with the Libyans, sensing that was what the Americans wanted. While in Tripoli, as a special envoy of the UNSG, Petrovsky would not discuss the Lockerbie issue in any serious manner. On the contrary, the Libyans noticed that he was "impolite, rude, arrogant and uncooperative." Petrovsky wanted one thing and one thing only. As soon as he arrived—and as if he were an envoy of the Americans, not the UN—he began to ask, "Where are the two? I am only here to get them." With that attitude, which was hard for the Libyans to digest, he met the Libyan leader. The Libyans had been told by Ghali that the mission was to confirm Libya's closure of terrorist camps. It seemed as if Petrovsky knew when he went to Libya that the United States and the United Kingdom, knowing Libya was not yet ready, wanted him to raise only the issue of the handover of the two suspects. Their approval of him was more important than any effort by his real boss, the Secretary General of the UN. The Libyans were right in that Petrovsky needed American support to keep his prestigious post. A personal ambition overrode international diplomacy.

However, this whole process would not mean anything unless the whole atmosphere of Libyan-Western relations could constitute a basis for a solution. The most important aspect left untouched was the political process not included in the issues of direct concern to the case, namely that of the United States and the United Kingdom, which would, in turn, lead to a change in the U.S. position.

The Libyans heard that agenda. Still, there were many issues that needed to be tackled. Those issues later became the guarantees which Libya obtained before finalizing the process of the solution.

One item on Ghali's agenda was eliminated. It was very devious of the United States to kill this process through technology, diplomatically, without a demonstration of any real positive results in Libya's favor. It is still not clear whether what the American pictures showed were real or the whole exercise was a game to preempt further moves by the Secretary General and Libya.

The political atmosphere was changing again, raising further complications and ambiguity. George Bush Sr. had just left the White House, and a new administration had moved in. The new president, Bill Clinton, was a Democrat. He knew less of world politics and came with an agenda focused on internal affairs, an agenda that defeated the "internationalist" Bush. Some Libyans thought the new Democrats would neglect the previous twelve years of Republican rule and build on relations and contacts they had with officials and relatives of the last Democratic president, Jimmy Carter. They had no idea that the absence of clear policies for the international scene, along with the deep-rooted influence of Jewish officials appointed to almost every national security post, would further a negative policy toward Libya: a continuation of containment through additional national and internationally sought sanctions, along with a willingness to ignore the wider political aspects of this issue.

Ghali noticed the new atmosphere in Washington. He thought it would provide him with more room to maneuver; thus, he decided to intensify his efforts.

On January 7, 1993, while in his native Egypt to celebrate the Coptic (Eastern) Christmas, Ghali met Omar Al-Muntasser, who became Libya's foreign minister after heading a committee established to deal with the Lockerbie issue. In that meeting, Ghali reported that Muntasser informed him he was going to New York, where he expected to take the entire affair in hand and find a rapid solution to the problem. That, in itself, left Ghali with the impression that the new Libyan foreign minister was more accommodating. He was surprised, he wrote later in his autobiography, to see that Muntasser "had completely changed his attitude" when he visited him in New York later that year.

Apparently one main reason for Muntasser's change of attitude was Ghali's rejection of an invitation by Qadhafi to visit him in Libya as a part of his North Africa tour, which he undertook in early April 1993. Muntasser, the Secretary General found, presented a new legalistic explanation of resolution 731, saying that it did not require Libya to extradite the two suspects. This explanation, which Libya repeated on many occasions, might have been true if the reader of the text expected the language to be totally unqualified by the references to other UN documents. In this case, the resolution referred to the letter of the United States, the United Kingdom and France in which they mentioned their request for the handover. Ghali asked for, and received, a legal opinion from the office of the UN's legal adviser. It confirmed that the letter of the three was an integral part of the resolution. Without question, according to the legal opinion, surrender was required.

When Muntasser came to New York, he was aware of new efforts by the United States and the United Kingdom to look into further sanctions against Libya. These efforts were official, for a new lobby was forcing itself on decision makers in Washington. The victims' families were mostly influencing Senator Edward Kennedy of Massachusetts, where most of these families reside. Kennedy had met the Secretary General and informed him of his pressure on the administration to impose an oil embargo. Ghali informed Libya of that effort while, with their colleagues in the Security Council, American and British diplomats were discussing strengthening sanctions through other means. They intended to make a proposal to that effect during the review of the sanctions, scheduled for April. The United States wanted an embargo on the export of Libyan oil, oil derivatives and equipment. The United Kingdom and France were more aware of European reliance on Libyan oil, which is of a special quality. Any transformation of refineries in these countries to accommodate replacement oil coming from other countries would require modification of existing refineries, costing around 800 million dollars. The British and the French were looking at other alternatives, including an incentive for Libya: a clear promise in any forthcoming resolution that all sanctions would be removed as soon as the two suspects were handed over. The American point of view, though modified, prevailed.

The whole process started to take a new turn by the middle of 1993. Libya had knocked on so many doors, and mediators had found the United States and the United Kingdom totally deaf to compromise; they insisted on the surrender of the two suspects, nothing less. It seemed, however, they were in no hurry to solve this problem. Everything, politically and diplomatically, was going their way, and Libya began to understand that the Arab countries would not breach those sanctions. Even Saudi Arabia refused to allow a breach for the Hajj (pilgrimage) flights while imposing further limitations on the number of Libyans wishing to fulfill this vital religious duty. That led Qadhafi, in a moment of anger at the Saudi rejection (and to the surprise of many of his colleagues in government), to send about two hundred Libyans on camels through Egypt for the pilgrimage to Jerusalem. Officially, the Libyan line was "a personal initiative of those persons and the Libyan leadership has no relation whatsoever with this issue."[9]

Meanwhile, efforts were being expended on different levels. The Secretary General of the Arab League, Esmat Abdel-Meguid, went to New York to try to help Libya lobby council members. He asked them to avoid escalation for at least the three months to come. Many leaders were undertaking similar efforts with a range of Western leaders they were visiting. These efforts were aimed at taming the first review of sanctions, which took place on April 8, and resulted in a routine extension of the sanctions.

U.S. economic experts advised against strengthening sanctions, as some officials wanted, for this would negatively affect the economies of allied countries, such as Japan and Europe. Still, President Clinton stated that the United States required Libya's full cooperation with resolutions 731 and 748, without such cooperation, Clinton warned, stronger sanctions were all but unavoidable.

American, British and French officials were continuing their consultations for strengthening the sanctions against Libya. Midlevel officials met in Paris in a setting similar to that arranged prior to presenting the issue to the council. By mid-July, they had managed to agree only on the necessity of such a move. Further, sanctions were too complicated an issue to be agreed on easily at their level. They decided to present the issue to their foreign ministers, who were due to meet within weeks at the Industrialized Countries Summit in Tokyo. Proposals for further sanctions ranged between those presented by France (such as freezing Libyan assets in other countries and prohibiting foreigners from working in Libya) and the reservations of the other two (that the proposals were not strong enough, especially since the United States had already frozen Libyan assets in 1986). The atmosphere was moving toward a strengthening effort that would have more publicity value than an actual impact.

Against these developments, Libya presented yet another compromise. On July 7, 1993, in an interview with the *Washington Times*, Qadhafi offered to cooperate with the United States in fighting terrorism. The United States immediately rejected that proposition, asking him to simply implement the Security Council resolutions.

Another review of sanctions was coming up at the Security Council. The three powers were continuing their discussions on how to strengthen the sanctions, holding another meeting, this time in London, on August 3, days after their ministers' meeting in Tokyo. Muntasser was in New York meeting Ghali and some ambassadors. He was getting a clear idea of what the three were discussing with their colleagues at the council. The feeling was that the only possible new element in the sanctions would be an embargo on oil equipment and spare parts. The intention would be to make it harder for Libya to find enough cash to pay for this equipment in the black market. The sanctions, then, would definitely hurt.

The Libyans went on a financial counteroffensive. They wanted to protect their finances and investments. Most of their foreign reserves were recalled and returned. Short-term investments were withdrawn. Some investments were transferred from countries likely to strictly abide by the new sanctions to countries that would be more flexible in protecting Libya's assets. Ownership of some direct investments was transferred to companies partially owned or invested in by Libya since the freeze might not be applicable in such complicated situations. The only assets left overseas were long-term investments since penalties on those early withdrawals would far exceed the benefit of returning them. That effort went on until the last possible moment before resolution adoption, with Libyan officials counting on the time difference between New York and Europe.

With regard to oil equipment and spare parts, Libya moved quickly into the market, buying the maximum possible to prevent the need during the following years of sanctions. That would save them some of the money they would have paid for those parts in the black market.

Diplomatically, however, a small window of opportunity was still thought to be open. After meeting Muntasser and other Libyan officials, Ghali came to the conclusion that Libya "accepted in principle" the requirement to hand over the two suspects. He made statements to that effect. The British government did not like those statements. On August 4, its foreign office issued a statement insisting, "We need deeds, not words." Meanwhile, in New York, the Libyan foreign minister was saying, "Libya implemented most demands of the Council and I hope Ghali would send a mission to Tripoli to discuss the implementation of the rest of resolution 731." In a letter dated July 28, 1993, to the Secretary General, Libya stated its readiness to receive a mission of the Secretary General's choice to verify the nonexistence of alleged terrorist training camps on its soil. It also added that it actively cooperated with Britain with respect to that country's special requests. It was clear that all parties were talking past each other.

On August 13, during a review of the sanctions that went ahead without any major action, the three informed the Security Council of their intention to present a new draft resolution to strengthen sanctions if Libya did not hand over the two suspects by October 1, 1993. The three went on to present Ghali with the first official draft resolution on September 9. Still, he tried to play a role, neglecting all political signs contrary to any softening of the campaign against Libya. He asked the three: "If the Libyans deliver the two suspects, do you plan to lift the sanctions?" The three responded that they would "suspend the sanctions pending the compliance of Libya with their other demands."[10] He requested two to three weeks before putting the new draft to a vote, in order to launch a new effort with the Libyans. He thought his rejection of the Libyan request for the mission would not reflect negatively on any further efforts he might undertake. He was wrong, for the Libyans, though not officially and publicly, began to feel that Ghali would not confront the three in any way imaginable. Efforts thereafter were mere diplomacy that was short on expectation of real success.

Still, on September 14, Libya's ambassador to Tunisia, Abdel Ati Al-Obeidi, met with Ghali and presented him with a list of technical and legal questions about the possible trial of the two suspects and the other elements of the Security Council resolutions, including the definition of terrorism.[11] Most of these questions remained on the table and consisted of the basis of discussions held in New York in 1998, putting the final touches on the deal reached to hold the trial.

American, British and French officials considered the Libyan questions a derogatory effort. They presented the Secretary General with a non-paper, asking him to convey it to the Libyans.[12] When the Libyan answers came, the three countries reacted by presenting the following talking points from the nonpaper:

> We have been able to take a preliminary look at the Libyan response to the tripartite non-paper. It still fails to address satisfactorily either the surrender of the two accused of Lockerbie or the requirements of the French investigating judge in the UTA case. We must make clear to Libya that these two issues are crucial. Without their resolution there can be no possibility of lifting sanctions.
>
> We have noted the Libyan assurances on complying with the remainder of SCR 731, and in particular on the renunciation of terrorism. You will understand if we remain skeptical of Libyan intentions. We do not exclude the deployment of verification teams (on which we would have views to be discussed with you in due course) after the Lockerbie two are handed over for trial in Scotland or the US and the French authorities are satisfied in their investigation of the UTA case. However, it is Libyan compliance with the requirements on Lockerbie and UTA that is the best assurance of Libyan good faith.
>
> We would welcome it if you would now probe Libyan intentions, as expressed in their letter, about handing over the Lockerbie two and co-operating with Judge Bugiere, and would back your intention to have such talks in New York.
>
> The three co-sponsors intend to issue a statement on 27 November, the first anniversary of the tripartite declaration of the requirements placed upon Libya in connection with the Lockerbie and UTA incidents.
>
> We should like to have your ideas on what further action would be required if Libya does not comply.

Ghali did not help the case since his answers to questions by the three on the seriousness of the Libyan questions diplomatically ignored the main answer they wanted to hear: that this was an effort by Libya aimed at preparing the grounds for a handover of the suspects. He later acknowledged not being encouraged by Libya's response, failing to read Libya's concerns and advising them of positions he would take in communicating with the three. In his autobiogrpahy, he wrote, "Personally I thought Qadhafi was stalling for time again. He did not want to surrender the two suspects," giving a reason, from Ghali's perspective, that one of them was "his relative." Ghali must have misunderstood the relationship since neither of the two is related to Qadhafi.

It appears that Ghali was playing some game against Libya. How could he not consider these major advances in Libya's positions, which proved to be the basis for the solution in 1999? How could he propose some action, only to back off when Libya responded? Was he merely satisfying Egypt's wishes for action while accepting the American pressure against any softening, believing he could succeed in satisfying both, or was he merely settling old personal grievances with Libya?

If Libya was "stalling for time," as Ghali claimed, it would not have been for those reasons. The Libyans saw another aspect in the developments of that month. They were eying the coming sanctions that would freeze their assets abroad. The more time that passed before the adoption of such a resolution by the council, the more those assets would be withdrawn and transferred to safe havens. That's what the delay was for. Not many outside Libya felt the urgency of, and the need for, such an effort, although a wise political reading and clever diplomatic maneuvering might have succeeded in dragging both parties to a solution, as was accomplished six years later.

Different efforts were still being attempted, aimed at calming the tension, only to meet escalation from the United States. One such effort was undertaken by President Mubarak, trying to work with Libya during a visit there in late September at the same time President Clinton addressed the forty-eighth Session of the United Nations General Assembly. In a speech delivered on September 27, 1993, Clinton emphasized that the issue of terrorism was high on the American agenda. Americans had watched that phenomenon reaching U.S. soil earlier that year when homemade explosives were detonated at the World Trade Center. Over fifty thousand people worked in those buildings. It would have been a catastrophe had the explosives brought the buildings down, as happened on September 11, 2001. The casualties were only six dead and about one thousand injured. Still, it was the biggest act of terrorism the United States had witnessed in its short history. In his UN speech, Clinton connected that incident with Pan Am 103, insisting the perpetrators had to be brought to justice. He was not about to show any softening in his first year in office, despite the widening efforts of Saudi Arabi, Egypt, Tunisia and Morocco, among others, to find a solution. With the danger of terrorism reaching home, the United States was not willing to waiver in its resolve by accepting proposals, such as a trial in a third country or a handover to the Arab League, the two main proposals of the efforts at that stage.

After a long delay, the Security Council met on November 11, 1993, and adopted further sanctions against Libya in Resolution 883. Those sanctions were to take effect on December 1, 1993, if Libya did not surrender the two suspects by then. The resolution said that the council:

> Decides that all States in which there are funds or other financial resources (including funds derived or generated from property) owned or controlled, directly or indirectly, by:
>
> (a) the Government or public authorities of Libya, or
> (b) any Libyan undertaking
>
> shall freeze such funds and financial resources and ensure that neither they nor any other funds and financial resources are made available, by their nationals or by any persons within their territory, directly or indirectly, to or for the benefit of the Government or public authorities of Libya or any Libyan undertaking, which for the purposes of this paragraph, means any commercial, industrial or public utility undertaking which is owned or controlled, directly or indirectly, by
>
> (i) the Government or public authorities of Libya,
> (ii) any entity, wherever located or organized, owned or controlled by (i), or
> (iii) any person identified by States as acting on behalf of (i) or (ii) for the purposes of this resolution.

It also imposed a complete prohibition on any dealings with the Libyan national airlines and their offices and any transactions regarding Libyan civil aviation. As for oil, the financial freeze would not affect financial transactions for sale of Libyan oil or gas, although the resolution imposed restrictions on the equipment and spare parts to be used in this industry.[13]

The resolution was adopted with the approval of eleven members and the abstention of four, with no negative votes.[14] The division between the members of the council became clearer: Western Europeans and the remnants of the Soviet Union supported the West, while many in the Third World supported Libya by abstaining.

Libya's representative, Ambassador Ali El-Houdeiri, made the following points and others in the council meeting, clarifying Libya's position:

> It is an attempt to destroy the Libyan economy by adversely impacting on our people's only source of income, as well as on the civil aviation structure on which my country depends for transportation.
>
> In its letter to the Secretary-General of the United Nations on 28 July 1993, my country confirmed that it was willing to discuss the procedures and arrangements relating to the trial of the two accused, with the mission the Secretary-General was about to send to Libya. It thus

becomes clear that out of our desire to reach a reasonable solution and despite the fact that the 1971 Montreal Convention gives Libya the right to try the two suspects before Libyan courts—question that is still pending before the International Court of Justice—the Libyan position has been extremely flexible. On the other side, there is the rigid and intransigent position based on nothing more than the logic of force.

My country will continue to do its utmost to cooperate with the Secretary-General of the United Nations in order to reach a final solution of this problem.

Nabil Al-Arabi, Egypt's representative to the UN at the time, addressed the council's meeting, saying:

Egypt calls upon the Security Council to keep in sight all the consequences that will impact negatively on the people of Libya and on the neighboring peoples of the region. Article 50 of the Charter stipulates that any State which finds itself confronted with special economic problems arising from the carrying out of enforcement measures against any State shall have the right to consult the Security Council. This means that the Council should today consider alleviating the economic suffering of Libya and of its neighbors that would arise from the adoption of the draft resolution under consideration.

Madeleine Albright, then U.S. Ambassador to the UN, countered the Libyan and Egyptian and other speakers by insisting:

The resolution is balanced and precisely targeted. Its hallmarks are an assets freeze, a limited equipment embargo against the Libyan oil industry and the tightening of earlier sanctions imposed under resolution 748 (1992). To those who say it is not strong enough, I ask this: Why did Libya try so hard to stop this resolution if the sting of its new sanctions is so mild?

Libya knows what it must do to comply. We await the turnover of those indicted for the bombing of Pan Am 103. We await the Libyan Government's cooperation with the French judiciary. We await compensation for the victims of Libyan terrorism. And we await the Libyan Government's clear and confirmed renunciation of terrorism.

What could possibly constitute the basis for a solution after all these developments? Libya's doubt of the existence of the hidden intentions of the United States and the United Kingdom, prior to the requests, was transformed into major worries and concerns after the strengthening of the sanctions. And while it could not afford to show any diplomacy short of resolve against terrorism, the unresponsiveness of the United States to the efforts of all mediators further enhanced the conspiracy theory in Libyan minds. For them, all these developments would only confirm that the Americans were not out for justice for the Lockerbie victims. They were out to destroy the Libyan revolution. Thus, protection of the revolution became the priority for Libya. Ghali, on his part, was further complicating his efforts and undermining any possibility for a successful mediating role for the Secretary General by aligning himself closer and closer with the U.S. position.

3

A Legal or a Political Problem?

Libya and many of its supporters felt the issue was being dealt with in the wrong forum. The authorities competent to deal with such cases were not consulted. They were the International Court of Justice and the Convention for the Suppression of Unlawful Acts against the Safety of Civil Aviation, signed at Montreal in 1971, widely known as the Montreal Convention. Politically motivated Washington and London never felt the necessity to resort to such forums, refusing any effort by any mediator to resort to them in order to find a solution. Libya, however, chose the legal path.

Libya claimed all along that the three Western states were using a legal problem for political purposes. A legal process was called for by the three on the national level. They did not, however, follow that process on the international scene, preferring the political route to achieve an outcome at the national level. The political process would serve a political purpose as well that would achieve two goals for the United States: justice for the victims' families, and containment of Libya.

Had that problem been dealt with as a legal case, Washington could have carried out measures called for in the UN Charter or the Montreal Convention. Libya had the right to try the two Libyans accused of the bombing or, at least, their case should have been presented to the International Court of Justice to try to resolve a conflict between the two/three countries. Secure, however, in its political power, the United

37

States used the United Nations Security Council to adopt measures reserved for different aspects of international conflict, such as their case against Iraq.

The two Libyans accused in the Lockerbie case were alleged to have committed what would amount to offenses defined by Article 1, paragraphs (a), (b) or (c) of the Montreal Convention. Furthermore, Article 5, paragraph 2, states quite clearly that a contracting state, Libya in this case, must take measures as may be necessary to establish its jurisdiction over such offense mentioned in Article 1: "in the case where the alleged offender is present in its territory and it does not extradite him pursuant to Article 8 to any of the states mentioned in paragraph 1 of this article." In other words, a contracting state must clearly either extradite an alleged offender or else prosecute the alleged offender itself.

Libya filed a case against the United States and the United Kingdom before the International Court of Justice aimed at challenging and nullifying the sanctions resolution adopted by the Security Council. The ICJ held that it had jurisdiction to hear the case.

The description of the case as "legal" or "political" was a major subject in debates in the Security Council and the ICJ and became the subject of studies undertaken by some scholars all over the world. Some argued that arbitration was the conventional method required to resolve such a dispute and that the Security Council's intervention had preempted that arbitration. Others held that Libya's presentation of the case to the ICJ led to a discussion of the actual legal ramifications of this issue. At the early stages, when the ICJ discussed the case presented by Libya, it became clear that circumventing the authority of the Court and hiding behind Chapter VII of UN Charter do not conform to the role of the principal organs of the UN, including the ICJ and the Security Council. It is not justified for any of these organs to override the constitutional framework set forth in the charter. One such argument was written by Judge Shahabuddeen, a member of the ICJ panel in 1992, saying:

> The question now raised by Libya's challenge to the validity of resolution 748 (1992) is whether a decision of the Security Council may override the legal rights of States and, if so, whether there are any limitations on the power of the Council to characterize a situation as one justifying the making of a decision entailing such consequences. Are there any limits to the Council's powers of appreciation? In the equilibrium of forces underpinning the structure of the United Nations within the evolving international order, is there any conceivable point beyond which a legal issue may properly arise as to the competence of the Security Council to produce such overriding results? If there are any limits, what are those limits and what body, if other than the Security Council, is competent to say what those limits are?[1]

In total contrast to what he was officially saying while in office, Ghali waited until after he left his post to announce his agreement with the Libyan positions on the legal issues, that is, the Montreal Convention and the role of the ICJ. He wrote:

> The Lockerbie outrage was precisely governed by an international treaty: the 1971 Montreal Convention for the Suppression of Unlawful Acts Against the Safety of Civil Aviation. Libya, the United States, Britain and France had all signed the treaty, which falls under the International Civil Aviation Organization (ICAO), as a specialized agency of the United Nations. The Montreal Convention requires a government to prosecute or extradite any person accused of placing on an aircraft "a device ... which is likely to ... cause damage to it which is likely to endanger its safety in flight."
>
> There were, however, no extradition treaties between Libya and the United States or Britain. The Montreal Convention speaks to this situation by declaring that each party to the treaty agrees that "if it does not extradite" those who are accused, it is "obliged without exception whatsoever and whether or not the offense was committed on its territory, to submit the case to its competent authorities for the purpose of prosecution."
>
> By doing so, Libya thus fully complied with the Montreal Convention. It arrested the suspects, notified the accusing states, asked for evidence, began an inquiry, and invited the United States and Britain to participate. Libya also responded positively to France by offering a high degree of cooperation between the investigations conducted by the two countries.
>
> In addition, the Montreal Convention provides recourse to the International Court of Justice for solving problems related to the interpretation of application of the Convention. The World Court would provide a very visible forum at which the United States, British and French evidence could be presented and assessed. If Libya refused to carry out the judgment of the International Court of Justice, it would be in violation of the United Nations Charter, and action by the Security Council could follow. But in this case the United States and Britain rejected Libya's offer to go to the World Court and instead went directly to the Security Council, requesting the Council to endorse the request for the surrender of the two accused Libyans.[2]

Officially, Libya first brought this case to the ICJ, the principal legal organ of the UN, following the Security Council adoption of Resolution 731 in 1992. It had two aims: to nullify the Security Council resolution and to look into the entire case. The court found no problem, then, in ruling against Libya with regard to the first aim. Nonetheless, many judges, members of the court, found, in their opinions, that although the Security Council resolutions are legal, the issue should have been raised at the court prior to its presentation to the council.

But since the council had already adopted its resolution, Libya had to abide.

The U.S. lawyer presenting his country's case was Edwin Williamson, the legal counselor for the State Department. His argument consisted mainly of a repetition of the accusations against Libya, adding, "The case is presented here because Libya wants to pressure the Security Council towards avoiding the sanctions resolution. Libya did not come here to the Hague to protect its rights, it came here as a result of a political decision to undermine the new Security Council resolution."[3]

In voting against Libya's position, Judge Shigeru Oda agreed with the argument that the Security Council resolutions "have nothing to do with the present case." He concluded his opinion by saying:

> The question remains whether the Security Council resolutions, particularly resolutions 748 (1992) and 883 (1993), which were adopted after the filing of the Application in this case, have any relevance to the present case brought by Libya. In other words, the question whether Libya's 3 March 1992 Application has become without object after the adoption of these 31 March 1992 and 11 November 1993 Security Council resolutions, is totally irrelevant to the case presented by Libya. If there is any dispute in this respect, it should be a dispute between Libya and the Security Council or between Libya and the United Nations, or both, but *not* between Libya and the United Kingdom (and the United States in its respective case).
>
> The effect of the Security Council resolutions (adopted for the aim of maintaining international peace and security) upon member States is a matter quite irrelevant to this case and the question of whether Libya's Application is without object in the light of those resolutions hardly arises.
>
> Even though I found that Libya's Application should be dismissed owing to the Court's lack of Jurisdiction, I nonetheless wanted to express my view that these Security Council resolutions, which have a political connotation in dealing with the broader aspects of threats to the peace or breaches of the peace, have nothing to do with the broader aspects of threats to the peace or breaches of the peace, having nothing to do with the present case, which could have been submitted to the Court as a legal issue which existed between the United Kingdom and Libya, and between the United States and Libya, before the resolutions were adopted by the Security Council.[4]

Judge Oda practically confirmed Libya's claim that this issue was raised by the United States and the United Kingdom as an element of the wider political and diplomatic conflict between the two countries and Libya.

After that early legal loss, Libya hoped the other part of its case would end in its favor: the authority of the court to look into the issue.

The United States and the United Kingdom disputed that right for the court, claiming it had no jurisdiction whatsoever. It took the ICJ about four years before exploding a legal and diplomatic bombshell: The ICJ ruled that it did have jurisdiction. That judgment, as will be seen later, had a major effect in helping Libya transform the positions of the majority of the states and regional organizations. Also, it presented the United States and United Kingdom with a new challenge: find a political solution to a case used politically, or face a political and legal upheaval. They chose the first, and the solution was found.

PART II

Libya's Response

4

Strategy from a Libyan Perspective

Against this backdrop of extensive developments, including the rejection of Libya's position by the ICJ, it is necessary to understand how the Libyans perceive their own country and its history and why they considered the imposed sanctions to be a culmination of events that dated back to the prerevolutionary period.

The Libyans are a people who see everything from a historical perspective. It is surprising to see the importance they give to Western books and publications on history. This insatiable hunger for learning and information related to current events, which might not bear any relation to history, made the Libyans consider every turn of politics as part of a great historical conspiracy that began during colonialism and continues today. Conversely, Americans and Western politicians and diplomats alike, may not consider history the most important element in evaluating events and drawing new policies, as they tend to rely more on a semipragmatic reading of current events.

Any realistic reading of events concerning the United States and Libya should start with the fact that the enmity between the two countries did not begin with the Lockerbie affair. It is part of a historical process that has mushroomed with different aspects and elements of geopolitical and economic events. When the United States, as an emerging world power in the aftermath of World War II, worried about its military bases in Libya, the confrontation took a major turn. These bases, American and others, played a very important role in providing a launching pad for the Western forces in their military campaigns in the Middle East and Africa. Hence, they played a major role in supporting Israel both in the tri partite attack by the United Kingdom, France and Israel against Egypt in 1956 and during the 1967 war in Palestine. The Libyan bases became one of the most important incentives for the revolution and continue to be a reference to the importance the United States and the West attribute to Libya.

At various times in its history, the territory that is now Libya was occupied by different powers. It was part of the Ottoman Empire from 1551 to 1911, serving in the eighteenth century as a base for pirates who, in return for immunity, provided large revenues to the local ruler. Libya was seized by Italy in 1911, but Libyan resistance continued until the 1930s. During World War II, as an Italian colony, it was one of the main battlegrounds of North Africa, passing under an Anglo-French military government when the Axis was defeated in the area in 1943. In accordance with a UN decision in 1951, the country gained its independence as the United Kingdom of Libya, with King Idris I as its ruler.

That situation lasted until the revolution of 1969. Since then in particular, Libya has continued to fear the colonial intentions of world powers, old and new alike.

In their account of their country's history, Libyans recount events dating back to a naval confrontation with the United States between 1800 and 1805. Indeed, "From the halls of Montezuma to the shores of Tripoli" continues to be the beginning verse in the hymn of the U.S. Marines. It was a proud moment for those Marines when they raised the U.S. flag on any part of the "old world." The song's reference to the Marines' 1805 landing in Libya leaves a foul impression in the minds of the Libyans, most notably among the revolutionaries and patriots.

The Libyans, of course, view that event differently, recalling that they destroyed the most important military ship in the American fleet, the USS *Philadelphia*, which led the Americans to enroll some mercenaries from the Western desert of Egypt to take revenge. Those mercenaries invaded Derna but were rebuffed later. That was the first confrontation between Libya and the United States.

The Libyans also note that, for most of the twentieth century, their country remained under the hegemony of four colonizers instead of one. France controlled the southern part because it was contiguous to its colonies in Algeria, Niger and Chad. In the east, near where Libya borders Egypt, Britain established land and air bases designed to ensure its control of the Suez Canal. The United States had established five huge military bases, in addition to other bases for communications and wiretapping, in the western section. Then, there were the Italian settlers who controlled economic life on the coast.

This situation persisted until the outbreak of revolution on September 1, 1969. The revolution's primary task, and one of its main motivations, was to liberate Libya from the occupying foreign presence, be it in the form of military bases and forces or the settlers who possessed the land of the Libyans as a result of colonialism. This first task was achieved when the British were forced to leave on March 28, 1970, soon followed by the Americans on June 11 and the Italians on October 7.

Libya has well-founded and fully realized sensitivities in terms of its strategic position vis-à-vis Africa, a continent at that time newly explored. Europeans had to cross the Mediterranean into North Africa before traveling by land to reach the sub-Saharan parts of the continent. Libya was a major crossing point of entry to Africa.

Libya's political situation as well contributed heavily to the launching of the Libyan revolution. At the time, Libya was a kingdom ruled by a politically conservative monarchy fully aligned with the West, which controlled its will through military pacts which led to the presence of foreign troops and bases on Libyan soil. The British base was so close to Egypt it was used to attack it. American bases existed throughout the country, the most important of which was Wheelus Air Base, the largest military base outside the United States. The Italians still had their old bases almost supported by a large Italian community controlling Libya's economic life.

These factors contributed to the awareness on the part of the Libyans (already fascinated by the beliefs of Nasser and his intentions) of the obstacles to the participation of their country in the calls for Arab unity, then on the rise throughout the Arab world. A group of Libya's youth, led by Muammar Qadhafi, established an underground political movement with Nasserite beliefs. Most members of this group, including Qadhafi himself, infiltrated the army and established the "Free Officers Movement," which in turn led to the 1969 revolution.

One of the aims of this revolution was to expel the foreign military bases, as well as the Italian community, from Libya and to revolutionize the country in order to transform it into a strategically important backyard for Nasser's Egypt, leading in turn to a merger between the two states to become the cornerstone of the ultimate grand Arab unity. This revolution did not aim, at the outset, to rule Libya. Its leaders considered their mission limited to the liberation of the country and unity with Egypt in order to protect the latter, knowing their land was used as a launching pad for attacks against Egypt during World War II as well as the 1956 and 1967 wars.

When the revolution was unable to achieve this fundamental aim due to the untimely death of Nasser in September 1970 and following the changes in the country during the rule of the late President Anwar Sadat, the leaders of the revolution began to learn the hard way some of the traditional ways and means to rule and manage the affairs of their country.

Following these surprises, the revolution involved efforts to formulate and implement economic and social programs in this mostly desert country. Schools, universities and hospitals were built, as well as modern roads and hundreds of thousands of modern homes. Huge industrial and agricultural projects were carried out. Tens of thousands of students were sent abroad for higher studies in developed countries, including the United States, Britain, France, Canada and others. The oil wealth was liberated from the control of foreign monopolies. The country's wealth was distributed fairly, vastly raising the standard of living of its citizens.

The leaders of the revolution could not adjust to a mix of principled ambitions and pragmatic government for short and long periods of time. And although Libya continues to consider itself a target of its enemies, Colonel Qadhafi succeeded in one of the most important accomplishments of his leadership: independent decisions in the most important of all fields, the international field. Some in the West consider these policies too independent for anybody's good. Some Arab leaders feel Qadhafi is one who has no room whatsoever for treachery, leading one to complain that "every leader has room for at least 5% of that, Qadhafi has none, making it very hard on anyone to find a median point between him and the West, to work on." This might have been enough to label him as "crazy," as Sadat did, or "unpredictable," as the elder Bush said, or even "hard to work with," as many Arab leaders have said. He has contributed to those feelings with fiery statements, publicly and privately. His actions, as an interpretation of the theory and philosophy he published in *The Green Book*, which rises to the level of "dreams of the idealistic society," have kept everybody guessing as to what he might come up with. That has led him, at times, to mistake reality with idealism, which has, in turn, led to misrepresentation and misunderstanding abroad, since it is very hard for the foreign observer to distinguish his intentions on either level. And while he might have done some abnormal things during his life, he seems to have become the most misunderstood leader in modern history.

Since the Qadhafi-led revolution in 1969, revolutionary fervor has not left the mind and life of this leader. "The leader of the revolution," as he is being called, continues to live the dream of that young patriotic officer in the army. When Nasser died about a year after the Libyan revolution, no one thought Qadhafi would seriously be left dreaming of the day when that theory would become reality, confronting other Arabs when they rejected his and Nasser's dream of the "one Arab nation."

Without a real experienced leader—sharing his and Nasser's ideals—at his side, the twenty-eight-year-old Qadhafi was shocked at Nasser's death. His address on that occasion reflected that "personal loss.... I am needier than you are for condolences. I feel very strongly today about the loss of Jamal Abdel-Nasser whom I was with yesterday, engulfing me in his big heart and courageous mind while shaking my hand, encouraging and assuring me, and bidding me a last farewell."[1] He took it upon himself to keep Nasser's ideals alive, mainly through continued efforts toward unity with Egypt and other Arab states. Nasser's successor had other plans, leading Qadhafi to intense frustration and further strengthening his feeling of personal loss.

The young revolutionaries were helped by what they discovered in the old regime's files to better understand their country's role and importance. They discovered reports regarding U.S. concerns in their country and region. These concerns were conveyed in a semiofficial manner to Libyan diplomats representing the Libyan royal family of the prerevolutionary era. The United States was, even then, anxious about any union or alliance that would give "enemy" states, such as Nasser's Egypt, which had strong relations with the former Soviet Union, control over more than half of the Mediterranean coast (1900 kilometers in Libya and about 1500 kilometers in Egypt). The result would be firm control over that vital sea, limiting the ability of the U.S. Sixth Fleet to maneuver in the area and practically cutting off a major route of support to Israel.

American fears intensified after the Libyan revolution, when a Libyan-Egyptian union was more feasible. Libya, however, saw different indications, one of which was based on a 1959 CIA report originally prepared for President Dwight Eisenhower but released in the seventies. That report played a very important role in the formulation of modern politics and policies in Libya. It described Libya's role as "a buffer between the Middle East and the Maghreb. It protects, though partially, the Maghreb from the pan-Arabism fever that emanates from Cairo.... And as long as Libya continues to be friendly with the West, the West could control the southern shores and parts of the Mediterranean..."[2] The report recommended intervention to help a regional ally, meaning Tunisia, thwart a coup d'état supported by Nasserite Egypt, against the royal regime.

With Sadat leading Egypt, eager to ally the most important Arab country with the United States and establish peace with Israel, a stunned young Colonel Qadhafi turned to aiding the Arab cause through heavy financial and material support to Palestinian and other Arab organizations and states fighting Israel. He supported, as well, many African causes such as the Pan-African Congress's struggle against apartheid in South Africa. Libya considered them national liberation movements. The United States considered them terrorists.

Qadhafi himself said:

> There is no liberation movement in Africa which Libya has not helped with training, arms and finance. They used to call them terrorist camps. They were Sam Nujoma's camps, Mandela's camps, Museveni's camps, Eyadema's camps, Sadiq al-Mahdi's camps, Turabi's camps, Rawlings's camps, Mugabe's camps and Mozambique's camps. All the African states which are now free and independent had camps in Libya. That is why they said that Libya was a terrorist state and it was setting up terrorist camps. If they are talking about terrorism, then Mandela, Museveni, Kagame, Rawlings, Mugabe, Mozambique, Kabila, Turabi, Sadiq al-Mahdi, Yasser Arafat are all terrorists. Yasser Arafat's camps were also in Libya. They said these are terrorist camps. Unlike Arab countries, African countries said we owe Libya favors and that it is important to the United States. Therefore, we cannot leave it to face America and Britain on its own. The impoverished Africans shouldered their responsibilities. Indeed, they made a decision and implemented it.[3]

Furthermore, Libya supported many other liberation movements in other parts of the world, some in Central and Latin America. The United States felt Libya's footsteps in its backyard, while Britain felt heat from Libya's support of the IRA. The threat was becoming too dangerous for America and Britain.

As politics always necessitate, the British and Americans changed their position and supported these same movements when they took control of their countries while working on the peace process in other cases, such as Northern Ireland and Palestine. And while U.S. presidents urged photo opportunities with these newly allied leaders, they still considered the Libyans terrorists.

At times, the Libyans have been fooled by some of the movements they have supported, for despite the sincerity of many of them, many others might never have existed beyond one or two persons. Some of Qadhafi's aides might have played games with that issue for personal financial gains, although many of them continue to be idealistic in their conduct and control of their departments' budgets. Overexpenditures and financing of some movements might have given Libya more exposure than reality could have provided. Since the idealism behind it all was totally unacceptable to the West, actions by organizations or states helped by Libya gave the impression that Qadhafi and his regime were fully responsible for those actions. And since Qadhafi considered them justified under the banner of liberation movements, he did not try to disprove many of those accusations. He became the leader of a worldwide network of terror by proxy, according to the West. For him, that was not such a shameful accusation, for his idealism provided for fighting oppression and occupation. However, his, or his regime's, involvement in much of what he was accused of was more slogans than realities. Western intelligence reports about what was considered irrefutable information about Libya's responsibility for one operation or another might not be much more than information about some Libyan official claiming responsibility for financial gain. That added to the burden Washington and London laid on Libya. Libya felt self-important for the attention the United States paid to its activities.

Libyan Oil and U.S. Interests

Another element contributing to Libya's policies was, and continues to be, oil. The wealth resulting from wider oil discoveries gave Libya the financial ability for self-support, self-reliance and independence. Libya no longer needed foreign assistance. On the contrary, it was able to employ oil income in providing support to its regional allies, instead of its being used by the occupying powers to support allies of their own. Such was the case since the days of royal rule which led to U.S. control of almost 90 percent of Libya's oil. The percentage changed later although U.S. companies continued to have a substantial share in Libya's oil industry, directly or through subsidiaries operating in other countries.

The role oil has played in the attitude of the United States toward Libya dates to the first days of the Libyan revolution. Five U.S. oil companies have been involved in Libya's oil industry (Occidental, Conoco, Marathon, Amerada Hess and W. R. Grace), providing over 10 billion dollars worth of oil as of 1984. Washington courted Libya as a huge oil field, not as an independent country, home to a people full of needs, dreams and ambitions.

Henry Kissinger, the National Security Adviser to President Richard Nixon and later his Secretary of State, accused the Libyan revolution of triggering the oil crises and raising the price of this vital commodity. The United States was directly impacted by such increases not only because many of its companies (most prominently Occidental) were involved in Libya's oil production, but also because of the reliance on oil imports growing from a convenience to a necessity: In 1947 the United States imported 8.1 percent of its oil consumption; in 1973, the amount grew to 36.1 percent. Stability in the oil market was maintained until the Libyan revolution. Until then, Kissinger remarked, the dominant role among the oil-producing countries was played by essentially conservative governments whose interest in increasing their oil revenues was balanced by their dependence on the industrial countries for protection against external (and perhaps even internal) threats. Qadhafi was free of such inhibitions. He set out to extirpate Western influence.[4]

Revolutionary Libya was not satisfied with mere nationalization of the oil companies and setting its own prices and policies. It moved to implement those prices through the Organization of Petroleum Exporting Countries (OPEC), forcing other oil-producing countries to follow suit, thus creating a new standard for the oil market. It gained the ability to link the sale of oil to political conditions, setting the norm henceforth for other oil-producing governments. It went so far as to initiate a boycott on the basis of those political positions, which led to the oil boycott of the United States and other countries supporting Israel during the 1973 Arab-Israeli war. Europe, depending on imported oil, mostly from Libya and the Gulf states, for 60 percent of its energy requirements, preferred to accept Libya's demands, leaving the United States alone in this economic battle.

This was the first ever-politicalization of this vital commodity. Libya stood to reap the benefits for the Arab people, thus increasing America's disdain. Since then, American and international oil policies have turned the oil market from one of the producers to one of the consumers: a great advantage to the United States.

Washington's worries about revolutionary Libya's oil policies were not principally dealt with on the basis of ideological differences that would turn into confrontations in the future. The U.S. State Department was of the view that third-world radicalism had frustrated Western liberalism. Politicians saw this as an extension of the East-West conflict over spheres of influence. None of those considerations were accorded to the Libyan revolution. Protection of the oil fields was the motivation and the goal.

An interagency paper prepared by a special group of officials in the aftermath of the revolution concluded: "We see no immediate threat to these [oil] interests, although such could result if the regime is threatened, or becomes increasingly unstable, or if there were a real confrontation over Wheelus [Air Base], or in the event of renewed hostilities in the Middle East." Thus, officials drafting that memo recommended by consensus a strategy seeking "to establish satisfactory relations with the new regime.... We seek to retain our military facilities, but not at the expense of threatening our economic return. We also wish to protect European dependence on Libyan oil; it is literally the only 'irreplaceable' oil in the world, from the point of view both of quality and geographic location."[5] Oil policies proved insufficient to deal with a new regime of rebels against the stagnant role played by the oil regimes prevailing in the region. The Americans either did not think the new regime would be able to fulfil its dreams or they were too preoccupied with the much bigger conflict with the Soviet Union in the Far East, mainly its war in Vietnam, so that such a change in a strategically minor country would not really be seen as affecting the balance of power.

Washington seemed to misunderstand the realities of the revolution. It was more concerned with any threat against its immediate interests there than with formulating a long-term strategic policy aimed at an alliance with the nations of the region. Thus, its aim of "retaining the military facilities but not at the expense of threatening our economic return" failed on both counts. Revolutionary Libya was able to set its own conditions for its oil production and sale, while insisting on the full evacuation of the U.S. military from Wheelus and other military bases, along with the evacuation of all other foreign forces. And since that goal was a primary task of the revolution, it then stretched its goal lines further and further while the United States was losing sight of the realities and motivations of this movement. The United States saw the region based on the sole understanding it was able to comprehend: internal politics in the United States, that is the Jewish votes necessitate one sole policy, the preeminence of Israel in the Middle East.

5

A History of Confrontations

The Americans never forgot this defeat in Libya and have maintained enmity ever since the Libyan revolution. Later policies adopted by Tripoli, based on its pan-Arab ideology, further distanced the country from the United States, while Washington struggled to formulate a policy toward Libya. It seemed that early strategic understandings of the area ignored the fact that small countries could still count politically. Washington appears to persist in the belief that the Middle East consists of only two states. These two, the Americans are right in thinking, constitute the only entities that embrace the basic components of a state or a nation. They both have long histories affecting the region. They both enjoy strategic locations and moderately large populations. They are Egypt and Iran. And while the United States was eying Egypt with the aim of distancing it from the Soviet Union, hoping to form an alliance with two states that would create a local claw around this economically important region, Libya was seen as nothing more than an oil field controlled by enemies that could be tamed by a U.S.–friendly Egypt. The United States was unaware that ignorance about Libya could lead to irritations that would later necessitate a containment policy or even confrontation.

Later developments in the Middle East, while further allying Libya with the anti-Israel camp, led the Americans to label this "oil field" as a radical state. Differences continued and added to America's hatred of

Libya and its leader. Libya's turn to European countries for economic and military relations proved hard for the Americans to accept. Thus, Washington decided it would not be able to ignore the revolution and moved to confront it. It developed a campaign to isolate Libya from the Arabs and the rest of the world. In turn, Libya was on a confrontational path as well. Those policies led to the first direct engagement between the military forces of both countries on March 21, 1973, when Libyan jet fighters fired on a U.S. reconnaissance aircraft over the Gulf of Sirt in the Mediterranean. An era of full-fledged American-Libyan confrontation had begun.

During the seventies and the eighties, with the ideological East-West conflict clouding the international horizon, the United States looked hard for any pretext to topple the Libyan regime or, at the very least, destabilize it. It held Libya responsible for many attacks launched against Americans overseas. It accused Libya of establishing a wide network of terrorists. It tried to link the Libyans to any affair it detested.

Then came the Camp David agreements between Egypt and Israel. Anwar Sadat, who ruled Egypt after Nasser's death, had never liked Qadhafi. He wanted to alienate Libya and minimize its ability to obstruct Egypt's peace with Israel. Remembering how supportive Libya had been prior to and during the 1973 war, financially, economically and militarily, Sadat noticed how opposed it was to the peace he was preparing to forge with Israel. And while he expelled the Soviets from Egypt, turning hastily toward the United States for all manner of support, he feared any Libyan effort to support any major internal opposition to his policies and rule, under some pretext of Soviet presence in "Egypt's backyard," although he and his intelligence knew very well how opposed Moscow was to the Libyan policies and how Qadhafi equated the Soviet hegemony to that of the United States, considering it "communist colonialism."[1]

Sadat moved his forces to the Libyan borders and started a mini-war, based mainly on Israeli reports conveyed in a meeting secretly held in Morocco between the directors of the intelligence services of both countries. In that meeting, held in 1977, the Israeli Mossad "produced an implausible story about a conspiracy to assassinate Sadat being hatched by Qadhafi. Sadat took it seriously enough to order what amounted to a brief war against Libya."[2] For nearly a week, Egyptian planes bombarded targets just over the frontier; the publicly announced excuse was that the Russians had been providing the Libyans with such quantities of arms that an invasion of Egypt must be imminent. Menachem Begin, Israel's prime minister in the late seventies and early eighties, mentioned the issue later in a letter sent in the summer of 1982 to Egyptian president Hosni Mubarak, confirming that account.

As if that were not enough of a confrontation between the then 45 million Egyptians and 3 million Libyans, Sadat supported some opposition groups and officers trying to topple Qadhafi. The Americans were not far away since they were presented with a major base from which to initiate an effort aimed at settling the score with the Libyan revolution. Sadat's Egypt was key to the anti–Communist crusade of the Reagan administration, as well as a prized source of effective intervention in difficult areas such as Libya, Chad and Zaire. Some of the American efforts against Libya were initiated from the Sudan as well. Libya was by then facing two of its most important friends and allies during the early days of the revolution: the Grand Egypt and the Sudan of Gaafar Nimeiri. Both were partners in the Union of Arab Republics. These events led Libya to become much more worried about U.S. intentions and presaged a full-scale confrontation on the horizon.

Throughout this period, the United States succumbed to some stories relayed by some leaders of the area who had personal or political agendas and considered Libya an obstacle, although some of those stories were too fictional to be true. One such story was conveyed by Sadat to Zbigniew Brzezinski, Jimmy Carter's National Security Adviser, claiming that "Qadhafi massacred his colleagues."[3]

In late 1979, after Iranian revolutionaries occupied the United States embassy in Tehran, holding its officials hostage for over fourteen months, Libyans attacked the U.S. embassy in Tripoli, setting it ablaze. They were showing support to the Iranian revolution and to the occupiers of the American Embassy. Those events did nothing but raise tension with Washington. The U.S. reaction was to take unilateral harsh measures against Libya. A series of sanctions was unilaterally imposed by the United States in 1981. They included prohibition of export of any military equipment and any equipment used in the aviation industry and import of Libyan oil or oil products. A travel ban was also imposed, severing diplomatic and other relations and freezing Libyan assets. These sanctions are still in effect and are the subject of discussions between the two countries to solve bilateral relations.

The Reagan-Thatcher Doctrine

Then Ronald Reagan came to the White House. This new president saw everything "the American way." He believed that Americans, simply by virtue of being Americans, could do whatever they set their mind to. The first meeting of his administration's National Security Council, on January 21, 1981—the day after his inauguration—put the issue of Libya on the agenda "among other urgent questions."[4] And while the tangibles—the accusations thrown almost daily at Libya—never changed, Reagan felt he should direct the heat straight at Qadhafi. The State Department looked into the issue immediately on an erroneous basis that considered Libya to be among the Soviet Union's proxy states. Secretary of State Alexander Haig worked on the issue personally.

While their efforts failed to topple the revolutionary regime, Washington never forgot its original intention but preferred to calm down as the Reagan administration worked on a bigger scenario: to chase all of America's enemies out of this world. Reagan referred to the Soviet Union as the "evil empire" and dreamed of protecting America from Soviet (and all other) attacks with a grand-scale missile defense system that the press took to calling "Star Wars." On a smaller scale, Reagan's administration conducted run-ins against small states like Libya, Nicaragua and Grenada, with a semiwar, by proxy mostly, against Iran and a politico-economic war against Cuba.

Reagan and his administration considered the fight against Libya one of the most important pillars of their agenda and an integral part of their overall doctrine: to confront the Soviet Union and eliminate its beachheads around the world. This doctrine of confrontation with the so-called evil empire, forcefully supported by Britain's Prime Minister Margaret Thatcher, was based on changing the previous doctrine of the West—containing communism—into putting freedom on the offensive and creating what the Reagan administration called a "worldwide campaign for democracy."

Thus, the new axis of the alliance, that is, Reagan and Thatcher, paid considerable attention to regional allies of Moscow. Libya was mistakenly considered one of those allies. It was labeled a country in the Soviet sphere of influence. An escalation of the confrontation was justified and necessary from that perspective alone. Libya's positions vis-à-vis Israel played only a minor role in the Reagan administration's assessment, publicly at least, although that was the single real problem Washington had with Libya.

To their surprise, officials of the Reagan administration discovered, when they raised the issue with the Soviets, that "Libya might be expendable." A U.S. delegation returned from Moscow to report hints from the politburo that they were not sure they could control Qadhafi. An important Soviet diplomat told a high-ranking U.S. official that Qadhafi was a "madman." Haig was surprised that Moscow "made it clear that Libya was an American problem."[5] This was another miscalculation on the part of the United States since the Libyan-Soviet relation was nothing more than a military client's relation with a supplier based solely on Moscow's financial necessities, not on identical ideological or political understandings or interests. This "new" information was not enough for the United States to back off from Libya. On the contrary, it contributed to a new way of thinking: Libya is a lone wolf, hated by regional and international leaders. Let the United States take care of Libya.

The most important aim to be served by the campaign against Libya would be to alienate it from the main issue in the Middle East: the Arab-Israeli conflict, with the Palestinian issue at its core. On January 17, 1979, David Newsom, a former U.S. Ambassador to Libya, wrote in the *Christian Science Monitor*: "The confrontation between the United States and Libya goes beyond being a conflict with one leader.... It is a confrontation between two fully different views of the Middle East and the world." Thus, the issue was not what Libya did in Libya. Ali Treiki, Libya's foreign minister at the time, recalled that the U.S. Secretary of State in 1980, Cyrus Vance, "informed me during an official meeting I held with him: there is no problem directly with Libya, the only problem we have is your efforts to undermine United States efforts for solving the area's problems."[6]

No other justification for countering the Libyan revolution was found by the Reagan administration. International legalities were on the side of Libya. Rumors about impending "terrorist" attacks by Libyans against Americans were never founded. Tripoli's support of the "liberation movements" was a political issue not directly involving the United States. American businesses in Libya were not threatened despite the daily rhetoric.

As for the British, Libya's support of the Irish Republican Army and the April 17, 1984, shooting of policewoman Yvonne Fletcher from inside the Libyan embassy building in London as the British government claims, though considerable misdeeds, were offset politically by the economic benefits British companies had in Libya. Diplomatic relations had to be, and were, severed, but other relations continued to exist as usual until 1992.

Historic considerations were there, but they did not severely affect relations between the two countries. After the revolution, the British were asked by the ex-king to coordinate with him in order to restore the throne. The British had signed a treaty to protect him in 1953. When the king announced his request, demonstrations in support of the revolution erupted in the streets of Libya while Nasser put his military on high alert. London, therefore, was convinced it had to deal with a new reality with the aim of protecting its economic rather than its military interests. It rejected the king's request and dealt with the revolution in spite of the ideological differences between them. That was more easily done by a country withdrawing from the international scene in favor of the new Western superpower, America, which would not be as wise.

The United States could wait no longer. The United Kingdom, especially under Thatcher, could refuse no Reagan request for support a few short years after Reagan had provided his friend with considerable support to defeat Argentinean military forces in order to restore British sovereignty over the Falklands, an island off Argentina's coast that was under London's rule, a rule which Buenos Aires never officially accepted until the early nineties. That support, ensuring British victory, was the catalyst in restoring Thatcher's popularity inside the United Kingdom and leading to her survival against efforts to remove her from office. That was not something easily forgotten. She was forever indebted to Reagan.

Another element played an important role in Thatcher's alliance with the U.S. president. Her popularity and internal problems were always negatively affected by the policies of the ever-so-strong National Union of Mineworkers, headed by Arthur Scargill. The union had been a power broker in Britain, and Thatcher had been looking for a way to minimize its influence. The opportunity arose when Scargill was pictured visiting with Qadhafi the same day Fletcher was shot. The "Iron Lady" accused her nemesis of receiving financial support from Libya, seized the opportunity, and decided to play that card to pay them both back. Externally and internally, she found personal justification to side with the Americans.

A confrontation with Libya was becoming much more feasible. The only viable issue the United States could raise was freedom of navigation in the Gulf of Sirt. The campaign shifted gear, setting the stage for a semiwar.

The Gulf of Sirt: Internal or International Waters?

While the confrontation became a daily fact of life in the early eighties, major military engagements did not take place until 1986. In a stirring up of old problems, the United States had begun, four months after closing its embassy in Tripoli in 1981, engaging Libyan forces in the Gulf of Sirt. On March 24, 1986, claiming once more that it did not recognize the line Libya had demarcated as the borderline of its internal waters, the United States began what officials called "military maneuvers" in the gulf. Raising the issue as a justification for a confrontation with Libya, the United States ordered its navy to constantly conduct naval exercises in the upper parts of the gulf. It considered the Libyan demarcation a "flagrant violation of international law and of freedom of navigation on the high seas."[7] That was the announced reason for that chapter of the conflict. Secretary of State George Shultz revealed the real motivation: "Qadhafi was a frightening figure to many governments in the region, so it was left to the United States Navy to deal with his unilateral claim to this part of the Mediterranean Sea. This our navy did by periodically notifying all concerned that our ships would, at a specified time, transit through the waters wrongfully claimed by Qadhafi."[8]

Once again, an issue between the two countries became a reflection of history and ambitions. For Libya, the issue of the legality of the demarcation of the line was put aside, despite the American position, shortly after its announcement of the demarcation in 1973. The United States did not materially challenge that position for thirteen years. The United States claimed the gulf should be considered international waters, meaning its fleet could sail in it without obstacles, and accepted only twelve nautical miles as territorial water off Libya's shores. Libya, in turn, considered any entrance into the gulf a preamble to attack. Libya's position was that there was no reason for any country to pass through that water unless it was coming to Libya's shores. It was a closed gulf. And since the United States had many ports on those shores during its occupation of parts of Libya, one of which was a very important communications base, any entrance of military ships into the area meant aggression. That is why Libya declared the gulf "internal water" with a legal status similar to any lake inside a country's territory. Still, Libya declared that only military ships were prohibited from sailing in the gulf, without imposing any prohibitions on commercial ships passing through the gulf or sailing deep toward Libya's shores and ports.

Legally, the norms of international law regarding such waters could justify Libya's position. The United States itself claimed that its territorial waters extend to twenty-four nautical miles, double the standard twelve nautical miles common for all countries of the world.

While any look at the map of the Mediterranean and the Gulf of Sirt leads to questioning the intentions of the United States in such "exercises" or "transit," the Mediterranean Sea provides all ships with an adequate route of transit without having to sail "down" into the gulf. Had that gulf not been Libyan, the U.S. navy would not have needed to transit through it. Another element of provocation was at hand. Libya considered the U.S. positions and maneuvers as efforts to encroach on its sovereignty. In his memoirs, Shultz implied that the United States was setting the stage for a confrontation with Libya. "We set such naval exercises for late March 1986, and we fully expected Qadhafi's air force and navy to respond aggressively. Some press accounts accused the administration of deliberately provoking Qadhafi by our movement into the Gulf of Sirt, but that was not the case."[9] Shultz and other officials failed to provide any convincing justification, for, despite the fact that international law was not on their side, the Libyan navy was not such an intimidating force as to endanger the U.S. Sixth Fleet. There is no other explanation but that of provocation in order to engage Libyan forces. The effort succeeded, leading to a series of confrontations that resulted in Libya's downing of an American fighter plane. Libya's losses consisted of one airplane and a naval boat. And although the atmosphere in the gulf later relaxed, the political and diplomatic escalation kept intensifying to the point where a major attack against Libya became inevitable.

The United States was satisfied that not many countries would cry foul. It used some private communications with some Arab officials as justifications for the escalation, while public statements from almost every government around the world criticized or condemned the American provocations. One of these private conversations was recounted by Shultz, who said that Esmat Abdel Meguid, then Egypt's foreign minister, told him in a meeting on March 28 in Rome, "I hope your blow to Qadhafi will temper his behavior."[10]

The U.S. provocation was a direct response to Qadhafi's declaration in 1986 that the line Libya drew as the border of its internal waters was a "line of death." The United States wanted to challenge a country facing regional and international enemies, including its immediate neighbors. Israel was involved as well. Its then prime minister, Shimon Peres, was playing a major role in the public relations campaign launched by Washington, while his government was providing all types of intelligence as well as technical and logistical support for the United States forces. Rumors floated about possible Israeli attacks against Libya under the pretext of its harboring of terrorists and responsibility for attacks in Rome and Vienna airports in 1985. Peres himself declared to the press in January 1986 that the aim of the United States and Israel was "to keep Qadhafi afraid so he would not frighten others."

Parallel to the military confrontation and American national sanctions, the United States and Israel called for international sanctions to be imposed against Libya. Reagan had increased American national sanctions against Libya, freezing all of its assets and limiting the movement of its diplomatic personnel at the UN to the five boroughs of New York City, although the United States continued to have businesses operating throughout Libya. The value of economic exchanges had exceeded 850 million dollars a year prior to that escalation. By 1984, that was reduced to 336 million dollars, with continued official pressure on the business community to cut economic relations entirely. These new numbers, then, would not substantially affect the United States economy in the way a European boycott of Libya would affect Europe's economy.

The United States called on the UN to adopt similar sanctions. No country accepted that call or followed suit. Even the United Kingdom considered them too harsh, or maybe too unrealistic, for such sanctions could damage its economy and other economies in Europe. Despite her allegiance to Reagan, Thatcher preferred to follow a line different from that of the Americans: political and military confrontation while preserving the economic relationship. This policy helped in keeping a line of contact that proved useful in the efforts of the late nineties. Furthermore, British companies took over many of the businesses the U.S. companies lost because of its national sanctions. Economically, financially and politically, the United Kingdom's wisdom proved more successful than America's angry reactions: Confront; do not boycott.

Looking for the justification for an attack was not a futile process. On April 5, 1986, a bomb exploded at the discotheque La Belle in West Berlin. U.S. soldiers in Germany were regulars at that nightclub. Two of them died while more than 155 were wounded. Barely three days had passed before U.S. officials concluded Libya was responsible for the attack. They claimed they had intercepted communications from the Libyan embassy in East Berlin to Tripoli, supposedly reporting the success of the operation. The United States found the justification it was longing for. It considered this information as the basis for a renewed campaign against Libya. However, no U.S. official revealed this information, on the basis of its "sensitivity." Although many Americans and non-Americans alike questioned the validity of the claim, the United States found an easy target. Its officials, including Vice President George Bush, Shultz and the U.S. Ambassador to the United Nations at the time, Vernon Walters (a former general and deputy CIA director), toured the world to explain their campaign. They noticed the absence of any substantial public statements of support for Libya, though many criticized the proportion of the U.S. response. Moscow, which was still expected to oppose American military adventures around the world, chose calculated silence to express its position on the issue.

The fervor of the revolution had not yet calmed in Libya. Its relations with neighboring states were neither as they should have been nor as they later became, that is to say, normal. Egypt was still feeling its way to balance its peace with Israel with its Arabism and needed leadership, leading to uneasiness with Libya. The Sudan was still a country ruled by an ally of Egypt, Colonel Gaafar Nimeiri, who was an ally of Qadhafi and his colleague in support of the late Nasser before he turned his full support to Sadat, thus becoming Qadhafi's enemy. The borders with Chad continued to be an issue of conflict that led to military confrontations between the two countries. France fully supported Chad prior to U.S. material help.[11] Chad had become the base for training and support for Libyan opposition groups and a launching pad for those trainees in an effort to topple the regime.[12] Tunisia was still considered too pro–West to have good relations with a revolution, and its then president, Habib Bourguiba, was not only getting old but also uneasy about the young revolutionary Qadhafi. Algeria never felt it could deal with Qadhafi, although their positions on general Arab issues were almost identical. In short, Libya was surrounded by conflicts that resulted in its inability to effectively confront the provocations and escalations of a superpower feared by all of its neighbors and the rest of the world, the United States of America. All these neighbors participated or acquiesced at one time or another in failed efforts to topple Qadhafi.

America's Might Is Right

On the morning of April 14, 1986, the UN Security Council met in response to Libyan and Arab requests to deal with the escalation of tension between Libya and the United States. Libya's representative, Ragab Azzarrouk, made a statement predicting a military attack against his country within hours. That statement explained the escalation of public attitudes taking place in the United States. In Washington, while policy and military planning meetings were preparing for the confrontation, the Soviet deputy ambassador was informing U.S. officials that his country understood what was happening but had to call on the Security Council to meet if an attack was launched. In turn, the U.S. officials understood the Soviet position and considered it positive. However, no Soviet requests were presented in New York. Even rhetorical diplomacy in support of Libya was something the Soviets could not accept. Libya faced a quagmire. It had to confront one superpower without the support or encouragement of another. Libya faced it alone.

Seven hours after the Libyan statement in the council, shortly after midnight Tripoli time, residents of the Libyan capital heard and felt huge explosions nearby. Using the La Belle incident as a pretext, the United States sent sixteen F1–11 jet fighters out of British bases to launch an attack against Libya. Thatcher acquiesced to America's requests to use its air bases, although she knew the British people were opposed to such an action. She had also participated in the public relations campaign justifying the attack. Thatcher advised Reagan to proclaim the attack an act of self-defense, using for justification Article 51 of UN Charter. President Reagan discussed the more important motivation in his address to the public at 9:00 P.M. Eastern Time on April 14, two hours after the attack, officially announcing it[13]: "Colonel Qadhafi is not only an enemy of the United States. His record of subversion and aggression against the neighboring states in Africa is well documented and well known." He went on to mention incidents where the policies of the two countries were on a confrontational course, including Libya's support of what the United States considered terrorism (the same type of activities that later, in Central America, the United States would call "freedom fighting").

The right of self-defense claimed by the United States, according to Article 51 of the UN Charter, was challenged inside and outside the Security Council.[14] Interpretations of that article insist the legitimacy of self-defense emanates from a consideration of the Charter as a whole since this Charter is aimed at organizing relations between states. It is conditioned on a clear military attack by one country against another, giving the attacked country the right to defend itself. Some American legal experts, such as Richard Falk in his book *War Crimes*, identified that attack as "the military forces of one country crossing the international borders." A statement by a senior American official claimed the attack was based on "preventive self-defense." There is nothing in international law called "preventive self-defense." One hundred and forty years ago, the United States explained self-defense as an "immediate and urgent necessity that does not allow enough time to choose the instrument." Where was this urgent need that allowed the United States to attack Libya on April 15, an effort planned and coordinated far ahead of any justification? The United States had intentionally distanced itself from any choice of possible instruments for a peaceful solution.

Following the direct aerial attack targeting Qadhafi personally, the United States continued its escalation against Libya through a combination of efforts. One issue that was raised was an accusation that Libya was building a chemical weapons factory in a town called Rabta. It later became known as the Rabta factory. At a later stage, when many neighboring countries, hoping to calm the situation in the region, gave the United States some type of assurance that the factory was not as claimed—that it was merely a pharmaceutical factory—the Americans settled down.

With the escalation of public rhetoric, many officials were concluding publicly that the attack had "tempered" Qadhafi and that Libya's involvement in terrorism was being reduced. They considered the aerial attack a success, though not the final blow. They were not satisfied that, despite the attack and the confrontations in the Gulf of Sirt, along with U.S. sanctions, the Libyan regime did not fall and Qadhafi weathered the storm and stayed in power. Thatcher, of all people, reflected on the attack, stating, "This initial response was probably too negative. Certainly the Americans thought so."[15]

When the Lockerbie crisis developed in the early nineties as the next major offensive against revolutionary Libya, many Libyans sarcastically referred to the raids as Locker (A) and Locker (B). Although the air raids of 1986 led some to raise voices asking whether "they will lead Qadhafi to become a statesman instead of a revolutionary,"[16] the Libyan leader was working on two fronts: rhetorically escalating the confrontation and adding another adjective to the official name of his country. Libya already had the longest name of any country in the world: the Socialist People's Libyan Arab Jamahiriya. The new name had the word "great" added at the beginning. The belief was: We were attacked by two great powers, so we must be great ourselves. The country's official name became "the Great Socialist People's Libyan Arab Jamahiriya."

PART III

The International Response

6

Libyan Counteroffensive

As the Libyans accurately perceived the prevailing international situation in the early nineties as the most important facilitator of the Western campaign and the eventual imposition of sanctions, the historical evaluation of that period would prove that, had the vacuum created by the disintegration of the Soviet bloc not existed, many countries in the UN Security Council would not have followed the United States and the United Kingdom in their call to impose sanctions against Libya no matter how strong a case they presented in their accusations regarding Pan Am Flight 103.

Since political circumstances provided the United States the opportunity to easily manage the achievement of what it longed for, different political circumstances proved the American case was not that strong, as was shown in the voting in the council to impose the sanctions. Had the United States waited a few years, or even a few months, or had it presented its case a few months or years prior to that period, such an outcome would not have been achieved.

Therefore, the timing of the accusations against Libya was quite important for Washington. The Eastern bloc had begun disintegrating in the late eighties. One European communist government after another was falling to demonstrators calling for the removal of the Iron Curtain. The Berlin Wall was destroyed in November 1989, officially signaling the end of the post–World War II era. A "new world" was emerging, culminating in the disintegration of the Soviet Union into fifteen independent countries and a move by the new governments in the countries that were until then members of the Warsaw alliance to align themselves with the West.

While these strategic evolutions were taking place throughout the world, Saddam Hussein of Iraq was committing another catastrophe. Two years after he declared complete victory in his war against Iran—a war he could not have won without U.S. support—he turned his attention toward Kuwait. Many theories exist to explain his new miscalculation, ranging from the need to employ his strong army somewhere outside the country in order to prevent it from moving against his rule to his need for hegemony over the gulf states in order to become the new shah of the region (a reason also given for his war with Iran). The United States, under the leadership of a foreign policy expert in the person of George H. W. Bush, would not trust him enough to allow such a privilege. Saddam moved on August 1, 1990, to take over Kuwait, a tiny country that had supported him financially, politically and logistically during his war with Iran. The Iraqi leader miscalculated the possible American response to his move. He thought Americans would not dare confront him in a land war and that they would accept Iraqi occupation of Kuwait as they did Syria's presence in Lebanon. To Saddam's surprise, the United States response was swift and confrontational. Tens of thousand of troops were flown to Saudi Arabia within hours in an operation called Desert Shield. Within five months, the United States had managed to round up half a million soldiers from thirty-three countries to participate in a new operation: Desert Storm. The aim was to liberate Kuwait. In the process, the Iraqi infrastructure was almost totally destroyed.

The Soviet Union, though facing major problems internally and with its satellite countries, was still a unified country in 1990. But because of these problems, which added greatly to its economic weakness, it was looking for a way toward coexistence with the United States in a reformed bipolar world. Thus, the Soviets had to give in to the Americans, hoping, in turn, to benefit economically either directly from the United States or through the international monetary and financial institutions heavily influenced by the United States. Saddam's illogical hope of reigniting the East-West conflict did not materialize. Moscow did not support him, resisting the temptation to reinvigorate an East-West confrontation that was giving way to an East-West political and economic detente. Moscow supported the United States with extensive military information about its longtime ally. The international scene was set for the so-called new world order, a Bush doctrine aimed at organizing the post–cold-war era.

Desert Storm was strikingly stormy in its success. The first war in the post–Cold War era was swiftly won by the United States and its allies, confirming its military superiority. In August 1991, less than five months after that victory, and while Moscow was preoccupied with a power struggle around the Soviet leader Mikhail Gorbachev, a group of military, intelligence and party officials felt they could restore the old and stagnant communist rule that had survived for eighty-five years. They were opposed to the reforms envisioned by Gorbachev, who was criticized by the reformists as well for not being swift enough in his endeavors. The group chose the timing of their coup to coincide with Gorbachev's vacation in the Crimea. They surrounded him and his loyal bodyguards, holding them hostage while they ordered the army to take over the streets, the official buildings of Russia and other republics of the union. While local support of the coup was weak, international recognition was limited to a handful of countries: Cuba, Iraq and Libya. The rest of the world either condemned or observed.

Little did the coup leaders know that the reformers would take over the streets themselves, refusing the coup and calling for measures Gorbachev had considered premature. Many army units refused orders to occupy official buildings, one of which was the so-called White House, the seat of the Russian parliament. The most visible resistance came from Boris Yeltsin, a staunch reformer who hated Gorbachev. Yeltsin defiantly stood over a tank sent to occupy his offices and defied the order. That was a strong sign of the inability of the coup leaders to gain full loyalty of the army. Washington noticed that the Russians were aligning themselves with Yeltsin. When the leaders of the coup acknowledged their failure, Gorbachev returned to Moscow. Yeltsin had other ideas and thus began a process to end the Soviet Union, humiliating Gorbachev before forcing him to resign on Christmas 1991, officially ending the existence of the "other superpower" by the end of that year.

While that turmoil was developing, the Bush administration was shaping its view of the new world. Bush had personally informed Gorbachev of his new doctrine on September 9, 1990, when, at the height of major transformations in the Soviet bloc and while the coalition forces led by the United States were amassing in the gulf, Bush and Gorbachev held a summit meeting in Helsinki. One of the most important items on the agenda was an introduction by Bush of his new world order. The context chosen by Bush for this introduction was the issue of the possible participation of Soviet forces in Desert Storm. Bush recounted: "I pointed out that United States tradition was to say the Soviets had no role to play in the Middle East. This policy had changed. The world order I see coming out of this is United States and Soviet cooperation to solve not only this but other problems in the Middle East, I said. The closer we can be together today, the closer the new world order.... I want to work with you as equal partners in dealing with this. I want to go to the American people tomorrow night to close the book on the Cold War and offer them the vision of this new world order in which we will cooperate."[1]

The cooperation Bush envisioned included the achievement of "a new era free from the threat of terror, stronger in the pursuit of justice, and more secure in the quest for peace. ...Today that new world is struggling to be born, a world quite different from the one we've known. A world where the rule of law supplants the rule of the jungle. A world in which nations recognize the shared responsibility for freedom and justice. A world where the strong respect the rights of the weak."[2] What Bush did not say was: a world where might is right; a world where the United States is the lone superpower; a world where everyone has to respect America's wishes.

Gorbachev shared the view that the United States misunderstood the developments of the world and dealt with them through conceptions "that did not point forward to the future but in many respects were anchored in the past; the past was their source of nourishment." He insisted that the language stubbornly repeated—namely that "the Western side was victorious and the East was defeated"—is accompanied by "arrogance as expressed in Western policies." Perhaps more expressive of U.S. policies is the last Soviet leader's comments that "problems of civilizations as a whole remained on a subsidiary or tertiary level as unpleasant matters that could be managed by taking measures of a partial nature that would not be burdensome for the United States."[3] Libya practically fits within the general framework of this description that Gorbachev saw Bush wanted to implement.

Finding Libya an easy target, the United States never missed an opportunity to identify that country with the rebels against the New World Order. Libya criticized Iraq's occupation of Kuwait but condemned Desert Storm. It continued to oppose the efforts led by the United States to launch a new peace process in the Middle East. It also criticized the New World Order for assigning the United States the role of international policeman. Its support of the coup in the Soviet Union was exemplified by the Americans. Nothing it said helped ease tension with the United States. The Bush administration itself made sure it would alienate Libya through its efforts to build the coalition to confront Iraq. The Libyans interpreted that as an effort intended to force them into the camp of the new rejecters of the world and label them, along with Iraq, Iran, North Korea, and Cuba, among others, as "rogue states." There was no effort to explore the possibilities of change. Libya felt endangered; it seemed that Bush's doctrine was nothing but a renamed and retooled continuation of Reagan's.

After Indictments, Libya Reviews the Scene

With the November 14, 1991, indictments came the latest chapter in the long confrontation with Libya. Many theories about this chapter of history can be justified. One thing can not be challenged: The United States found the momentum it was looking for. Justly or not, some evidence led investigators, one way or another, to accuse two Libyans of committing the crime of placing explosives on Pan Am Flight 103 while en route from Europe to the United States. Libya's press and private investigations challenged the evidence to no avail. However, a United States emerging from major historical victories was not about to let this opportunity to severely punish Libya slip from its hands.

Libya needed to review this situation from all aspects. A political analysis was conducted in preparation for a response to these developments. Days of meetings and exchanges resulted in one unanimous conclusion: Revolutionary Libya is the target.

The Libyans concluded that their revolution was a major obstacle to the implementation of what they perceived as a Western plan for the Arab nation. After all, Libya had, for a long time, effectively opposed all actions aimed at the implementation of the "Arab surrender plan" through the Palestine cause, commonly known as the Middle East problem or the Arab-Israeli conflict. Accordingly, whatever happened since the 1973 war was directed toward one end: for Israel's requirements to reach Libya.

This view might require an explanation to many in the West. The Libyans and all nationalists in the Arab world believe that every political process in the area, be it cause or effect, must involve Israel. The United States, especially since 1973, has not tried to dispel such notions. Libya noticed that, since the occupation of Palestine, the Zionists have called for direct negotiations and secure borders, while the Arabs called for the liberation of Palestine until 1967, after which time the call became: eliminating the effects of aggression. Then came the 1973 war, which did not succeed in answering either call. All that was achieved was direct negotiations and the beginning of Arab talk about secure borders. The Arab-Israeli war realized Israeli demands, starting with the Egyptian-Israeli negotiations at "kilometer 101," leading to the Camp David process and its results.

Despite regional tensions and many problems with their neighbors, the Libyans believed they managed to overcome the problems forced upon them, forcing the West into a direct confrontation. Since Libya did not cease its support of the Palestinian movements and the support of other national liberation movements in Africa, Asia and, most important, Central America, a direct confrontation with the West became a reality. This conflict was built around the previous provocations in the Gulf of Sirt and the support of the national liberation movements labeled as terrorism. The whole effort grew to a climax called the Lockerbie issue, which emerged as Libya's best tool to achieve what they had failed to accomplish through other means. The international scene after the fall of the Soviet Union made that much more possible.

With regard to the core of the Lockerbie issue (the request to hand over the two suspects), the Libyan officials considered it, in the big picture, a small part of the whole process of escalation against their country. Although they did not oppose the principle of the handover with the right conditions, they considered any handover, under the then-prevailing atmosphere and conditions, a major surrender which could lead to a whole new effort to topple the regime. Their attention was directed at creating those right conditions while trying to avoid the storm that was blowing over the world: the new world order.

Libya's Internal Considerations

Much has been said about the internal considerations preventing the handover of the two suspects to the West. Other than the direct threat to the regime if those two were to be forced to cooperate with Western intelligence, many in the West spoke about tribal complications preventing the Libyan leadership from surrendering them for trial. Yet, surprisingly, this tribal factor was not an obstacle to the handover in the early stages of the issue and definitely not when the actual handover took place. The external dangers the regime faced if it handed over the two without guarantees far superseded any other internal considerations.

For Qadhafi and most Libyans as well, it was hard to underestimate the dangers they would have faced had they been too negligent in their response to this crisis. The United States had played a significant role in trying to topple the regime. It had trained some Libyan opposition groups in Chad and in the United States to implement such efforts. The CIA had recruited most of these opposition groups along with some individuals in order to topple revolutionary Libya. That effort never ceased, and Tripoli watched how frequently some of those individuals would report to the United States, claiming knowledge of the regime's involvement in terrorism. The Lockerbie case included testimony the United States claimed was provided by two former Libyan officials. The trial itself proved one Libyan dissident to be unreliable in his claims against the accused. What would prevent the Americans from trying to force or incite the accused to cooperate on this or other issues, fabricating testimony similar to what the United States already had? The guarantees were an important necessity, and it became clear that without them Libya would never agree to a handover.

To deal with the legalities concerning the two suspects, Libya began an effort at assembling an international team of defense lawyers. The group met in Tripoli during the early weeks of October 1992. The focus of their effort was discussing details and arrangements needed in case the suspects were to be tried by a Scottish court. Scottish law seemed acceptable; the venue, however, would continue to be a problem. A trial before a U.S. court seemed out of the question. The Libyans felt that the negative media attention could influence not only jurors but defense attorneys. Libya witnessed a ferocious public attack against an American lawyer when it was thought he might participate in giving counsel to the accused. The defense attorneys were deeply concerned over the possible prejudicial effect publicity in the United States and Scotland would have on prospective jurors and about the absence of the usual arrangements for extradition due to the prosecution's refusal to reveal the evidence it intended to use in the trial. It thus became clear that the concerns of the defense attorneys were rational and justified.

Libya Prepares for the Counteroffensive

As far as the Libyans were concerned, the United States was not acting on a legal basis in looking at the Lockerbie case. They considered the action political, while the case raised was supposed to be legal. They felt the United States was actually stating three requirements, none of which involved the Lockerbie case. They required that Libya should:

1. cease all types of support to national liberation movements considered by the West as terrorists;
2. cease opposition to the surrender process—a term Libya used to describe the Middle East peace process—since Libya's objective voice was irritating to some Arabs who supported the U.S. initiative;
3. cease any effort to build any self-relying military capabilities.

These requirements were communicated to the Libyans through many official and semiofficial channels and meetings, as well as through some mediators' efforts. This is what Libya strongly believed, and that's what Libyans built their counteroffensive around.

To deal with this problem, the Libyans formed a committee of top officials to manage the issue. Headed by Muntasser, its members were Muhammad Azwai, then ambassador to Morocco; Abdel Ati Al-Obeidi, then deputy foreign minister; and Colonel Yussuf Al-Debri, then head of the intelligence service. The formation of this high-level committee reflects its mission, which was to tackle this issue from all perspectives, explore Libya's situation and friendships around the world and launch a counteroffensive in order to reach a viable and favorable solution. The committee led Libya's efforts to consolidate and strengthen this previously misunderstood situation.

The committee and other Libyan institutions moved quickly to work on both external and internal fronts. On the external front, Libya's first step was to deal with its immediate neighbors. To normalize relations with Egypt was most important to prevent it from being used against Libya in the event of military attacks. In a matter of weeks, Libyan officials worked with their Egyptian counterparts to achieve bilateral agreements in many fields of interest for the Egyptians, mostly economic. What helped was that relations with Egypt had moved during the late eighties, after president Mubarak settled the tensions his predecessor had created all around, from enmity to mere absence of relations. At the height of the escalation during the previous years, Libya had arranged for the revitalizing of relations with Cairo, leading the Egyptians to play an important role in calming the United States regarding some issues, one of which was the Rabta factory.

As for other neighbors, relations with Tunisia had not faced any major problems since the new president, Zein el-Abedine bin Ali, had come to power in November 1987. Meanwhile, Algeria was facing the early stages of its internal turmoil and was unable to interfere even if it wanted to. Relations with Chad had become very friendly, and Chad could no longer be used as a base against Libya. In the Sudan, a new regime was taking over following the fall of president Nimeiri. The new leaders would not allow their country to be used against Libya.

Countries in southern Europe, such as Italy, France and others—even as far north as Germany—were too reliant on Libyan oil to get involved in military confrontations.

On the internal front, Libya moved to consolidate the popular base and support for the government, preparing the population for a long battle since the only winning card Libya had was the time factor. This time factor was considered by the Libyans to be the only way out. Officials felt it advisable to wait while reorganizing their relations with other countries and their overall situation. The post–cold-war world was, Libya felt, divided into three camps: the afraid, the surprised and the stunned at what did, and will, happen. No one could say no to the United States, including Russia, which was living one of the most unsettling periods in its history. There was a need to await its eventual mental return to reality. Europeans and others needed to formulate new policies for the new international situation, realizing the aspects and consequences of what was happening while studying the possible forthcoming dangers before adopting new policies that could be considered closer to being correct—not necessarily fully correct. Then and only then would this whole process reflect itself on the political scene, including Libya's case. Only time, Libya officials felt, would help Libya with the United States.

In order to normalize the international community at the UN, Libya chose Azwai as its representative in New York. A calm and realistic man with a charming personality, he was always looking toward modernization while understanding the realities of his country, all while holding to his (and the revolution's) principles. The late king of Morocco, Hassan II, described the choice of Azwai as extremely important for that period of the conflict. Azwai's mission was to explain Libya's position to the international community, making sure it stayed calm while his colleagues were working on their program, preparing the grounds for the inevitable solution. He later concluded: "After the long years of the committee and the country's work, Libya and the West were surprised to discover that Libya's enemies were not as numerous as previously thought, and its friends were much more than previously thought to be."

After completing his assignment, Azwai went back to his old post as justice minister in 1997, contributing mightily to the legal efforts while still politically involved in the committee's work. He was later assigned to represent his country in London as a high-level ambassador to the United Kingdom, the first since the solution was reached and a choice that provided assurance to London that Libya was serious in its endeavor to improve relations to the utmost. He contributed as well to the tripartite negotiations with the United States and United Kingdom and later bilaterally with the United States.

One element, however, was not working in Libya's favor: the situation in Russia. Only a few months had passed since the coup d'état there was defeated. Some Libyan officials had gone to the Soviet embassy in Tripoli to congratulate the new government. That support made a negative impact on the victorious leaders in Moscow, who were at that time looking very hard for American support. Both factors of support, combined with the historical distaste in Moscow for the revolutionary Libya, led to a Russian role supportive of U.S. moves. The Libyans had to wait while making sure Russia would not fully align itself with the West against them, hoping that further transformations in the world would lead it back to opposing the United States. At the same time, Libya would not expect itself to be a reason for enmity between the United States and Russia.

Libya Begins Implementation

Libyans planned and executed a layered, increasingly sophisticated response. It would follow two tracks: satisfy the demands of the Security Council resolutions (other than the handover for the time being) while asking the regional organizations to adopt a favorable position strengthening Libya's stand vis-à-vis the West. With the issue of a handover of the Lockerbie suspects on the back burner, awaiting developments on the international scene, work had to concentrate on contributing to this transformation in order to turn the table around: the United States and the United Kingdom would be isolated, then Libya would be able to claim international support.

The results of such an effort would lead to a change of attitude. Steadfastness would turn the present situation into a different reality. The pariah state, as Libya was labeled by the Americans, would become one they could deal with.

Some changes had to take place. The image of Libya had to be transformed in order to enable the country to adjust to the new realities in the post–cold-war era. The substance of Libya's policies, therefore, would have to adjust to these realities without any surrender of the basic principle: Israel was not a state Libya could deal with, despite what Libya called the "surrender of the Palestinians."

One major aspect of the American-Libyan problem, the issue called terrorism, was due to face inevitable changes contributing later to the solution. Most liberation movements in Africa became ruling governments, and their relations with the United States were later based on government-to-government relations, with the United States more actively seeking those relations. And while the Palestinian Liberation Organization (PLO) headed toward peace with Israel, consequently gaining American recognition, the other Arab "liberation movements" had become almost nonexistent, except for Hezbollah in Lebanon, whose situation was totally different; it almost fully relied on Iran and was in no need of Libyan support. What remained of movements in the area were mostly Islamists which Libyan ideology could not deal with due to their enmity with the vital basis of that ideology: that is, Arab nationalism. In the rest of the world, most movements either gave up or turned into a political struggle from within the existing political systems. The very few countries still opposed to the United States were too busy trying to survive U.S. econo-political offensives with the absence of the umbrella that provided them with some security, however nominal that security might have been.

However, one terrorist continued to be a minimal obstacle until 1998. That summer, press accounts talked about the well-known Sabri

Al-Banna, better known by his nom-de-guerre, Abu Nidal, arriving in Egypt and being held there. Later, it was said Egypt had sent him away from the country. His whereabouts continued to be a mystery, as they had always been—that is, until he was killed by the Iraqi regime while in Baghdad, weeks prior to the U.S.–led war toppling Saddam Hussein and his regime. However, one fact is confirmed. The Libyans asked him in the summer of 1998 to leave Libya, and he did. That was the last actual contact Libya had with those labeled terrorists. No accusations were directed at Libya for harboring terrorists after that. In 1999, the U.S. State Department's annual report on terrorism shyly acknowledged, "There is no evidence of Libyan involvement in recent acts of international terrorism."[4] That same report said that Abu Nidal is believed to have moved to Iraq in 1998.

Libya with Britain: IRA and Fletcher

Toward the end of 1993, as part of their efforts to satisfy demands, the Libyans asked Ghali to arrange for the first Libyan-British meeting in order to provide the information needed by the United Kingdom on Libya's support of the IRA. It took the two countries over two years and five exchanges of questions and answers before the British authorities felt satisfied.

At the outset, it was clarified by the Libyans in their direct communications with Ghali that, in the absence of trust, they should know in advance what they would get in return for their cooperation with the British government. Libya was concerned that the United Kingdom would not have a positive reaction to this cooperation since it would prefer to accommodate the United States. Ghali halfheartedly managed to convince the Libyans that all they would be able to get would be, as he remembered in his autobiography, "a receipt, a document declaring that this case is closed." He could not get that commitment from the British at the outset, since he had asked for it only passively. What he promised the Libyans was nothing more than his personal expectation.

The Libyans had no alternative but to engage in the process. All Libya could hope for was that the British would oblige them after they proved their seriousness. Five secret meetings were held, mainly in Cairo. Libya provided the British government the information and documents it needed regarding its relationship with the IRA. The issue was settled, although the British government was not quick in responding to Libya's requests for an official document stating that fact.

Ghali was asked by the Libyans to press for that "receipt." However, it wasn't until December 1995 that the British government agreed to provide a positive response to Libya's cooperation. Originally, Hurd did not agree to provide a British letter. He provided only a verbal message while the UN Secretary General "would provide Libya with a written document." Finally, and after Libyan insistence, the British ambassador to the UN informed Ghali on November 20, 1995, that his country had received all the information it had requested from the Libyans "but insisted that my letter not imply that Britain had dissociated itself from the United States case." Ghali responded: "It is my letter, not yours. Therefore, I am responsible for its contents, not you."[5] Later, the British Government elected to issue that acknowledgment in a document of its own, saying that, qualifying with:

> There remain gaps and omissions in the information given to the United Kingdom, but when the Libyan disclosures are considered in their entirety, we are satisfied that they have largely met our expectations. We acknowledge that the Libyan readiness to answer our questions is a positive step towards its implementation of the relevant Security Council resolutions, in particular towards its renunciation of terrorism, a path which we hope it will continue to follow.

The British government made sure this statement was not, on its own, to be considered a call for lifting the sanctions.

> Libya has answered our questions in the context of just one of a number of demands placed on it by the post-Lockerbie Security Council Resolutions. We remain committed to the United Nations sanctions against Libya until such time as Libya has complied with those demands, in particular that it must surrender those accused of the Lockerbie bombing for trial in Scotland or the US.[6]

After the closure of the IRA file, Libya continued to clean up its act in preparation for the more important solution. Slowly, the negative labels were removed from Libya's name. A British internal review noticed this change in Libyan behavior on many issues, one of which related to the accusation that Libya was trying to acquire weapons of mass destruction. The United Kingdom, and consequently the United States, were satisfied with Libya's actions in this field. However, no positive signal was revealed until February 10, 1996, in the House of Commons, when a member asked Robin Cook, the foreign secretary:

> MR. FLIGHT: What information, if any, does the Foreign Secretary have on the production of biological and chemical weapons in other parts of the Near East? I am thinking in particular of Syria and Libya, which are a factor in the stability of the area and the peace treaty.
>
> MR. COOK: I am not aware of such production in Syria. Libya, as the

Honorable Gentleman knows, is also subject to very tight sanctions, one of the aims of which is to ensure that there is no possibility of that country developing any chemical or biological weapons.

Another issue remained on the British-Libyan agenda: the Fletcher case. London never included this issue in its conditions presented at the UN, nor did it present it to Libya when discussions were held on the IRA issue. This case would resurface in 1999 only after Libya handed over the two suspects in the Lockerbie case. It became a focal point in the effort to resume diplomatic relations between the United Kingdom and Libya.

In the summer of 1999, London passed a message to the Libyans, through both countries' ambassadors in New York, expressing willingness to discuss the remaining bilateral issues. It suggested the Libyan side be represented by Obeidi, who was by then ambassador to Italy, while the director of the Middle East department in the foreign office would represent the British side. Libya did not hesitate. It took both countries no more than three short meetings before Obeidi visited London and the final touches were made to the agreement. Diplomatic language was drawn through which London would claim full Libyan responsibility for the shooting of Fletcher, while Libya would accept only certain partial responsibility for the fact that something had happened in front of its embassy.

On November 22, 1999, Cook informed the House of Commons that Libya had paid compensation to the Fletcher family. Therefore, the last obstacle was removed, and ambassadors would be exchanged between both capitals. The British ambassador went to Tripoli the following month. Prior to that announcement, many British companies returned to Libya. British Airways, which had never flown to Libya prior to the 1984 break in relations, had already added that destination to its schedule in September. British businessmen became regular visitors to Libya. Normalcy seemed to prevail.

Libya with France: The UTA Flight

The UTA problem took a little longer than expected before a solution was reached. One obstacle at the time was the ambiguity of France's requests to Libya. Although the process of exchanging information regarding the UTA flight was gaining momentum, Paris did not have a clear idea whether that was all it wanted from Libya or whether other issues should be raised. Libya moved early to find a solution to the UTA issue with France. In the spring of 1993, Libya handed the UN Secretary General a file on their enquiry. Ghali transferred that file immediately to the French government. It was not satisfied. A letter from the French judge in charge of that enquiry, J. L. Bruguière, concluded that "the content of the documents produced as constituting the Libyan file on the enquiry are inconsistent and the documents therefore have no probative value. There are even anomalies in some documents."[7]

Many exchanges followed, including contacts at the highest levels. In March 1996, Qadhafi sent a letter to the French president. In that letter, the Libyan leader undertook to respond to the French demands. He stated that the French judge would be allowed, by Qadhafi's own authorization, to continue his inquiry freely in Libya, and guaranteed that he would be accorded "every facility and assistance during the necessary duration of his mission." In response, the French government informed Libya it was sending Bruguière to continue his investigation and that he was traveling to a Tripoli maritime port aboard a French military vessel. The Libyans reacted furiously: Did Bruguière, they wondered, imagine he was coming as some sort of liberator? Libya refused this arrangement. The French realized their mistake and arranged for the judge to travel through Tunisia. Had they insisted on their arrangement, the whole process would have been aborted by the Libyans. Bruguière's mission was successful.

The political will and legal possibilities provided for a quick solution. Politically, France had come to believe that Libya had changed. The issue of the Ouzo strip on Libya's southern borders with Chad came to a solution acceptable to all parties, including France and the United States, while the newly elected French president Jacques Chirac was looking to recover his country's old standing in Africa. A solution to the UTA issue would lead to improved relations between the two countries and could put them arm in arm in the new French endeavor.

As for the legal aspect of this issue, the French judiciary system provides for trial in absentia, meaning the more complicated issue of handover would not be insisted upon by the French authorities. The Libyans accepted such a trial because they only looked for the closure of a file that was one of the requirements of the resolutions that imposed sanctions. This file was officially closed, in Libya's view, although the French created a blunder later on when discussions were held in the Security Council to adopt the British-American acceptance of a Lockerbie trial in the Netherlands. The French ambassador insisted then that the new resolution include a call on Libya to fully satisfy French demands. Everybody was surprised, including the ambassadors of the United States and the United Kingdom. A sentence to that effect was eventually included. The Libyans raised the issue with Paris but were satisfied with an answer confirming this would not mean new demands but an assurance that all items were inter-connected.

It was on November 6, 1996, that France officially informed the UN Secretary General that the Libyan "judicial cooperation satisfied most of the French demands, although some of the them have still not been met. It enabled me to make significant progress by giving me the opportunity to issue two additional arrest warrants for Libyan nationals and to complete the file on the inquiry. It has opened the way, as permitted under French law, to the trial in absentia of the six suspects."[8]

Less than three years later, and after a three day trial, six Libyans were convicted in absentia in a French court on March 10, 1999. They were sentenced to life imprisonment. The six were Qadhafi's brother-in-law Abdallah Senoussi, Abdessalam Issa Shibani, Abdessalam Hammouda, Abdallah El-Azragh, Ibrahim Naeli and Musbah Arbas. After some French victims' families issued angry statements requesting a handover of the accused, the government issued a statement claiming the investigation was not over and Qadhafi would be indicted. The French have yet to move on this indictment, and although they issued warrants for the arrest of the six Libyans, listing them with Interpol as well, they did not move seriously toward that end. The French have effectively closed this file, especially since barely four months after the verdicts, on July 16, Libya transferred more than 200 million francs ($31 million) to compensate the families of the 170 people killed in the bombing in 1989. The French court ordered the payment. In a statement from its foreign ministry, Libya announced that "French authorities note with satisfaction Libya's payment of this indemnity, a payment expressing an acknowledgment by the Libyan authorities of the responsibility of their citizens, in accordance with the rulings of French justice."

Still, when France found out that the Lockerbie victims' families got higher compensations than the UTA victims' families, they tried holding back approval of the official lifting of sanctions in order to renegotiate those amounts.

The most important fact here is that another of the demands of the Security Council resolutions has been implemented by Libya. It is officially over.

7

Libyan Gains

ICJ's Decisions

By the time Libya had satisfied two of the most important demands of the Security Council, it had become convinced that the remaining demands required a more intensive political effort. Libyan efforts turned to concentrate on the two facets of the Lockerbie issue: The political and diplomatic aspects were tackled through regional organizations while the legal aspect was dealt with at the International Court of Justice (ICJ).

On March 3, 1992, Libya had filed two separate actions with the ICJ against the United States and the United Kingdom. The case put several principal questions before the court:

1. Whether the destruction of the Pan Am aircraft over Lockerbie is governed by the Montreal Convention, to which Libya, the United States and the United Kingdom are all signatories;

2. Whether the United States and the United Kingdom have a right to compel Libya to turn over the two Libyans to a court in the United States or the United Kingdom for trial;

3. Whether the intervening resolutions issued by the Security Council—Resolution 748 (1992) and Resolution 883 (1993)—rendered moot or have priority over all rights and obligations arising out of the Montreal Convention.

The courts came to the same conclusions in both cases, with large majorities and only two or four judges in opposition to the majority decisions, as follows:

1. The ICJ has jurisdiction to deal with the merits of the cases.
2. Since Libya's Application was filed before the two (2) Security Council Resolutions were adopted, the Court retains the jurisdiction it had, as of the time the Libyan Application was filed.
3. The Court would not rule on this question at this time and will decide this issue when it deals with the merits of the case, for to do so now would be premature.[1]

When the ICJ decided it had jurisdiction over the cases filed by Libya, this decision was another fact that the United States and the United Kingdom had to face, adding to the pressure to find a compromise solution to Lockerbie and Libya.

Western and Libyan Reactions

Not only were the United States and the United Kingdom surprised by such an outcome, Libya was surprised by the judgments as well. Although Libya felt the legal requirements favored its case, it thought the Western pressure on the members of the court would culminate in some vague outcome that would not totally reject the United States and United Kingdom positions. The previous ruling of the court on the legality of Resolution 731 was still fresh in the minds of Libyan officials. Therefore, a new strategy had to be prepared for Libya to be able to take full advantage of this victory and integrate it with the diplomatic progress they were achieving with the regional organizations.

The official American-British reaction to the ICJ judgments were given only on March 16. In a letter both governments sent to the president of the UN Secretary General, they stated, "Our two Governments, out of the high respect they have for the International Court of Justice, will proceed in the light of its findings that it has jurisdiction and will avail themselves of their full rights to deploy further legal argument rebutting Libya's claims at the merits state."[2]

However, the letter clarified:

> It is important to be clear what the cases before the International Court of Justice are not about. They are not a determination of the criminal case against the accused. The Court has no jurisdiction to try criminal cases and has not asserted such jurisdiction. The case against the two

accused can only be determined once they are brought for trial in a criminal court. And the cases are not about the International Court of Justice deciding where the criminal trial should be held. The Court does not have jurisdiction to decide on the appropriate manner for the accused to be tried. Instead, the Court has held that it has jurisdiction to determine, under the Montreal Convention, whether our two Governments' demand for surrender of the accused (endorsed by the Security Council) are or are not in breach of Libya's rights under that Convention.

Libya responded to this position on March 24. The Libyan ambassador to the UN noted that the U.S.-U.K. letter "ignores the fact that, by the judgment(s), in which it rejects the objection to jurisdiction, the Court determines that there is a dispute between the parties concerning the interpretation and application of the 1971 Montreal Convention." He also said, "The Court thus has yet to rule on the effect of the Security Council resolutions on the Libyan applications.... The judgment of the Court is not entirely procedural because it implies an order relating to resolutions 748 (1992) and 883 (1993)."[3]

Voices rose both in Washington and London, doubting whether they should continue to refuse a negotiated solution and await a final decision of the ICJ on the substance of the issue. The signs were not that good; opposition by British and American judges meant that the rest of the world believed this was not an issue for the Security Council to deal with. It was a legal problem, as Libya had said at the outset. American and British qualification of the judgments as "procedural," having no effect on sanctions, was technically correct. Their importance, however, emanates from the fact that such judgments pull justification from Security Council resolutions. And with the diplomatic gains Libya was already making, these judgments provided further momentum and justification for those still reluctant to support Libya publicly to do so.

In press statements issued in New York on February 27, Libya offered its immediate reaction to the judgments included the following points:

> —This is a judgment in Libya's favor. It was adopted almost unanimously, not by a simple majority;
> —It is not only a victory for Libya. It is a victory for justice, for reason and for international law;
> —It means the issue of the Pan Am 103 incident is a legal case, 100 percent, not a political one;
> —The forum responsible for dealing with such an issue is the ICJ, not the Security Council;
> —The Montreal Convention [of] 1971 regarding protection of civil

aviation is the legal basis for judging this issue, which is what Libya has been saying;

—This judgment means, as well, that sanctions imposed against Libya, based on SCR 748 and 883, are illegal. They should be immediately annulled, or canceled at the very least;

—Based on the aforementioned, we reaffirm what we have been saying to the Security Council in official documents, and to the victims' families through letters and personal contacts: the responsibility for the delay throughout the years falls on the governments of the United States and the United Kingdom. Had they agreed at the beginning to resort to the ICJ, as we communicated to them officially through letters to the Secretary of State and the Foreign Secretary, the court would have issued its ruling on the issue by now, not only judgments on its jurisdiction:

—Those who do not abide by today's judgment are the ones refusing international law, which we fully accept.

The same day, the Libyan foreign minister sent letters to some of his counterparts in countries that were council members. The letters presented the ICJ judgment and concluded:

We look forward to your Excellency and to your country to take the initiative to begin practical measures to terminate these sanctions which are not justifiable anymore, particularly when the World Court emphatically expressed the illegality of those resolutions; and to energetically support our demand that the Security Council issue an immediate resolution to nullify them and put an end to the suffering of the Libyan Arab people.

Libya's Diplomatic Buildup

Libya moved quickly to transform its gains in the ICJ judgments and exploit them diplomatically. A new review of the sanctions was coming up at the Security Council on March 6. Libya vowed not to let this opportunity pass without a major demonstration of its diplomatic and political gains, while pushing the previously "shy" supporters to come out in the open and leading the other previously announced supporters to move ahead with stronger demands. That effort helped further consolidate Libya's position and added once again to the pressure on the United States and the United Kingdom. Many countries, as a direct result of the ICJ judgments, declared their opposition to the way Washington was pressing its policies around the world, especially after the United States became the lone superpower. Much public reaction was a reflection of those feelings. Libya struggled to keep those feelings up, encouraging many to turn away from the sanctions.

Libya's demands prior to the ruling were advancing toward calling on the Security Council to adopt "transitional temporary measures." These measures were outlined in a common letter sent by the secretary general of the Arab League, the secretary general of the Islamic Conference, and the chairman of the Arab Parliamentary Union:

> Pending a definitive peaceful and just settlement of the crisis based on one of the three proposed solutions, we hope that the Security Council will take measures to help mitigate the negative consequences of the air embargo against the Libyan Arab Jamahiriya by lifting the ban on certain flights carried out by the Libyan authorities, namely:
> —Flights of a humanitarian nature, medical evacuations and importation of medicines;
> —Special flights to transport material assistance provided by the Libyan Arab Jamahiriya to other countries;
> —Individual flights for religious purposes.[4]

The ICJ decisions came a few days prior to a scheduled review of the sanctions by the Security Council. The reviews were usually held in private meetings. After this victory, Libya raised the stakes and demanded that the review be held in a public session and that such a debate should discuss as well the ICJ decisions and their effect on the sanctions. Libya was looking for ways to translate legal victories into further diplomatic advantages: the weakening of sanctions.

The political demands Libya presented were included in an explanatory letter from Libya's UN representative, Abuzed O. Dorda, to the president of the council.

Referring to the ICJ judgment of February 27, 1998, Dorda suggested the council should refrain from renewing the sanctions; that the two resolutions should be rescinded; that the two cases before the ICJ should be considered the only means for settling the dispute; and, finally, that the two Security Council resolutions be suspended.[5]

The regional organizations that supported Libya moved at the UN to adopt most of its positions and demands. The first move was to support Libya's demand to hold an open official meeting of the council. That would mean airing all criticisms against the United States and the United Kingdom, which the two, with the support of some council members, on technical grounds, opposed. However, as a result of mounting pressure, they approved holding an open meeting to "discuss the problems between the Libyan Arab Jamahiriya and the United States and the United Kingdom, regarding Lockerbie, in light of the rulings of the International Court of Justice and according to articles 31 and 32 of the Charter." The African group at the UN went further to express its "wish to see the sanctions against the Libyan Arab Jamahiriya either suspended until the dispute is finally settled, or lifted altogether."[6]

A flood of letters from Libya's supporters reached the Security Council, adopting its positions in full. The council had no possibility to refuse the open meeting, although it was willing to accept the American and British pressure not to adopt any resolution changing the sanctions regime so long as the two Libyan suspects had not been handed over. One interesting request, dated 4 March 1998, came separately from the representative of Saudi Arabia, expressing his government's "support of ... the request presented by the Libyan Arab Jamahiriya to hold an open meeting during the coming review of the sanctions." It seemed that, other than Prince Bandar bin Sultan, the Saudi ambassador to Washington, and the leaders of his government, only the leaders in Libya knew what the letter was all about. An Arab request had already been presented, and the Saudis had never involved themselves openly in such efforts. It was unusual. Saudi Arabia, it turned out, was trying to convince the Libyans that the Saudi kingdom was on their side.

The aforementioned letters came mostly from four committees established by the Organization of African Unity (OAU), Arab League, Islamic Conference and the Non-Aligned Movement. These committees were established in order to follow daily work on the Lockerbie issue, based on the resolutions adopted by these organizations. The Arab letter (like the others dated 4 March) was signed by the members of the Arab League committee (Tunisia, Egypt, Algeria, Morocco, Mauritania, Libya and Syria). It said:

> Upon instructions from our Governments, we, the members of the Arab Committee of Seven in New York, have the honor to request, as a matter of urgency, pursuant to Articles 31 and 32 of the Charter of the United Nations, the convening of a formal meeting of the Security Council to consider all aspects of the dispute between the Libyan Arab Jamahiriya and the United States of America and the United Kingdom of Great Britain and Northern Ireland in the matter of the Lockerbie incident, especially in the light of the two Judgments delivered by the International Court of Justice on 27 February 1998.

After a long process of corridor negotiations and arm twisting, the review was held privately, as usual, on March 5. The council members officially decided to hold a public meeting on March 20 as an accommodation by the two for the growing pressure from other member and nonmember states.

Despite the acceptance of the open meeting, many members spoke in the private review meeting in full support of the Libyan position, calling for either the lifting of sanctions or, at the very least, suspending them due to the judgments of the ICJ. The results of the review were a clear expression of differences of views. The council used to issue a simple statement saying, "After hearing all the opinions expressed in the course of consultations, the President of the Council concluded that there was no agreement that the necessary conditions existed for modification of the measures of sanctions established in paragraphs 3 to 7 of resolution 748 (1992)." No statement, however, was issued after this review, since most members wanted some positive language in support of Libya, which led the United States and the United Kingdom to consider the absence of a statement more beneficial than one with any positive language regarding Libya's legal and diplomatic gains.

The following two weeks witnessed a full diplomatic offensive from Libya and its supporters on one side and the United States and the United Kingdom on the other. Libya wanted some type of a resolution. The United States and the United Kingdom were opposed to any outcome of the public meeting, threatening the use of their veto powers to prevent any resolution from being adopted. All they would accept was a meeting in which Libya could show off its gains while the United States and the United Kingdom swallowed their pride and kept silent about the agreement they had already reached privately on a revised policy: accepting Libya's proposal of holding a Scottish trial in the Netherlands. Had they hinted at this change, some of Libya's supporters might not have expressed such staunch support. Thus American and British diplomats at the UN were kept on the defensive for almost a year. Among themselves, those diplomats wished they could dispense with public meetings until an announcement could be made. It was an exceedingly difficult diplomatic maneuver.

Keeping in line with the public policy of no change and continuous attacks against Libya, Martin Indyk, Assistant Secretary of State for Near-Eastern Affairs, repeated his country's position the day before the council's meeting. He accused "Libya and its supporters of having engaged in myth-making on both the question of Libyan involvement and the effects of sanctions on the Libyan people." He once again repeated the accusations against Libya regarding the Lockerbie issue and made a strange demand: "When the suspects are handed over, compensation paid, and Libya ceases their support for terrorism, the sanctions can be suspended, as the Security Council provide, but not until then."[7]

Indyk was intentionally either raising the stakes or moving the goal post. These positions or conditions for lifting the sanctions turned out to be the position the United States had followed after the handover, despite the fact that the council's resolutions themselves called for suspension of the sanctions as soon as the two suspects were handed over and for the lifting of them when the other demands were met. Bearing in mind the American enmity of Libya, whatever the latter did, it seemed realistic for such conditions to be added as such, leading Libya to wonder about any real possibility for a solution. Some in Libya went so far as to call for a halt of the diplomatic and positive efforts toward the United States. Fortunately, those voices did not succeed and the positive efforts continued.

There remains one last note on the legal aspect of this case. One of the arguments presented by Libya was confirmed in three major incidents in which the United States applied double standards. One of those incidents involved a Rwandan indicted by the International Criminal Court (established by the UN on a recommendation by the United States, to try war criminals of Rwanda). This Rwandan clergyman, Elizaphan Ntakirutimana, who was being sought by Rwanda and by the International Tribunal for Rwanda (established by the UN Security Council) on charges of having been involved in the interethnic war crimes committed in Rwanda in 1994, resides in Texas. He followed the legal procedures of the United States leading to the refusal of a U.S. judge, Marcel C. Notzon, the federal magistrate in Laredo, Texas, to hand him over to the UN tribunal. The judge released him on grounds that the 1996 agreement between the United States and the International Tribunal for Rwanda was unconstitutional.

The other case concerned a young American Jewish man, Samuel Sheinbein, who committed a murder in Maryland, where he resided. He fled to Israel, claiming his father's Israeli citizenship would provide him with citizenship as well as protect him since Israeli law prohibits extradition of any Israeli citizen. While Israel refused him citizenship, it protected him and refused to extradite him, conducting instead a nominal trial leading to conviction and minimal punishment. Despite many expressions of anger from federal and state prosecutors in Maryland, the U.S. government failed to press Israel for his extradition or to even apply sanctions on Israel.

The third case concerned a U.S. national, Richard Bliss, accused of spying in the Russian Federation. He was released on parole by Russian authorities on humanitarian grounds in order to spend the Christmas holidays with his family in California and failed to return to the Russian Federation at the agreed time to stand trial. In this connection, the Associated Press, on January 8, 1998, quoted a U.S. official, who spoke on condition of anonymity, as saying that forcing Bliss to return to the Russian Federation for trial would have been impossible because there is no extradition treaty between the U.S. and the Russian Federation.

Libya had argued strongly about the absence of reciprocal extradition agreements between Libya and the two countries involved in its case. It asked: How could the United States Administration fail to recognize that Libyan nationals, such as the two who are merely suspected of involvement in the regrettable Pan Am Flight 103 incident at Lockerbie, have the same constitutional, legal and humanitarian rights conferred on American nationals and even on some who are not? The Libyans asked, as well, for their citizens' rights to be the same as those granted an American citizen, Timothy McVeigh, who blew up a federal building in Oklahoma City in 1995. His trial was moved to Denver, Colorado, under the pretext of the impossibility of a fair trial in Oklahoma. The Libyan argument was that their citizens would not receive a fair trial in the United States or in Scotland, thus proposing the move to the Netherlands.

8

Arab and African Regional Organizations and Their Effectiveness in the Security Council

In Africa and the Arab world, Libya capitalized on the two successes it had achieved by then in solving the bilateral issues with the United Kingdom and France, as well as those with its neighbors and the ICJ judgments. It moved toward laying the groundwork for a solution to the more comprehensive issue. It would be in a better position than it was in 1991, when (and if) a solution appeared. And although the world was moving away from the U.S.-U.K. position, the two successes would not, by themselves, deliver the comprehensive solution. The Libyans needed to improve the positions of those who had not moved yet.

With a political stalemate on the Lockerbie aspect of the Security Council demands prevailing between 1993 and 1997, the international political scene witnessed the renewed activism of many countries. Russia was trying to assert itself on the international stage, though minimally compared to the Soviet Union it had replaced. China was preparing itself to occupy a higher level of international standing, though its opposition to the United States would continue to be more verbal and symbolic. The third-world countries were detecting the limits of United States influence as the sole superpower, leading them to look for margins within which they would be able to maneuver without striking the anger chord of the Americans.

Implementing that aspect of its original strategy, Libya moved in 1997 to concentrate its efforts on regional organizations. Since they represent more than two thirds of the countries and populations of the world, these organizations were starting to put themselves on the international stage in the new world order. Possibilities arose when they all considered the Libyan issue an instrument to be used to achieve a status of influence short of confrontation with the United States. This issue provided them with an opportunity to discuss the reorganization of the world and to raise their voices while debating and studying issues such as the use of force and the imposition of sanctions.

A combination of Libya's aims and the wishes of the members of the regional organizations culminated in the achievement of a new set of rules in the world. UN Security Council resolutions, especially those adopted at the height of the world's transformation, were no longer necessarily untouchable. A major distinction was made between situations where international peace and security were threatened, such as the situations of Iraq and the former Yugoslavia, and situations that were mere differences of opinions, such as those regarding Libya and the Sudan. Somewhere in between were situations that involved timely and limited international action, such as those regarding Haiti.

Consequently, the principle of imposing sanctions became a major issue of debate around the world. Different interpretations of that item on the UN Charter were presented in many forums. The discussion intensified as well regarding the issue of national sanctions, that is, sanctions imposed by a specific country against another without the approval of the UN. The United States was always the target of these discussions since it was the country that most often used sanctions as a tool of its policies, to an extent rejected by close allies of Washington, such as the West European countries. That was the case when the U.S. Congress felt it could extend its authority to force other countries to abide by the sanctions it imposed unilaterally, despite the rejection of the UN of such measures, adopting what was known as the Iran-Libya Sanctions Act (ILSA). ILSA intended to boycott European countries and companies that continued to deal with Iran and Libya,[1] ignoring U.S. sanctions against them. Another law was imposing similar actions with regard to Cuba. That effort failed when Europe as a whole rejected it and continued to deal with that country along the line of the UN resolutions. ILSA backfired at the UN as well. Cuba, Iran and Libya managed to get the UN General Assembly to adopt resolutions rejecting the U.S. position, with an overwhelming majority.

The growing dissatisfaction with the American abuse of their new status in the world led the regional organizations to accept Libya's call for new positions, finding it the most opportune issue to softly confront the United States with. The OAU, the Arab League, the Organization of the Islamic Conference (OIC) and Non-Aligned Movement (NAM) supported Libya's position. They adopted various resolutions throughout the years of the conflict. The tone of their resolutions was gradually escalated from an original call for restraint, to propositions of compromise, such as a trial in a third country and, finally, to threats to breach sanctions, thus undermining the authority of the Security Council, the body the United States needed to legitimize its actions as the sole superpower.

The final stage of these efforts became the main incentive for the United States and the United Kingdom to change their policies and accept the compromise. That chapter began when the OAU summit of June 1997, held in Zimbabwe, adopted a forceful resolution on the subject.

First, it recognized that Libya had rejected terrorism and was ready to cooperate in eradicating it. Second, it acknowledged that extradition of the Libyan suspects was impossible. Third, it condemned the impact the sanctions had had on the Libyan people as well as on other Africans. Three options were proposed for resolving the political impasse:

1. Try the suspects in a third, neutral country selected by the Security Council.
2. Try the two suspects by Scottish judges at the ICJ in the Hague with Scottish Law.
3. Establish a special tribunal at ICJ headquarters in the Hague to try the two suspects.

The OAU justified its position by stating that:

> The Libyan Arab Jamahiriya had fully met the requirements demanded by the Security Council as contained in resolution 731 (1992) of 21 January 1992. As a matter of fact, the Libyan Arab Jamahiriya had unequivocally condemned terrorism in all its forms as well as those perpetrating or encouraging it, and had made clear her readiness to give all necessary cooperation to the international community with a view to eradicating that heinous phenomenon. However, the Libyan Arab Jamahiriya had found it impossible to extradite its two nationals allegedly implicated in the bombing over Lockerbie in 1988."[2]

The African leaders went on to say:

We take note of the fact that the Government of the Libyan Arab Jamahiriya has accepted the initiative of the League of Arab States supported by OAU, the Movement on Non-Aligned Countries and the Organization of the Islamic Conference, to the effect that the two Libyan suspects be given a just and fair trial by Scottish judges and according to Scottish law at the headquarters of the International Court of Justice (ICJ). We remain convinced that this initiative, if accepted, constitutes a practical solution and should guarantee a just and fair trial whereby the interests of the concerned parties would be taken into account. Indeed, the objective of resolution 731 (1992) is not to violate the sovereignty of the Libyan Arab Jamahiriya but rather to serve the cause of justice and reveal the truth. We strongly deplore the fact that one or two concerned countries have so far shown indifference to the initiatives presented to them with a view to a just and equitable solution to the crisis. This has led to an impasse and, as a result, the entire Libyan people have not only been held hostage for five years, but have also been subjected to collective suffering because of accusations none of the two countries concerned have been able to substantiate.

After repeating the three alternatives for a solution, the OAU leaders concluded by calling on the UNSC to adopt one of them. They even went so far as to challenge the council, mainly the United States and the United Kingdom:

We appeal to the Security Council to lift the sanctions imposed on the Libyan Arab Jamahiriya. This has become imperative, more so as the sanctions are having an increasingly devastating effect on the people of the Libyan Arab Jamahiriya as well as on the country's economy. In this connection, we endorse the position expressed by the Council of Ministers at its sixty-fourth ordinary session, held at Yaoundé, Cameroon, from 1 to 6 July 1996 and at its sixty-fifth ordinary session, held at Tripoli, the Libyan Arab Jamahiriya, from 24 to 28 February 1997, to the effect that continued imposition of sanctions might lead African countries to devise other means of sparing the Libyan people future suffering. In this respect, we mandate the Secretary-General of OAU to prepare a practical plan of action."

Although this was not exactly what Libya had hoped for, that was the immediate action by the Africans to cease their compliance with sanctions, and the first time some states had warned the UN Security Council against its positions. It transformed the theoretical process from the Council imposing its positions on states to the more realistic norm: states telling the Council what it should do. In reality, it was the Africans addressing the United States and the United Kingdom indirectly through a message directed at the Council. Both countries heard the African call but refused to abide by it; they were not used to African words turning into deeds.

Many African leaders and delegations implemented their summit's resolution and began to fly directly into Libya. The travels were sporadic and, intentionally, with minimal flare since the Africans were still not sure how the United States would react. Some were afraid the American forces might shoot down planes. Others were afraid Washington would cut the assistance they receive. Nothing major happened. Libya intensified its dealings with the Africans that breached the sanctions and went on to send its own airplanes on certain flights it considered exempt from the sanctions, such as Hajj flights and other trips for religious reasons, one of which was a trip by Qadhafi himself to the Niger to attend a gathering of Muslim organizations.

Furthermore, Libya succeeded in getting seven other African countries to form a new alliance with it. The leaders of Mali, Chad, Niger, Burkina Faso, the Sudan, Eritrea and the Central African Republic breached the UN sanctions, flying to Libya to meet with Qadhafi between August 15 and August 17, 1997, forming the Sahel and Saharan States Grouping. The attending states issued a separate statement expressing their "concern regarding the continuation of the sanctions which have negative effects on the economies of their respective countries, and special concern regarding the human and material losses suffered by the Libyan people as a result of those sanctions. The presidents salute the position and initiatives of Libya and issue an urgent appeal to the international community to support all efforts and measures in order to find a just and final solution to this conflict, and they especially call on the UN Secretary-General Kofi Annan to send a special fact-finding delegation to Libya to examine the suffering of the Libyan people."

Following the OAU summit, the UN Security Council conducted its sixteenth review of the sanctions against Libya on July 10, 1998. It was the first to be conducted while the new labor government was in office in London. It was, as well, a review that was taking place under Arab, African, and other pressures to change the policy and possibly lift the sanctions, while London was conducting its own review and trying to keep it as private as possible. The British and American delegations to the meeting were in an uneasy situation.

In that review, the pressure was extreme for sending a delegation to Libya to examine the humanitarian effects of the sanctions on the Libyan people. The United States and the United Kingdom were facing political pressure as well from the Africans who were carrying the resolution of their summit calling for a change of policy. The Western response was repetitive: Libya did not comply and sanctions should remain. They were stunned, however, by the weak support their position was receiving.

That same day, President Mandela was visiting London. One of the main issues he discussed was the Lockerbie issue. He was lobbying strongly for the trial to be held in a third country. He was faced with all the obstacles—both technical and constitutional—that the British government constantly claimed it faced in accepting such a compromise. He was not informed of any results of a British internal policy review, but he left with an understanding that the issue was still open for possible changes. The timing of these events, as well as their contents, was significant in showing the new British government, especially its foreign minister, that support for sanctions was weakening; that there was no chance of strengthening the sanctions in order to compel Libya's compliance; that simply keeping the status quo was impossible and that Libya's isolation was broken. The United Kingdom realized it needed to regain the initiative, and began a review process toward that end.

Libya Disappointed by the Arabs

In the Arab world, the rejection of sanctions never reached the level Libya had hoped for. During the early years, such neglect was understandable, for the region and the whole world were still waking up to the two major developments they faced: Desert Storm and the fall of the Eastern bloc. That period seemed endless. The Arab people were more occupied with the continuous crises Iraq instigated. Saddam's policy of keeping up pressure, hoping that would lead to a major Arab revolt, was failing, but he never gave up. The Arabs kept their attention on that part of the world for two reasons: Iraq is far more important than Libya in the strategic sense (the Libyans never challenged that fact), and Saddam did not give up until early 1998, when he reached what could be considered a conviction that sanctions would never be lifted from his country as long as he ruled it.

The Libyans were disappointed. Their support to various Arab groups and countries since the revolution should have won them some sympathy, if not full-fledged support. However, no Arab country showed any willingness to announce full support, let alone act on it. Many governments in the area had complained of the Libyans' revolutionary tendencies and their efforts to export them. They had reached a stage they did not pass, where they had to follow the United States without any questioning. Even when the rest of the world was questioning U.S. actions and policies, the Arabs considered their survival dependent on either befriending the Americans or, at least, avoiding their enmity. They felt that the presence of Israel in their region would keep the Americans as a watchdog, always ready to interfere directly if their interests were threatened. The experiences of the October 1973 war, the Iraq-Iran war and the Iraq-Kuwait crisis were examples of U.S. willingness to forget about its problems, internally or in other parts of the world, and directly and substantially intervene in the Middle East. This was further exemplified when the United States invaded and occupied Iraq in 2003 under the pretext of eliminating the danger Saddam's regime presented to America.

The intellectual connection between the sanctions imposed on Iraq and those imposed on Libya, along with the failed efforts to impose sanctions on the Sudan, brought realization for the necessity to face off this new burden of international politics. This realization, in turn, brought, public pressure, encouraging the governments to show change in their public stance. Noticing that the Libyan issue was not so strategically important on the international scene, the Arab governments were willing to provide Libya with public support in order to fend off the pressure on the more strategic and dangerous Iraq issue. In order to translate that minimal change into action, the Arabs accepted Libya's call to adopt a resolution at the Arab League. That would be the least controversial step they would take since none of them would implement it. The ministerial council of the Arab League met for its annual session on September 2 and adopted a resolution "calling on Arab States to take measures to ease the level of sanctions against the Libyan Jamahirya until a peaceful and just solution to this conflict is achieved, by exempting" certain flights from the sanctions, and other actions that were not practically implemented. That was the first vital position adopted by the Arabs in support of Libya. As expected by everybody, it continued to be a resolution no one was courageous enough to implement.

This Arab decision was met with anger by both the United States and the United Kingdom, and by the UN Secretary General. Diplomats meeting with Annan and Cook over dinner on September 21 revealed that the Secretary General spoke of "a fear that the Arab League move could weaken the United Nations by encouraging others to defy the world body." Cook agreed adding, "There is no justification for the move. It sends the wrong message on fighting terrorism and it makes the United Nations look weak if some countries ignored what was agreed upon collectively."[3]

As if Arab incompetence were not enough, Washington and London, angered by such a decision, pressed Saudi Arabia and Kuwait to change their position. Both countries sent letters to the Arab League secretariat requesting their positions be changed to some type of abstention in the official records. The Arab League responded negatively, saying no such procedure existed in its rules. The votes were left unchanged. The resolution, unlike that of the OAU, remained words, not deeds. The Libyans, while receiving African leaders flying into Tripoli on a regular basis, became more convinced they would never see an Arab challenge of the sanctions.

Within days, Qadhafi was ready to declare once again that Libya would turn its back on the Arabs and rely on Africa. All governmental efforts were geared in that direction. He wrote the African leaders, explaining the international situation and concluding that he became convinced that "under the slogan 'Africa is for the Africans,' the salvation of Africa and the creation of a prosperous future must be done only through the Unity of Africa, as was the case of the United States of America." He later, on many occasions, called publicly for the establishment of "the United States of Africa."

Libyan efforts to implement this slogan are still going on. They range between mediation to solve the continent's regional conflicts—a move received positively in the United States and many other countries—and the provision of financial support to different public groups, such as a $200-million fund Libya established in 1999 to provide scholarships to African students. Moreover, Qadhafi declared to his African colleagues that their citizens would be able to enter his country without a visa. They would need only their national identity cards. A few months later, he began revoking that privilege from many Arab nationalities.

The Arabs and the Africans Move United

With these decisions at hand, both Arab and African organizations began an effort by their secretary generals, Esmat Abdel-Meguid and Salim Ahmed-Salem. They both sent a common letter to the president of the Security Council advocating that council members accept one of the three alternatives. They went even further, requesting that "pending the final and peaceful solution of the crisis and the adoption of one of the above-mentioned proposals, we urge the Security Council to undertake the following measures which, we believe, will go a long way in mitigating the severe impact of the air embargo, by exempting flights that may be run by Libyan authorities:

> (i) Fights for humanitarian purposes of medical treatment and the importation of medicines;
> (ii) Special flights to send material assistance from the Libyan Arab Jamahiriya to African countries;
> (iii) Flights for religious purposes;
> (iv) Flights related to participation in official missions."[4]

The British reaction to those letters was transformed, at the time, into a confrontation between Abdel-Meguid and the British UN representative, John Weston, in a bilateral meeting they held on June 26 at the office of the U.K. mission in New York. It was Weston's personality to talk nervously when dealing with others, concentrating on unnecessary details and losing sight of the big picture. Contributing to his uneasiness was the fact that London was witnessing the Libyan gains without a clear new policy of its own. In that meeting, Abdel-Meguid started to present the positions he was carrying. According to persons present at the meeting, Abdel-Meguid had barely begun when Weston interrupted him, saying that the U.K. would deal only with Libya itself, and therefore he had nothing to talk to Abdel-Meguid about. Stunned, Abdel-Meguid walked out. Weston later called Abdel-Meguid to apologize. But the substance of the problem was never revived between the two; the British and the Americans claimed the Arab League and its secretary general had their own agenda, totally different from those of the international community. They tried to alienate the Arab body on this issue, insisting any exchanges should be conducted through the UN Secretary General. What is noteworthy here is that the American, British and UN reactions to the positions taken by the OAU were never as harsh as those directed at the Arabs, although the latter's were not as strong as those of the OAU.

With African leaders flying into Tripoli and Libya getting more involved in the affairs of the continent, the OAU held its next summit in Burkina Faso in June 1998. The resolution they adopted moved the whole process to a dangerous new level. The African leaders decided they would ignore the sanctions in the beginning of September, if the United States and the United Kingdom did not accept the trial in a third country, while threatening further actions. At the Security Council, meanwhile, diplomatic business went on as usual; that is, the United States and the United Kingdom were losing support during reviews of the sanctions and were still unable to respond with the results of their bilateral discussions.

Prior to the OAU resolution, Libya had managed to get the OIC summit meeting, held in Tehran in March of the same year, to adopt a series of resolutions in Libya's favor, some of which gave even stronger support to Libya's other problems with the United States. Then Libya turned to the NAM, gaining, for the first time, the adoption of its position at a ministerial meeting held in Cartagena, Colombia, from May 18 to May 20. The Libyan delegation played its cards, ranging from technical tricks to political savvy, successfully achieving an outcome similar to that of the Africans', that is, a certain deadline by which the movement would move toward undermining the sanctions. The ministerial conference welcomed the decisions of the International Court of Justice. The ministers and heads of delegations called for the immediate suspension of the sanctions until the ICJ decided on the issue. They recommended that the twelfth summit of the movement make a decision to not continue complying with the sanctions resolution on the basis of Article 25 of the UN Charter because they were in violation of Articles 27 (3), 32, 33, 36 and 94 of the charter. That summit was to be held in late August in South Africa. Such a decision was all but confirmed to be adopted, but the U.S.-U.K. announcement came days prior to the summit.

The OAU Summit of 1998

The OAU summit of 1998 was very important. It provided the first-ever public challenge of any grouping of states to the Security Council. Not only did the summit support Libya, it clearly and directly threatened the Security Council. The African leaders had just witnessed the judgments of the ICJ and accepted Libya's call to build on them.

In their resolution, the African leaders called upon the council "to adopt a resolution on suspending the sanctions imposed on the Libyan Arab Jamahiriya under Security Council resolutions until the International Court of Justice pronounces its verdict on the issue." They decided "not to comply any longer with Security Council resolutions on sanctions, with effect from September 1998, if the United States of America and the United Kingdom of Great Britain and Northern Ireland refuse that the two suspects be tried in a third neutral country" and further decided "on moral and religious grounds and with immediate effect that the Organization of African Unity and its members will not comply from now on with the sanctions imposed against the Libyan Arab Jamahiriya related to religious obligations, providing humanitarian emergencies or fulfilling statutory obligations of the Organization of African Unity."[5]

That resolution was an important turning point. It further confirmed to the United States and the United Kingdom what they already knew: They should change their position. They were, in fact, ready to do so but could not announce their change in time to affect the OAU resolution, although they hinted at that change while lobbying the Africans, who would not accept anything short of an official declaration.

The Americans were very angry at the OAU resolution. The anger emanated mainly because Washington had lobbied strongly against such a declaration. Clinton himself toured Africa in March and raised the issue with the leaders he met, urging their patience. Secretary of State Madeleine Albright and her assistants at the State Department went so far as to threaten certain cuts in assistance the United States provided them. The OAU dismissed the U.S. warnings. Most notably, the official reaction announced by the State Department came to anger Africans, for it was drafted in a manner they considered insulting. The statement attributed to the spokesman of the State Department, James Rubin, issued on June 10, 1998, called on the OAU to "rescind this irresponsible resolution." This is the text of the statement:

> In a June 8 resolution, the Organization of African Unity heads of state called on African nations to suspend compliance with United Nations Security Council sanctions on Libya immediately, for religious and humanitarian reasons, on OAU-related Libyan flights, and to ignore sanctions entirely beginning in September if the U.S. and United Kingdom have not by then agreed to one of Qadhafi's third-country trial options.
>
> We are extremely disturbed by this short-sighted action, which constitutes a direct assault on the authority of the Security Council and its binding resolutions adopted under Chapter VII of the Charter of the United Nations. It is, thus, an attack on the United Nations system itself. The integrity of United Nations Security Council sanctions, and the requirement that the sanctions regime be universally observed, were essential to resolving African conflicts in Mozambique, Angola, and South Africa. For sanctions to remain an effective tool in resolving disputes everywhere, countries cannot pick and choose which sanctions they will observe. We also note that under existing United Nations resolutions there are already procedures for approving appropriate humanitarian and religious flights.
>
> This decision makes it less likely, not more likely, that the Lockerbie matter will be resolved, because it may lead Qadhafi to conclude mistakenly that he no longer has to comply with Security Council resolutions. In order to resolve this situation as quickly as possible, the OAU should instead focus its efforts on urging Libya to comply with Security Council Resolutions 883, 731 and 748 immediately.
>
> We call upon OAU members to fulfil their United Nations charter obligations to abide by the binding decisions of the United Nations Security Council and to disregard this action by the OAU, which cannot in any event affect those obligations. We also call upon the OAU to rescind this irresponsible resolution.

The language of this statement was more important than its substance, for such a U.S. rejection was expected, based on the Africans' assessment of all the American lobbying before and during the summit at Ouagadougou. However, the threats it contained were shocking. The Africans could not understand how the United States could call them "irresponsible" and ask them to renege on a resolution of their own without any official and public acceptance of what the Americans were communicating in private. They responded with a statement issued by the OAU, rejecting that language and reiterating the substance of the resolution, which was seen as a real expression of anger by the United States after it lost another battle with one of the most important elements of the international community.

The Africans responded by sending another flood of flights to Tripoli. Many could not wait until the deadline they set at the summit. But since the policy decision was already made in London and Washington, those flights only added to the aggravation of the U.S. and British officials, who were not able to counter those breaches without any revelation of the process underway. The U.S. government, however, was in the most critical position. The U.S. Congress was pushing for action against countries breaching the travel ban. The administration knew any such punishment would only be heaped on the already-existing animosity those Africans had toward the U.S. position. But nervousness was prevailing among Washington officials, who issued statements they later regretted.

9

The Victims' Families

As diplomatic and legal gains were adding up on Libya's side, one more battle had to be decisively won: the public relations battle. This battle had two forums: the UN, mainly the Security Council, where advances had already taken place, and the victims' families, since they had always played an important role in lobbying their governments, though from different perspectives, on how to achieve justice for the loss of their loved ones. The press was never as important a tool in this battle; its role was marginal compared with the effects it had on related issues.

Early on, the United States and the United Kingdom tried to play the families card as a counterattack against Libyan gains. They arranged for representatives of the families to attend the open meeting of the council in March 1998 and hold press conferences inside the UN headquarters. That effort proved futile as well; some families turned against their governments after they witnessed, at first hand, the realities at the council.

The differences between the groups representing the families were clear from the early days of this conflict and led to a division among the families on national and intranational levels. With the British families constituting a minority while being represented by one group, the American families were divided into three camps. The differences among all of the groups were quite deep, although the U.S. government spared no effort at representing a "unity" that never existed. The Americans never acknowledged the differences until the announcement of the solution, when it needed the groups on board.

The three camps of the American families had three positions: one supporting the government, whatever it did; a second always calling for harsher measures against Libya; and a third practically asking the government to accept the compromise solutions and call Libya's bluff.

The families' positions tended to represent their respective countries' worldview. The Americans tended to believe they could do whatever they wanted in the world, while the British felt diplomacy would achieve better results. The British families openly expressed dissatisfaction with the stagnant positions of the United States and the United Kingdom, calling on them to accept the trial in a third country. They concluded it was the only possible trial that could be held.

On the margins of the council meeting of March 20, 1998, the British delegation was embarrassed by the representatives of the families it invited as part of its strategy drawn with the Americans to counter Libya's increasing support after the ICJ judgments. After meeting some of them privately, the mission canceled the press conference it had called. Jim Swire, who headed that group, was more accommodating of Libya's compromise offers and wanted to call for the acceptance of their argument, favoring holding a Scottish court in a third country. The British government was not ready to humiliate itself on its own official premises, since the press conference was called for by the mission, meaning the government was sponsoring the conference. Swire found another venue for his press conference. He managed to be invited by the United Nations Correspondents Association (UNCA). The association had its own room on the third floor of the secretariat building, which housed the offices of the Secretary General's spokesman and his staff, as well as offices of correspondents.

In his conference, Swire accused U.S. Ambassador Bill Richardson of being "economical" in the facts he was providing. He felt that the current position of his government "had led to a deadlock, contravened treaties and did nothing to obtain truth and justice in honor of those who fell at Lockerbie."[1] On a previous occasion, Swire tried, in vain, to publish his opinion in the United States, sending letters to some newspapers. One of those included a harsh criticism of the United States, claiming, "So far we have been unable to find an American official who will claim that if two American citizens were wanted for alleged destruction of a Libyan airliner, their country would surrender them for a trial in Libya." Swire and his group also played an effective role during the period when his government was studying new aspects for a solution. He visited Tripoli on April 18, 1998. Although this was not his first visit, it was one of the most important, for it substantially affected the general atmosphere, pressing for a solution, and the positions of many American families of the victims, pressing them further toward acceptance of a compromise.

Swire was accompanied on this trip by Robert Black, a lawyer and lecturer at the University of Edinburgh. Black is credited with having come up with the idea of a Scottish trial in a third country, as early as January 1994, when he and Swire were visiting Libya for a second time. They had noticed the impasse facing the parties. That is why Black, based on his expertise in Scottish law, expressed in a proposal dated 10 January 1994 the idea "that a trial be held out with Scotland, perhaps in the premises of the International Court of Justice at The Hague, in which the governing law and procedure would be the law and procedure followed in Scottish criminal courts in trials on indictment."

Black's comprehensive proposal dealt with all the details. He suggested that "the prosecution in the trial be conducted by the Scottish public prosecutor, the Lord Advocate, or his authorized representative; that the defense of the accused be conducted by independent Scottish solicitors and counsel appointed by the accused; that the jury of fifteen persons, which is a feature of Scottish criminal procedure on indictment, be replaced by an international panel of five judges presided over and chaired by a judge of the Scottish High Court of Justiciary whose responsibility it would be to direct the panel on Scottish law and procedure; that any appeals against conviction or sentence be heard and determined in Scotland by the High Court of Justiciary in its capacity as the Scottish Court of Criminal Appeal."

To everybody's surprise, these elements would later serve as the basis for what the governments of the United States, the United Kingdom and Libya would agree upon, despite early rejections by the two Western countries. In a letter to Black dated January 12, 1994, Dr. Ibrahim Legwell, who was the head of the legal team defending the two suspects until 1998, stated that this scheme was wholly acceptable to his clients and, if it were implemented by the United Kingdom government, the suspects would voluntarily surrender themselves for trial before a tribunal so constituted. In a letter of the same date, the deputy foreign minister of Libya stated that his government would place no obstacle in the path of its two citizens they elect to submit to trial under this scheme.

After Swire and Black's latest visit to Tripoli, with a stopover in Cairo, where they met officials from the Arab League and Egypt, they sent a letter to Cook, which was an alternative to a meeting Cook had refused. What Cook and his assistants did not give as a reason for their rejection of a meeting was that Cook felt such a meeting might give the impression, later, that the new position was a response to the families' pressure as well. Furthermore, he felt he would be under pressure, in such a meeting, to reveal the discussions taking place with the Americans and the Dutch and, since Swire and Black were on good terms with the Libyans, he was afraid they might reveal the information to them or even to the press. He rejected the meeting and responded to their letter in writing, softly repeating old positions, without giving a hint about what was going on behind the scenes.

During the 20 March meeting of the UN Security Council, the invited U.S. representatives of the families were mostly from groups extremely opposed to any compromise. It seemed as if the U.S. mission intended to invite the most hawkish of those families in order to let them vent their frustration while the private diplomatic efforts were taking place. U.S. Ambassador Richardson, being the politician he is, also felt that such an exposure would help him politically, for he thought those groups reflected the public's position, as was always indicated by his former colleagues in the U.S. Congress, especially fellow Democrat Senator Edward Kennedy. Richardson was hoping to be vice-president in 2000.

At their press conference held while the Security Council was meeting across the hall, the families expressed outrage at the level of support Libya was receiving. One of the families' representatives, George Williams, said, "We simply do not understand how nations who say they oppose terrorism can support nations who practice it." Williams reacted as well to the issue raised by most speakers in the meeting, that is, the humanitarian suffering of the Libyan people as a result of the sanctions. He insisted, "We are the victims, not the Libyan people. The Libyan government made United States victims and Qadhafi and his agents made the Libyan people victims." These expressions of anger might have been intended to indicate the lack of support the United States and the United Kingdom were getting, opening the eyes of the American families to the realities of a world that is not always reflected within their country.

The Libyans had lobbied these families since the early days of this conflict. Most of them were receiving Libya's positions directly, though some did not accept Libya's communications. First, the Libyans bought advertising space in U.S. newspapers, presenting their position. Then they began sending the families letters explaining developments. The effect of this campaign proved fruitful when the United States and the United Kingdom finally changed their positions. Many of the American families were more receptive to that change; they had become aware that their old positions had led to stagnation.

A few days after the council's meeting, Libya's mission to the UN sent yet another letter to the families. It all but ignored the press conference some of their representatives had held. In that letter (dated 7 March 1998) the Libyans noted:

> The meeting of the United Nations Security Council on the 20th of March 1998 was another opportunity to prove that the claims of the United States and the United Kingdom governments of international support are nothing but a misrepresentation of facts.

The letter went on to say that the meeting proves, among other things, that:

> the United States and the United Kingdom governments are not interested in finding the real criminals in this case. The editorial of the Washington Post on 3/25/98 is another proof of that. Here is what it says: "The families, for their personal loss and for their weight in public opinion, have an undeniable claim to be heard by American and British policymakers. Still, a broader public interest lies in doing what seems most necessary as a nation to combat and deter terrorism…. But 10 years is also proof of necessary stamina to stay engaged in the pursuit of a terrible crime for however long it takes." Translation: the aim is not justice to the families. It is fighting Libya. Is that not a political issue? Is the aim anything other than the continuation of the sanctions against Libya and the suffering of its people as well as that of victims' families?

The conclusion of that Libyan position was to reaffirm that:

> the only way to end the suffering of both the Libyan people and the families of the victims is accepting to hold the trial in a neutral country. Justice is what you want. Justice is what we want.

As a result of this Libyan campaign, Swire's efforts and the inability of the American and British policy to deliver justice sought by the families, the announcement of the changed position around mid-1988 was, consequently, the breaking point in changing the tone of most American families. Their differences came out in the open and, for the first time, this conflict was publicized. Since the U.S. government had always claimed that its position was based mostly on the families' wishes, this change managed to help the officials accept and present a compromise. On October 17, the Associated Press ran a report on its tickers, noting that some of the families were now willing for a trial to take place in the Netherlands or another neutral country. One relative was quoted as asking the president to show some backbone, to bring

this matter to a resolution by agreeing to the trial in a neutral country."
The article continued:

> Still, some other members were, for other reasons, opposed to the compromise. Susan Cohen said I am outraged. For anyone to suggest that we're calling Gaddafi's bluff by giving him what he wants is totally outrageous—it's doing his work for him.
> "Gaddafi has launched an enormous propaganda campaign and has succeeded with the British families," she said in a telephone interview.
> "I am concerned about Americans being duped by Gaddafi," she said.

It was interesting that one expression was the central theme of that report: "calling Qaddafi's bluff." This expression was at the center of Libya's advertisements, letters and statements directed to the families. It was a major element of doubt in the minds of both British and American officials. They thought that these Libyan positions were nothing more than a maneuver to break the international community and that the two suspects would never be handed over. Libya was responding, "Call our bluff, indeed!"

PART IV

The Reactions of the United Kingdom and the United States

10

Conflicting Signs of Impending Solution

The Blair-Clinton Doctrine

It is necessary to assume that had the parties directly involved not reached that stage of frustration leading to a willingness for a solution, the positive outcome of the many efforts in play might not have been reached.

As the new world order doctrine lost momentum, the Clinton administration, which wanted to pay more attention than its predecessor to internal affairs, left most international issues without clear policy guidance. The United States and the United Kingdom witnessed Libya's gains without any major movement on their part. This almost total preoccupation with internal affairs led Clinton to surround himself with aides who possessed little or no experience in international affairs. Those few who did, such as National Security Adviser Anthony Lake and Secretary of State Warren Christopher, nevertheless lacked the personality needed to impose U.S. international leadership. Thus, the Americans might not have clearly seen or understood the changing world picture that left the United States on a weaker path of leadership. They were not able to fully envision the value of the historical role they were playing. Most of their policies were slogans lacking depth.

Witnessing the change in Libyan behavior and its diplomatic successes in the international forums put the Americans and the British on the defensive for years. It was a battle they were losing, with the momentum shifting rapidly and cumulatively in their adversary's favor. Failed efforts to strengthen the sanctions were replaced by failed efforts to even maintain what existed of them. They needed to change their policy if they were to maintain relevance.

The other factor playing toward a solution was the involvement of some mediators who forced themselves on the problem. Despite their preparedness to play a vital role, those mediators faced resentment and fear from the United States and the United Kingdom. They had to force themselves on them, although their effort was fruitful in raising Libya's morale in the process. Those mediators were none other than President Mandela and Prince Bandar, who turned out to be catalysts for the solution, as much as the Blair-Cook factor was a catalyst for the new thinking in the west.

Stagnation had prevailed until the Labor Party won the May 1997 elections in Britain, bringing Tony Blair to the post of prime minister and the Scottish lawyer and politician Robin Cook to that of foreign secretary. Blair and the labor government wanted to put their stamp on the policies of their country. Signs of change were emanating from London, leading Qadhafi, in a television interview, to consider the new prime minister "a revolutionary like me." Although this was typical overcharacterization from the Libyan leader, it showed a willingness to open a new page with a new leader. He had also welcomed Clinton's youthfulness on that same occasion.

It was becoming clear to all that a new group of people would be calling the shots in the West. Most important was the fact that Britain was now led by someone who was understood for what he was and was not. His personal approach, or vision, covered whatever possible shortcoming existed in the official and institutional position of the government. Blair was not Thatcher, meaning he did not look for force to implement his visions. He did not carry the heavy load Thatcher had (and her successor, John Major, had for her role) in the 1986 American bombing of Libya. Clinton himself was not Reagan or Bush. He did not look for many external confrontations as Reagan and Bush had, although he had to do it reluctantly a few times in order to deflect attention from his internal problems. And then there was Qadhafi. Although he is now very much the same man, with the same principles, who has led Libya since 1969, intellectually and politically he had changed.

The new Labor government in Britain, following a tradition in reviewing its predecessor's policies in order to formulate its own, ordered a full review of their country's policies as soon as it took over from the

Conservatives in early 1997. The full review was conducted between May and July 1997. Because pressure in the House of Commons and from the victims' families was increasing, the review included the British policy regarding the Lockerbie case. Blair, however, did not officially announce the existence of such a review until June 18, when addressing the House of Commons, seeking to restore his country's influence and standing in the newly formulated Europe. This goal, in turn, required restoring Britain's international policies. The Labor government moved to sort out many of the problems left from the previous era, including, among others, the improvement of relations with Cuba and reestablishing relations with Iran.

It took the new British leader more than two years to be able to formulate his new vision of the world. What turned out to be the "Blair Doctrine" was at last announced to coincide with the fiftieth anniversary of the establishment of NATO. Blair explained:

> For Britain, the biggest decision we face in the next couple of decades is our relationship with Europe. For far too long British ambivalence to Europe has made us irrelevant in Europe, and consequently of less importance to the United States. We have finally done away with the false proposition that we must choose between two diverging paths— the transatlantic relationship of Europe. For the first time in the last three decades we have a government that is both pro-Europe and pro-American. I firmly believe that it is in Britain's interest, but it is also in the interests of the U.S. and of Europe.[1]

Blair reiterated the conflicting theories about globalization and non-interference:

> The most pressing foreign policy problem we face is to identify the circumstances in which we should get actively involved in other people's conflicts.
> Non-interference has long been considered an important principle of international order. And it is not one we would want to jettison too readily. One state should not feel it has the right to change the political system of another or foment subversion or seize pieces of territory to which it feels it should have some claim. But the principle of non-interference must be qualified in important respects. Acts of genocide can never be a purely internal matter. When oppression produces massive flows of refugees which unsettle neighboring countries, then they can properly be described as threats to international peace and security. When regimes are based on minority rule they lose legitimacy— look at South Africa.

Clearly, Blair was providing his views of the world, which he called "the Third Way." He was trying to combine the theories that ruled the world up until the end of the cold war, squeezing out of them a new theory that provides more conciliation intended at paving the way into economic globalization. This big picture provided guidance for efforts to eliminate the obstacles under the slogan "We can only survive in a global world if we remove barriers and improve co-operation." Without saying so directly, the Lockerbie issue—and, by extension, relations with Libya—is but one of those barriers he sought to remove.

Results of Blair's Review

One result of that review of British policies was the emergence of ideas on the Lockerbie case. And since this was a cross between international concerns, Blair and Cook raised many questions about the existing policy, demanding answers. The gist of the questions was:

Is there any doubt we could win this case in court?
Is the evidence strong enough to be presented in court?
Is this a poison chalice we are inheriting from the Conservative government?

The directives were for Cook to look into the diplomatic aspect of the case and for the lord advocate to look at whether there was a legal case. Diplomatically, the result was that a need for a change in policy was necessary, at least cosmetically, to face the growing support Libya was receiving.

Legally, the answer was simple: Yes, we have a case.

Another aspect of the review of the policy on Libya was the continuing considerable public and parliamentary interest in this issue. The families of the British victims were very active and receptive of the Libyan and Arab offers to find a compromise, mainly the one in favor of holding the trial in a third country or at the Hague. In the parliament, one member stood out. He was consistently asking questions about the lack of progress and, later, the lack of a positive response to the international evolution in positions calling for a compromise. That member was Tam Dalyell.

Despite the work toward change on the general aspect, London still had to face daily efforts by Libya and its supporters at the UN. The UN Secretary General was facing African and Arab pressure to send an envoy to Libya to study the humanitarian effect of the sanctions on the Libyan people. The secretary general of the Arab League came to New York to lobby for such a mission and for a trial in a neutral third country. The secretary general of the OAU raised the issue with Annan on many occasions. The reaction to such a request was favorable among many countries, except the United States and the United Kingdom.

With the initial results of the internal review, the British officials began drawing the new policy. It was very difficult for them to imagine the technical possibilities to make the necessary decisions for such major changes in policy and procedures, especially when taking into consideration how hard it was for the U.S. government to face the internal lobbies opposing any change. London could not face such a challenge alone. There was a need to formulate a presentation to the U.S. It was supposed to be sharp enough not to create an immediate rejection, yet dynamic enough to find acceptance among Libya's supporters and possibly Libya itself.

Officially, until the end of 1997, the Labor government insisted its review was neither unusual, nor did it bring about anything unusual. Cook denied there was any change in his country's position, as reported by some newspapers and other media which contemplated something about a change. On September 22, 1997, after a meeting with Albright at the residence of the British ambassador to the UN, Cook said: "I'm glad to have the opportunity to put the record straight. There has been some quite mistaken reporting of the British government's position. I've had a number of meetings on this in the Foreign Office. I have discussed it with my Prime Minister. Our position is quite clear; this was an act of mass murder. It cannot be laid to rest until there is a court hearing and justice is seen to be done. And we will continue to insist that those two men should stand trial in the Scottish jurisdiction where they will get a fair trial."

Albright, standing next to him, could not offer anything new. Her statement was simple, echoing previous statements: "We believe the Libya sanctions need to stay in place until the Libyans turn over the suspects for the Lockerbie bombing."

The difference between the two was in the last sentence of Cook's statement. He did not mention the trial should be held in Scotland but "in the Scottish jurisdiction." Not many noticed this change, and the media took the general statement as expressive of the British position without notice of the change in tone—or maybe just thoughts in his mind—leading later to a changed position. Albright did not reject or correct Cook's statement in this regard.

Cook's Firsthand Experience at the Security Council

In an atmosphere of gloom, stemming from American and British anger at their continuing diplomatic losses, both countries witnessed yet another setback at the UN, with a higher degree of intensity than that at the sanctions review by the UN Security Council. The council held a ministerial meeting on Africa on September 25, 1997. Madeleine Albright, who had just become the Secretary of State at the beginning of the year, had proposed the convening of this meeting in order to enhance her standing with the Africans. She and Cook, like many others, thought the meeting would be nothing more than a ceremonial discussion of the general issues of a continent emerging as a focus of many people in the world. To their surprise, Libya managed to get many member and nonmember speakers to raise the Lockerbie issue. Some speakers went so far as to call for the sanctions to be lifted. Had Albright foreseen what would happen, she would not have called for the meeting, for it signaled yet another diplomatic victory for Libya.

Albright responded angrily to the African statements. She inserted the following into her previously prepared statement (and later attached it to the text distributed):

> Let me say today that there can be no compromise with Libya when it comes to terrorism. With respect to the case of Pan Am 103, the responsibility for the effect of this Council's actions on the people of Libya rests squarely on the government of Libya. We must be united in our demand for full compliance with this Council's resolutions. To do less is to insult the memory of those who died so tragically and to deny the victims' families the demands of justice.

Cook's similar insertion in response was the following:

> Let us be clear about the intent of those who placed the bomb on the Pan Am flight which exploded over Lockerbie. Their intention was to wipe out every passenger on that plane. All of us round this table travel frequently by air, we above all people have an interest in stopping airplanes being used as a vehicle for terrorism. The charge sheet against the two Libyan nationals who have been indicted is a full one which compellingly sets out the evidence that they must answer and can only answer if they appear on trial. I welcome the statement by President Mugabe that he wishes that trial to take place under Scots law. The only place they can face trial under Scots law is Scotland. There is no legal authority for Scots court to meet outside Scotland, there is no legal authority in the law of the Netherlands for a court of another jurisdiction to sit in the Hague. We are, though, conscious of the international interest in this case. That is why we have recently invited Libya, the Organization of African Unity and any other country around this table who wishes to send international monitors to attend any trial in Scotland. Justice we know must be seen to be done but justice must also be carried out. A fair trial which protects the innocent but provides for justice against the guilty is an important basis for universal human rights.

Cook's reference to the call for observers came hastily. The plan was for it to be announced separately and with some flare. He wanted to counter the Libyan-Arab-African-Islamic position claiming, "There would be no fair trial in Scotland." It became a necessity "to flush those arguments out." But when the Security Council had such proceedings, he retracted. He did not want to be seen compromising as a result of the African campaign. That is why he once again said the trial should be held in Scotland, and his aides worked hard to convince reporters that what he said "was not new." One month later, the offer became a new official proposal. In a confirmation of that proposal, the British UN ambassador, on October 31, sent a letter to Annan calling on him, "as we did the Secretaries-General of the OAU and the Arab League," to send observers to attend the trial in Scotland and asking them to send two representatives to Scotland as soon as is convenient for you. If your chosen representatives are persons with experience of legal procedures, you may subsequently wish to appoint them as observers at the trial. They will visit Scottish prison and court facilities and meet United Kingdom representatives to discuss the modalities of a trial in Scotland in the presence of international observers.... We would welcome the presence of international observers from the United Nations at the trial of the suspects in Scotland. Observers will have full access to the suspects before and during the trial (if the suspects agree), will be able to witness all the court proceedings and will be provided with administrative and reporting facilities."[2]

Meanwhile, the UN Security Council continued its reviews of the sanctions, every 120 days, as called for in the resolutions. Those reviews added to the burdens of the United States and the United Kingdom. They witnessed increased support for the Libyan position and felt further pressure. After one such review, on November 9, 1997, the Chinese ambassador, who was presiding over the council during that month, walked out of the council to make a statement to the press revealing that major differences of opinion were presented and that his country wanted the sanctions lifted. Although some Western diplomats attending the meeting said he did not make such a forceful call inside the meeting room, the fact that this statement was made showed the beginning of a major break in the body responsible for such decisions, despite public statements to the contrary made by the British representative and his American colleague, both of whom claimed that the council unanimously opposed lifting the sanctions." It was clear they were both stunned by the development.

Libyan Humanitarian Suffering and Legal Review

One very important element raised and discussed during that review was the humanitarian situation in Libya that followed sanctions. The issue of the suffering of the Libyan people was further explored by Libya, who sent its health minister, Dr. Suleiman El-Ghammari, to New York in early September to meet members of the Security Council and the Secretary General, presenting them with detailed reports of the suffering. This was another effort by Libya to increase pressure on the United States and the United Kingdom, knowing full well the new General Assembly session was about to begin and the ministerial meeting of the Security Council was being planned to contribute politically.

In that same review, the humanitarian issue was discussed intensively when Egypt and other member countries raised it. El-Ghammari had explained the situation to the members. He provided detailed information to the secretariat and requested that a delegation visit Libya to examine the situation. Most council members supported such a delegation, but the United States and the United Kingdom rejected it. No one could doubt that Libya's efforts were continuing to gain ground. Still, the UN Secretary General would not oblige. He was facing different pressures. The United States and the United Kingdom wanted him to send a delegation to Scotland, rejecting any to Libya. Libya and many council members wanted him to send a delegation to Libya while seeing no necessity for a delegation to Scotland. The UN Secretary General later decided on both.

During that review, Ambassador El-Arabi of Egypt presented strong legal and political support to Libya's position, leading Washington to complain to Cairo about his statements. Egypt was in a unique position during its tenure as a nonpermanent council member in 1996 and 1997, for it exchanged turns with Libya, which faced a major offensive against its membership for those two years.[3] Moreover, El-Arabi was very active in coordinating the efforts of the African members in the council, leading to a very effective line of diplomacy which made these members force some of their positions on the other members and on their positions. The support Libya was receiving in the UN Security Council was not solely Arab-African anymore. The Non-Aligned Movement and China were contributing heavily, while Russia and France and other Europeans began to show some tough, limited flexibility.

After this latest review, Dorda sent a letter to the Chinese ambassador thanking him for his support and that of other members who "turned the Council's consultations into a serious meeting in the course of which they addressed the practice of the automatic and routine renewal of sanctions and clearly placed on record the positions adopted by their countries in support of rectitude and of my country and its demands. I should also like to express appreciation to those who preferred silence in the Council, inasmuch as their silence was more eloquent than any words. By their silence they too stood by my country, which was not present in the Council."[4]

While Annan accepted the invitation to send a committee to Scotland, the OAU and the Arab League rejected it. Libya was disturbed by this British maneuver and by Annan's hasty acceptance (while still refusing to send the long-sought humanitarian delegation to Libya). It issued a statement on November 3, reiterating that "Libya does not doubt the honesty or fairness of the Scottish judicial system. This particular matter, however, has given rise to biased publicity campaigns carried on in the media and through statements made by senior officials in the countries concerned. The result has been a social and psychological climate that is loaded against the two suspects, who have effectively been convicted in advance. This means that there is no possibility that they would be given a fair and impartial trial in Scotland, especially since Scottish courts use the jury system, which requires that all jurors must be unbiased and not personally prejudiced against the accused. Moreover, there are serious grounds for regarding the accusation against the suspects, who are held to have been responsible for the Lockerbie incident, as unsound."[5] This position proved to be a smart countermaneuver in response to a shrewd one. It succeeded in keeping Libya's supporters, the actual target of the British proposal, on Libya's side.

The Secretary General felt the Libyan answer would not satisfy Britain, which was pushing this "presentation idea" to counter Libya. For him to neglect such an effort by a permanent member of the Security Council would expose him to many accusations. He had to accept the British invitation while looking for ways to satisfy the African and Arab pressure regarding the humanitarian aspect. He decided on both. The final phase of what could be considered stage setting for the solution, unintentionally of course, came with the reports the Secretary General presented on the work of the delegations he sent to both Scotland and Libya. However, the way both delegations conducted their work, and the reports themselves, reflected the old status of the powerful and the weak.

The delegation sent to Scotland consisted of Dr. Enoch Dumbutshena, former chief justice of Zimbabwe, and Henry G. Schemers of Leiden University, the Netherlands, as the Secretary General's representatives, accompanied by legal experts from the UN. Their mission was simple: to visit Scotland and to study the Scottish judicial system.[6] The delegation visited Scotland and presented a report full of technical details such as floor plans and measurements of Dumfries

Sheriff Court, the special holding facility in HM Prison Barlinnie, the High Court of Justiciary in Glasgow, the holding cells of the High Court of Justiciary in Glasgow and the High Court of Justiciary in Edinburgh.

While it is still unclear what purpose these measurements served, the report explained how the trial would be held, as well as other procedural details relating to the holding of trials in Scottish courts. The report concluded "that the accused would receive a fair trial under the Scottish judicial system. Their rights during the pre-trial, trial and post-trial proceedings would be protected in accordance with international standards. The presence of United Nations and other international observers can be fully and easily accommodated. A trial by jury would not prejudice the accused's right to a free trial. If, however, the accused could reasonably establish that their right to a free trial would be prejudiced by a jury trial, we suggest that the idea of dispensing with the jury be pursued with the Government of the United Kingdom."

The "humanitarian" delegation visited Libya from December 13 to December 18, 1997. The Secretary General presented the report on this mission in such a way as to give the impression he did not endorse all of its contents.

This report was issued March 6, 1998, and, "according to the Government of the Libyan Arab Jamahiriya," an effort was made by Petrovsky and Annan to distance themselves from substantially adopting the details it contained about the suffering. It explained the effects of the sanctions on three sectors: economic, health and psychological. The report concluded:

> It was apparent that the sanctions had a psychological effect on the Libyan leadership. It feels isolated, targeted and unjustly subjected to a form of collective punishment even before the guilt or innocence of the two suspects had been established through an appropriate judicial process. The Libyan officials underscored that the stigma of a rogue State was hurting the people at large, and the damage to national pride has been grave. They noted that the psychological impact also constrained other countries from dealing with the Libyan Arab Jamahiriya in areas outside the purview of the sanctions. They also seemed perplexed that the initiatives and alternatives proposed by the Organization of African Unity and the League of Arab States, among others, to facilitate a resolution of the problem were not accepted by the Security Council.[7]

In addition to political demands for the Security Council to accept a compromise, the report identified the demands in the humanitarian fields as

> specific exemptions that they would like the Security Council to

approve, particularly urgent requests of a humanitarian nature relating to the health and social sectors. Those include: permission to operate flights to carry medicines, vaccines and blood specimens; an increase in the number of countries where patients may be taken by Libyan medical evacuation aircraft for treatment; permission to purchase aircraft for use in medical evacuation inside and outside the country; permission to operate direct flights for humanitarian and religious purposes; and permission to acquire spare parts, emergency equipment and equipment and services directly linked with civilian air traffic control. The mission emphasized that many of those requests could not be addressed within the existing mechanism and would require a decision of the Security Council.

In total contrast to the norms of reports presented by the Secretary General to the council and to that by the legal team on its visit to Scotland, this report did not include any conclusions or recommendations. That was an accurate acceptance of the American and British pressures against any interference by Annan. They were not about to accept any type of mediation short of the handover. Petrovsky himself adopted such a position in the report when he referred to his response to the political demands presented by the Libyan officials, insisting that the Security Council was the sole venue for discussion.

Despite their public lukewarm reaction to the humanitarian aspects of the report, Libya's officials were disappointed. The report did not present them with the political support they sought to continue this battle, and the Secretary General was not as supportive as they had expected him to be. Their original fears about Petrovsky were confirmed. The result was that they had lost a major diplomatic battle for the first time since 1992. As for Annan, the two reports practically offset each other. He managed to get out of a delicate situation.

An Unlikely Battle of Letters

While the presentational idea proved insufficient to provide the United States and the United Kingdom with the momentous shift they were seeking, Libya's foreign minister and other officials pressed on touring Africa for support. Libya's energetic UN ambassador kept his lobbying efforts at the highest possible level. He moved to implement aspects of the regional organizations' resolutions by holding meetings of the committees they established. The new effort concentrated on holding an official meeting of the UN Security Council to discuss the issue publicly. It was geared toward putting further pressure on the United States and the United Kingdom. The Libyans were succeeding at the UN and in other countries and forums.

The anti-Libya lobby in Washington was witnessing these developments with dismay. The ILSA was not providing any results affecting Libya's economy and its political decisions. The most hawkish of the victims' families kept asking for stronger sanctions against Libya, with the administration regularly paying lip service. Senator Kennedy faced the most pressure. He decided to act once again, knowing in advance there would not be a positive international response. All he could manage was to get fifty-four of his fellow senators to sign a letter dated May 19, 1997, which they sent to Richardson in New York, acknowledging, "There is no reason to believe that the current sanctions will be sufficient to persuade the Government of Libya to turn (the accused) over for trial in the future." They asked for an oil embargo to be imposed by the UN, especially since they expressed their "concern that the United Nations sanctions against Libya are often broken with no repercussions, and no public pressure brought to bear on those responsible." With that senatorial letter, which could be considered the most official acknowledgment of defeat, disappearing in the drawers of the U.S. mission to the UN, it became clear that all efforts to impose further sanctions against Libya had failed due to the economic necessities of Libya's European partners and a change in the atmosphere at the UN, where Russia, China and France prevented further use of sanctions (against the Sudan, for example) and were calling for an easing of the sanctions imposed on Iraq. A new atmosphere was emerging, putting Libya in a better position at the UN. That letter, however, was further proof of how much harder it was for the United States to adopt a change in policy. The opposition to change, by Kennedy and some of the victims' families, was enormous and continued to be, even after the handover and during the preparations for the trial in the Netherlands.

Libya played that "letter game" with the Americans. Dorda, to the surprise of all, wrote privately to Kennedy as well as to Richardson and U.S. Attorney General Janet Reno. In his letters, which were sent during the last week of May 1997, the Libyan ambassador offered to "assure you of my country's total readiness to immediately engage in the process of investigations and trial. I am personally ready to enter into negotiations over the procedural details of this question.... The economic boycott will not solve the problem, it would only make the waiting of the families of the victims longer than they have already endured." None of the U.S. officials responded to Dorda's letters.[8]

New Ideas to Counter Libyan Gains

At the U.S. State Department and in other circles around Washington, ideas were floating on the desperate necessity to do something to counter Libya's gains. The debates taking place around the world and at the UN were helping those calling for a change, no matter how cosmetic, in U.S. policy. During the daily briefing of October 6, 1997, James Rubin was asked about the dispute going on at the UN over where the suspects should be tried. His answer reflected continued stagnation, mingled with a sour feeling for losing the support of the international community. He said: "I don't think there's that much of a dispute. When the Secretary was in New York—the occasional comment does come up about exploring the option of going to a different format. But Foreign Minister Cook was very clear that you can't have a Scottish court and Scottish justice if you're in another country. We are looking to the international community to continue its support of the United States and the United Kingdom, to bring to justice those responsible for the Lockerbie terrorist incident; and that requires them to be handed over for justice in either Scotland or the United States. That position has not changed."

He was right in saying that the position had not changed. He did not say, however, that many in the State Department and in Albright's inner circle, including himself, were calling and working for the change, if for no other reason than to call Libya's bluff. He failed to reveal as well that, while ambassador in New York, Albright had commissioned some think tanks to look into a possible change in policy but had never brought the issue to her superiors in Washington. She was personally convinced of that necessity but was not willing to face the political heat while preparing herself for the more important position she wanted and got.

Despite this official caution, the American diplomatic assessment was that Libya would never hand over the suspects. Therefore, the United States decided to present a new position, which they did not expect Libya to accept. When Libya refused—so the plan went—the United States could argue in favor of further sanctions. The new position, that assessment went on to say, would make it easier for the United States to get Libya's friends back on the American side, and stricter sanctions would be feasible.

The British government seemed more willing to take that political risk, believing that Libya had grown tired of the sanctions psychologically, economically and politically, while the whole world had grown politically and diplomatically tired of the principle of imposing sanctions and the insufficient unilateral leadership of the United States. Libya was flying some of its airplanes in breach of the sanctions. Many African leaders were flying constantly into Tripoli's international airport in similar breaches. Washington was getting furious at this challenge to its will. Trying to embarrass those supporting Libya, U.S. officials were spreading rumors about Libya offering payoffs to African leaders to get them to fly in. Congress was threatening cuts in assistance to those countries breaching these sanctions, although action was never taken, for it would be costly for the Americans on other issues. Sanctions were becoming almost impossible to keep and enforce.

In other words, the argument first used by the British, and later by the Americans, urging the change, was that for them it would be a win-win situation. If Libya did not hand over the suspects, it would lose the support it had acquired. If it did, the problem would be solved. Either way, the United States and its allies would have escaped a quagmire.

Madeleine Albright, then U.S. secretary of state, admitted diplomatically to this American need for such a dramatic move while meeting her colleague, attorney general Janet Reno, to convince her on this initiative. She recalls saying to Reno, "If Qadhafi turns over the suspects, that's good. If he refuses, it should be easier for us to maintain or even strengthen sanctions." Albright comments that after a long discussion with her colleague on January 15, 1998, she concluded that Reno was "unconvinced but agreed" to discuss details with State Department officials.[9]

Libya's efforts and developments in the UN Security Council further contributed to the forthcoming change. For the first time, this conflict was publicized.

11

Western Attempts to Regain the Initiative

Regaining the Initiative? But for Libya: Their Efforts Continue

As far as London and Washington were concerned, nothing they did, not even Libya's loss on the humanitarian issue, seemed to halt the Libyan offensive. In the field, African leaders continued to fly into Libya while, on the diplomatic front, momentum kept shifting Libya's way. The Security Council's resolutions seemed to become almost obsolete, with regional organizations' resolutions becoming the legitimizing force behind the breaching of sanctions by the Africans. And despite the fact that Arab leaders were providing only verbal support, refusing to fly into Libya, London felt the African actions were dangerous enough on their own. More and more earnestly, regaining the initiative grew to become one of the top priorities of the British government.

The first moment for the actual and semiofficial effort toward that aim came toward the end of 1997 when the presentational proposal to invite observers to Scotland did not achieve its goals. Cook was still contemplating this firsthand experience in witnessing Libya's gains at the UN and moved to discuss this common experience with Albright. The opportunity was a private meeting held around Christmas, when he invited his American counterpart to spend a few days with his family. The atmosphere was cordial. No other officials were sitting around restraining the discussion. It was the best opportunity to explore fresh ideas.

Cook explained his views and the results of his government's review of policy. He urged Albright to adopt a new common position revolving mainly around the idea of holding a Scottish trial in a third country. Since thoughts were already explored at her office, Albright did not hesitate to agree with the necessity of finding a new way. They both agreed to start a common exploratory process through a dialogue based on the need to reach for a new initiative that would either lead to a trial or call Libya's bluff, leading in turn to restraint in the support Libya was increasingly receiving around the world. Would it be safe to assume that the conclusions presented by Cook included the fact that Libya was "not what it used to be," thus making it much easier to move toward a change of policy?

Officials in London were divided into two camps. One, a minority, thought Libya would hand over the two suspects under the OAU–Arab League compromise, with some conditions. The other was more in line with the general American view that no handover would ever take place. Either way, a change of policy was urgently needed, and the process began, albeit slowly. They could wait no more. The Libyan–African–Arab–Nonaligned tactics had begun to move away from the simple demand for a third country trial to the threat of totally ignoring the Security Council resolutions and breaking sanctions. The key thought was that the current policy would not make progress in bringing the suspects to trial and would lead to the disintegration of the authority of the UN Security Council. Cook was consistent, with his objective being the trial; he insisted that Britain had no hidden agenda.

At last the final work began. It was an intensive effort. Many small incidents led to doubts in minds on all sides. Washington was in the most inconvenient situation. Many of its top officials wanted a change, while others were more receptive to the pressure of the different lobbies.

On the ninth anniversary of the Lockerbie incident, spokesmen in Washington and the U.S. representative in New York made the usual statements accusing Libya of intransigence. Libya's reaction to those statements came in a letter from its foreign minister and later became a central element in the British-American identification of Libya's position, on which the revised policy was built. In that letter, addressed to the president of the Security Council, the Libyan foreign minister said:

> As is well known, the Libyan Arab Jamahiriya has left no stone unturned in seeking a peaceful solution to this dispute. All it has sought

to do is to ensure the right of the accused to a just and fair trial at a venue where they have not been found guilty in advance. There is no such place in the United States of America or in the United Kingdom. Libya has proposed many initiatives, and it has accepted many of the suggestions made by regional and international organizations. It accepted the proposal of the League of Arab States that the two suspects should be tried by a court in a neutral country and then the League's proposal, as endorsed by the Organization of African Unity, the Organization of the Islamic Conference and the Movement of Non-Aligned Countries, that they should be tried at The Hague by Scottish judges and in accordance with Scottish law. It also supported the options proposed to the Security Council by the Secretary-Generals of the League of Arab States and the Organization of African Unity. Those options met with wide support not only from international and regional organizations but also from distinguished international leaders and personages, who viewed them as a realistic and workable way to resolve the dispute in a manner satisfactory to all parties. The options were as follows:

—That the two suspects should be tried in a neutral country to be designated by the Security Council;

—That the two suspects should be tried by Scottish judges at the International Court of Justice at The Hague in accordance with Scottish law;

—That a special criminal tribunal should be established at the seat of the International Court of Justice at The Hague to try the accused.

The Libyan letter concluded:

Accordingly, the General People's Committee for Foreign Liaison and International Cooperation sees no justification for fabricating excuses, for any delay in holding the trial or, indeed, for prolonging the sanctions and the suffering of the families of the victims.[1]

In the early days of January 1998, contacts between British and American officials began on two levels: diplomatic and legal. While thoughts concentrated on finding a compromise, the officials picked up on what London considered the most feasible idea: the African-Arab proposal to hold a Scottish trial at the Hague, the seat of the ICJ. But instead of accepting that idea as a whole, they picked the first part and made changes to the second. They would accept holding a Scottish trial in the Netherlands, the country that hosted the ICJ, but not on the court's premises. The exploration process began to look into the legal possibilities and relevant procedures.

While those meetings were taking place, Clinton received Blair at the White House. The issue of Lockerbie was not raised at all during that meeting. The only discussions they touched on were the situation in Kosovo and, of course, the Monica issue, which was taking most of the American president's attention. Still, Clinton made a statement after the meeting, held on February 7, 1998, raising the Lockerbie issue. He said, "We haven't forgotten the victims of the bombing of Pan Am 103 in the skies over Lockerbie, Scotland, or their loved ones. We'll not rest until Libya complies with the requirements of the world community and surrenders for trial in the United States or Scotland the two Libyans accused of that brutal crime." Blair, on his part, did not say a word about the issue during that press conference.

That statement was reflective of the internal official quagmire in the United States: the victims' families. In December 1998, the tenth anniversary of the crash would be observed with some flare. The president would have to attend. If he managed to get an agreement on a trial, he would be in better standing. This date continued to guide many of the American efforts for the rest of the year, at times threatening the possibilities for a deal.

So far, no country other than the United States and the United Kingdom knew of their discussions. However, almost everybody felt something was moving in that direction. The only signals to that effect came on two fronts: some type of assurances from the two to their allies that they were trying to change their policy, and some contradictory statement made by some officials in both countries, showing a certain dissatisfaction with the imminent change. It was still extremely hard for Libya to believe a change was about to take place. But the atmosphere was full of speculations and generalities without any direct hint at the substance.

During that period, the American-British technical work was continuing. The experts reached an agreement on the political and diplomatic specifics of what they later called their "initiative," bypassing the U.S. Department of Justice, which was publicly insisting on holding a trial in the United States for procedural and technical reasons while acknowledging privately they had no case. The Department of Justice accepted that proposal only after the White House put its weight behind it. By the end of March, both governments had moved to consult the Dutch government on the legal and technical possibilities. The discussions there faced technical and political obstacles, leading to a slow process. On the technical side were questions related to transferring a certain piece of Dutch land to the British authority for it to be compatible with the legal requirements. An agreement could not be reached immediately since the Netherlands was facing elections, meaning the country had no real effective government in office, that is, until late August.

On the political scene, the process was facing incidental obstacles that did not necessarily relate directly to the issue, although they might have briefly affected the willingness of the American and British officials to seem compromising when they were supposed to show resolve. The Iraqi issue was facing growing complexities, taking most of the time of the principal officials in London and Washington and at the United Nations and further diverting the efforts on Lockerbie. Meanwhile, two American embassies in Africa—in Tanzania and Kenya—were blown up by terrorists of Al-Queda, an Islamic group led by Osama bin Laden, adding to the worries about the wider issue of confronting terrorism, with some accusing Clinton of being soft in his confrontation.

The Libyans were watching with concern. What if a change of policy came, with the sole intention of depriving them of the international support they were getting? What if that change led the regional organizations to turn their pressure against Libya even though a new proposal would not be along the lines of what they proposed? What if they insisted on a handover without guarantees? Are we about to lose five years of progress, having implemented all other demands in return for one single reward: no immediate military attack?

The only signal Libya was getting was limited to the insistence of the American and British officials, in their public statements, on the old conditions. This would lift the burden from Libya's shoulders. Libya would not have to retract its demands from the international organizations to consider sanctions null and void. It would not have to cease its requests to other countries to fly into Tripoli. Most of all, it would not have to hand over two of its citizens into the bleak unknown.

At the Security Council, Libya was continuing its battle as usual. It managed to raise the stakes one more time: asking for a lifting of the sanctions. The council was preparing for another review of the sanctions, a review in which the United States and the United Kingdom would face yet another offensive without any ability to reveal that an agreement had been reached between them on a new position. It was hard for the British and American diplomats to stand tough, repeating old positions, while aware that what they were saying was not going to stand for long.

The review was held on July 2, 1998. All parties were repeating old positions, for as yet there was no official change of policy by the United States and the United Kingdom. Libya, having seen signs of what was coming, was playing its cards diplomatically, avoiding a confrontation, as was noticed in the letter of their friends the day prior to the council meeting. The committees established by regional organizations[2] sent letters to the president of the Security Council in support of Libya. They both contained two main demands:

1. Immediately lift the sanctions imposed on the Libyan Arab Jamahiriya by accepting one of the options submitted by the Organization of African Unity, the Arab League, the Non-Aligned Movement and the Organization of the Islamic Conference; or

2. Suspend the sanctions imposed on the Libyan Arab Jamahiriya pending the decision of the International Court of Justice on the question.

The letters included an explanation best expressed in the letter of the Non-Aligned Movement. It said:

> We, as members of the Committee of Six established by the Cartagena Ministerial Conference, and in the name of all the members of the Non-Aligned Movement, call upon the Security Council to suspend immediately the sanctions, and to await the substantive decision by the Court of the dispute. We call upon the States permanent members of the Security Council, which are party to the dispute, to have the ability to strike an equilibrium between considerations of national interest and their international responsibility, and not to impede the Security Council in taking the right decision, which represents the interest of the international community and expresses the will of the majority of Member States, on whose behalf the Security Council is supposed to act.
>
> The resolutions adopted by the conferences of the Non-Aligned Movement in this regard are in fact in defense of the United Nations and its Charter. They are, at the same time, in defense of the judgments of the International Court of Justice and international law. Member States of the Non-Aligned Movement view the disregarding of the Court's judgments, as well as ignoring the will of the international community, as leading to a constitutional crisis that would involve the principal United Nations organs—the General Assembly, the International Court of Justice and the Security Council—thus damaging the credibility and the image of the United Nations.
>
> In the light of all this, the majority of the Member States, led by the Non-Aligned Movement, expect the Security Council to take the necessary action to strengthen the United Nations and its credibility and act according to the will of the majority of United Nations Members, in accordance with the Charter.[3]

Libya, for its part, presented a stronger position. For the first time, it was registering a strong request for compensation. However, the letter sent by Dorda to the council left the door open for "a solution to the dispute through one of the peaceful means stipulated in the Charter of the United Nations and the Montreal Convention, or await the decision of the International Court of Justice."[4]

These efforts furthered Libya's position while the isolation of the United States and the United Kingdom was further confirmed and strengthened. Russia, for the first time, began to move to Libya's side with the first clear expression of support for a compromise based on the Arab League and OAU proposals. Although that move was not clear in the statement of Russia's representative in the private review, the Russian foreign ministry issued the following statement on July 7:

> On July 2 of this year the United Nations Security Council conducted a regular review of the regime of sanctions in respect of Libya. The comprehensive discussion of the situation around that country became a logical continuation of the principled and substantive discussion that was started during the previous review on March 6 and the subsequent formal meeting of the Council on March 20. The study of the "Libyan question" highlighted the growing displeasure of most United Nations Security Council members with the absence of genuine progress in its resolution, something that is damaging to the Council's prestige. The desire of the international community to see a more vigorous search for compromise solutions concerning the Lockerbie case is increasingly evident.
>
> It is of fundamental importance that in the discussion the accent was made on the expediency to make more active use of the potential of the United Nations Secretary General to facilitate a resolution of the "Libyan problem." An appeal to Kofi Annan to continue his efforts to promote the speediest implementation of the relevant United Nations Security Council resolutions was included in the statement to the press that was made by the Chairman of the United Nations Security Council after the meeting. It is also of substantial importance that most speakers at the meeting supported the idea of expanding the list of humanitarian exceptions from the existing regime of sanctions. Along with this, most members of the Council clearly underlined the unacceptability of attempts of a one-sided withdrawal from regimes of sanctions.
>
> The Russian side confirmed, within the framework of fulfillment of the relevant resolutions of the United Nations Security Council, its support for the search of compromise variants of resolving the "Lockerbie case" on the basis of proposals made by the Arab League, the OAU and the Non-Aligned Movement, for the advancement of humanitarian exceptions from the regime of sanctions and for sending a fact-finding United Nations mission to Libya. The hope is expressed in Moscow that the review will give an additional impetus to stepping up the work to find a way out of the present impasse with the "Libyan file."

Russia, it seemed, knew that some new position was about to be announced by the United States and the United Kingdom. It did not want to be left out but could not get itself to move fully to Libya's side, even on an issue similar to that on Iraq, where Russia had taken a position totally contradictory to that of the United States. The Russian position on Iraq put it on a confrontational course with the United States since Moscow felt there were many benefits, both financial and economic, with regard to Iraq. Although Libya owes Russia about $2 billion, Moscow preferred to stay on the margin, since Libya is not as important geographically to Russia as an Iraq that has to keep Iran worried about its western, instead of northern, borders.

A large group of African leaders flew to Tripoli to visit the Libyan leader. Most of them did not even bother to ask for permission from the UN Security Council sanctions committee. Two leaders, however, did. Their position was extremely expressive of the political situation. The Africans fully supported Libya and demonstrated their support by breaching the sanctions, while Arabs fully abided by the Security Council resolutions. The two requesting permission were President Mubarak and PLO chairman Yasser Arafat. Mubarak received approval to fly under the pretext of taking with him some Egyptian doctors to help treat Qadhafi, who had broken his hip. Arafat's request was denied. He abided and went by land from Tunisia.

Mubarak's visit, though officially approved by the Security Council, received more attention than about a dozen breaches of sanctions by other African leaders. Still, while Egypt continued to insist on respecting Security Council resolutions, the Americans made sure to play two themes in public. The first was the humanitarian reasons for permission. The second was that Mubarak respected the resolutions, and, given his importance in the worldwide community, the leaders of other African nations should consider following suit. It was clear, however, that even when respecting the sanctions, a leader such as Mubarak would not be spared criticism. Those who broke sanctions received only minor expressions of criticism.

On July 10, the Egyptian foreign minister was visiting with Albright in Washington. After the meeting, the press asked them both about Mubarak's trip. This is how the exchange went:

> QUESTION: Madame Secretary, I wonder if you could tell the United States what the US thinking was in not opposing President Mubarak's decision to visit, despite a United Nations ban, to go to Libya to pay his respects to Muammar Qadhafi. I understand the fact that Egypt's Health Minister is in Iraq right now. I mean, Egypt, you've projected them as a friend and, of course, they're always projected as a moderate force. Is there any conflict here? The mother of one of the victims called this, this morning, a betrayal; and said that the Administration just seems to have lost interest in the American victims of Lockerbie. What is Mubarak doing in Libya with Qadhafi that you can tell the United States?

> SECRETARY ALBRIGHT: Well, first of all, let me say that President Mubarak went through the procedure at the United Nations, through

the Sanctions Committee, saying that he had wanted to make a humanitarian visit, that he had a doctor going with him; he approached it through the appropriate channels. We felt that a one-time humanitarian visit was appropriate, but we are not going to go along with any further visits by anyone for the purpose of just paying courtesy calls on Mr. Qadhafi. So we did believe that this was a humanitarian effort, and that President Mubarak had gone through the proper channels in order to secure the appropriate permissions for this.

Let me say that we have not nor do we ever forget about the victims of Lockerbie.

QUESTION: Mr. Foreign Minister, just to follow up on the earlier question—why is Egypt reaching out at this time to Libya and Iraq?

Especially when you're talking—two countries that are considered pariah states by the United States and its allies—when you have this strategic dialogue?

FOREIGN MINISTER MOUSSA: Well, on Libya we have been reaching out or trying to reach out since long time in order to discuss with the Libyan leadership the ways and means to resolve the Lockerbie issue, and to enlist the support by Libya of the goals by the Security Council.

Ever since this involvement by Egypt and by President Mubarak, in particular, a lot of changes have been noticed, have been entered into the Libyan position. We believe that it is always useful to dialogue, to talk. The Secretary was just saying that nothing is resolved without dialogue between the parties. So we see no inconvenience. We see, in fact, that it is useful to talk and to try to find a solution for the problem, as the families themselves suffering would also benefit from it.

As for the latest visit, it lies within the parameters of Arab traditions and of neighborly relations when there is a certain, say, circumstances that would necessitate a visit, especially within the humanitarian framework, we do it. Also, there are channels and this is within the framework of legitimacy and the resolutions of the Security Council on that matter. So Egypt has acted within that parameter, as the Secretary has just underlined.

It was clear that Moussa was not about to align with the OAU resolution. Instead he talked about a "framework of legitimacy and the resolutions of the Security Council." Because of these statements and other futile efforts since sanctions were imposed, Libya would feel later that Egypt could not play a major role in bringing about a solution. Reliance fell almost fully on Mandela and Bandar. Libya did not give Egypt the privilege of even announcing a solution after the process had led to the handover.

More important were the threats made by Albright:

> We felt that a one-time humanitarian visit was appropriate, but we are not going to go along with any further visits by anyone for the purpose of just paying courtesy calls on Mr. Qadhafi.

IV. The Reactions of the U.K. and the U.S.

Libya's UN mission reacted on July 13, saying that the statements

> confirm, once again, that sanctions against Libya are Americans, not
> international. The Security Council has to prove its independence from
> American decisions and positions. These positions do not take into con-
> sideration but the US's interests. The Security Council has to prove, as
> well, it works on behalf of the international community which refuses
> to abide by the control of one country abusing this international orga-
> nization as a tool for its foreign policy.

The statement ignored Moussa's comments.

12

A Solution Nears: Leaks,
Fears and Anxiety

While secrecy enveloped all efforts and the agreements reached and everybody waited for the new Dutch government to be formed, some officials felt they could not hide the existence of such an agreement. Some general facts were leaked diplomatically, others were leaked to the press apparently with the hope of creating enough of a storm to kill the deal.

In diplomatic circles, the Libyans were told that some type of change was coming. Two possibilities were raised. One was that the United States Congress would soon debate the sanctions issue, leaving certain impressions that the debate would help the administration retract its position on Libya and possibly abandon such a policy. The discussion, however, was held, concentrating on the issue of U.S. sanctions against China, more than anything else. There was some debate regarding the benefits of U.S. national sanctions, rather than UN sanctions. Many studies revealed those sanctions were hurting the U.S. economy. However, the U.S. Congress was in no mood for change. On July 20, 1998, the influential Senator Jesse Helms (R—N.C.) reaffirmed his commitment to the sanctions weapon, saying, "There are three basic tools in foreign policy ... diplomacy, sanctions and war." This left no room for any change in this abuse of the principle of sanctions. A saying in Washington holds that in the Senate, 90 (out of 100) senators think they can do a better job as Secretary of State, and in the House, 90 percent of the representatives think there is no need at all for the post of Secretary of State. In other words, Congress would not help prepare the way for the administration.

The other possibility was directly connected to some governmental change of policy. No details were known, but fear of the new counteroffensive of the United States and the United Kingdom to sell their new position would lead to a weakening of Libya's position at the NAM Summit. Anxiety prevailed.

Press leaks raised anxiety among all concerned, officials and families alike. The most important leak came on July 21, 1998. The *Guardian* newspaper in London published an article containing the following:

> Britain and the United States have decided that two Libyans accused of the Lockerbie bombing can be tried in The Hague under Scottish law, reversing their position that justice can only be done under their jurisdiction—and shifting the onus on to Colonel Qadhafi to hand them over.
>
> Robin Cook, the Foreign Secretary and Madeleine Albright, the United States Secretary of State, are to make the announcement simultaneously in London and Washington in the next few days, the Guardian has learned.
>
> The two allies reached agreement earlier this month but the announcement has been held up pending a new government in Holland, whose approval is required for the trial to go ahead.
>
> Libya has not yet been informed of the new position, which is likely to follow closely a proposal made by the Arab League and the Organization of African Unity, which have said Colonel Qadhafi will accept a court operating under the Scottish legal procedure. Under this proposal, it would have an international panel of judges instead of a jury, presided over by a senior Scottish judge appointed by Tony Blair.
>
> The Hague is home to the International Court of Justice and the Bosnia War Crimes Tribunal. If the two men are handed over, and convicted, special arrangements will have to be made for their imprisonment.
>
> Diplomats believe it is unlikely that Colonel Qadhafi will agree to surrender the men but argue that if he does not, it should be easier to reinforce the sanctions.

The way the story was leaked confirmed one fact: Whoever did it was either not directly involved in the formation of the new position or was intentionally trying to give inaccurate details to keep himself (or herself) away from any doubts. Other explanations included a certain leak "by coincidence," where the reporter received a vague indication of the discussions but was unable to confirm the full extent of the real story, leading him and the newspaper to prefer the publication of a story not fully accurate over waiting and losing an advantage when somebody else might get the real scoop and publish it.

Two main elements in the story were not accurate: the venue for the trial and the panel of judges. The trial was not at the Hague but in another part of the Netherlands—Camp van Zeist; it wouldn't be an international court presided over by a Scottish judge but a panel consisting only of Scottish judges.

That story was a definite journalistic coup. For the next few days, almost every media outlet followed up with details and inquiries. The official response to the story was more important, since it was extremely hard for anyone to deny the facts in their entirety while confirmation would entail a follow- up both London and Washington were not quite ready for.

In London, Blair's chief press spokesman denied that any decision had been taken and said there would be immense legal, diplomatic and technical complexities in staging a trial in a third country. But he added: "We are willing to explore any option which would bring justice to the families. Discussions on such options have been taking place for some time. We will maintain close cooperation with our allies on these options."

The next day, July 22, 1998, the spokesman, Alastair Campbell, came out with a clearer and more accurate position, which gave the first detailed, public explanation of what was going on. He said Britain had never accepted criticism of the Scottish system but was prepared to look at alternatives in the interest of justice for the families of the victims. He failed to state that criticism was not made (by Libya, at least) of the Scottish judicial system but of the venue.

Campbell went on to say, "That is why we did launch discussions with the United States some months ago and more recently with the Dutch about the possibility of a trial under Scottish law with Scottish judges—not, as has been said, an international panel of judges." After noting the existence of legal and technical difficulties, he said, "We do think they can be resolved and should be resolved reasonably speedily."[1]

In the United States, the first official reaction that same day showed the complexity it faced in its internal process. National Security Adviser Samuel Berger and Albright had a conference call with ten representatives of the victims' families to explain the situation in light of the *Guardian* story. At the State Department, spokesman Jamie Rubin had a prepared statement that reflected more uneasiness in the urgency of his department's reaction to the story. At the daily briefing that day, he read:

Let me start by saying that we have worked very hard for 10 years to impose and then keep on an effective sanctions regime against Libya, pending their compliance with U.N. Security Council resolutions requiring that these suspects face Scottish or British or American justice.

And we have been exploring alternative ways to meet that objective—that is, again, to bring the suspects who committed this heinous crime, where over 180 Americans died, before a trial, an effective trial, before an effective justice system.

To date, we have not found practical alternatives to a trial in the United States or in Scotland. Our bottom line is simple; the accused perpetrators of this heinous crime must face justice before U.S. or Scottish courts. We are working to achieve that goal. It has been 10 years, and this delay of justice has been a denial of justice. And we have been working very hard to see whether there is a way in which it is practicable to hold a Scottish court outside the United Kingdom, and what steps would be necessary to make this possible. Determining whether such a proceeding might take place and how it might take place without affecting the integrity of the judicial process has taken a great deal of study and reflection, as well as extensive consultations with other governments. It will take a great deal more effort to make this procedure happen. We are exploring it, but let me emphasize, very clearly, we have made no decision on this matter. What we are doing is seeing whether the question of a Scottish court in a third country, with Scottish judges, Scottish procedures, and Scottish justice, can be arranged logistically and legally. And if that happens, then it will be up to Muammar Qadhafi to comply with the Security Council resolutions which state that he must allow for a U.S. or Scottish justice.

Rubin also made the following points:

—The accused are not going to negotiate the tribunal in which they're going to be tried. Let me try to state this again. The question is geography, not the quality of justice. We are not suggesting there would be any change in the quality of justice. The question is whether that justice system with the same procedures, the same prosecutors, the same law, the same process by which justice is provided in a Scottish court would occur, but in a different place. And that is not allowing the suspect to choose the venue; the venue is a Scottish court. If it were in another location, it's still a Scottish court. It's a de facto Scottish justice system, ...the point is to bring them to justice.

—It is our view that not only do the suspects have to be provided, but the Libyan government has to cooperate in the trial, that appropriate compensation has to be paid, and they have to stop their ... support for international terrorism. Those are the requirements and those haven't changed.

—It is our view that compensation ought to be paid, and if these nationals from Libya were involved, the four issues that I mentioned are our requirements for sanctions to be lifted. It's not enough to just hand over the suspects. There's a level of cooperation in the trial, in the evidentiary proceedings and all that goes with that would be required, as well as a flat change in Libya's policy of supporting international terrorism.

—We have not made a decision. And I hope all of you who are covering this issue accurately reflect the fact that we are exploring something. We have not made a decision. We are exploring a creative way to deal with the fact that justice delayed is justice denied, and that a change of geography does not mean a change in the quality of justice.

—The question ... is once we make this arrangement—and this is not a negotiation; what we are talking about is a take-it-or-leave-it package that puts a Scottish court in a third country and presents that to the United Nations as an alternative way of meeting the objectives of the U.N. Security Council resolutions. And I'm sure we'll find out very quickly whether the Libyans are going to put their money where their mouth is, or whether they were bluffing.

The U.S. president was asked about the story at a public appearance that same day:

Q: Mr. President, your administration's making a new push to end the standoff with Libya over the Lockerbie bombings, including possibly holding a trial in a neutral country, under US or Scottish jurisdiction. Are you optimistic that this time it might help? And what has brought on this new push?

PRESIDENT CLINTON: Well, we have always said that our first goal was to bring the perpetrators of the Pan Am 103 murders to justice. That's our first purpose. And ... since I got here, we've been looking for ways to do that. We have had conversations with representatives of the British government as well. We've always said we thought that there had to be a trial under American or Scottish law. There may be some possibility of standing up a Scottish court in another country, but there are lots of difficulties with it as well, apparently.

All I can tell you is that its one of the things that we have explored, with a view toward accelerating the day—it's been a long time now; it's been a lot of years since that terrible day when Pan Am 103 crashed over Lockerbie.

And we're looking at it, but I don't know that it can be done. ...Our people have spent a lot of time on it. We've talked to the British at great length about it. We're trying to find some way that has real integrity that will work, but there are all kinds of practical difficulties in it that I'm sure our folks can explain. I don't know if we can do it, but we're working on it.

Q: What brought it up now, I mean what—all of a sudden, after so many years?

PRESIDENT CLINTON: I don't know why—I don't know why it is just now coming into the press, but it's not just being brought up now, I mean, we have literally been working for years. I have personally been engaged in this for years ... trying to find a way to get the suspects out of Libya into a court where we thought an honest and fair and adequate trial could occur. And, you know, in a case like this, like every other case, as the years go by, you run more and more chances that something will happen to the evidence that is available, to any witnesses that might be available. ...We've had a sense of urgency about this for some time.

But my guess is that it has come to public light because of the significant number of conversations that had to be held between the American and the British authorities, and between others in potential third-party venues, like the Netherlands. And I know there's been discussion of that, but it has not been resolved yet.

The Americans, apparently, were willing to confirm the general facts but not the timing or the details. Berger and Albright, among other officials, discussed what their reaction should be, coordinating that reaction with their British counterparts. In a case such as this, public reaction should normally be used to soften the position of those families that are extremists, although they represent a minority compared to the wider group that leaves such decisions and positions to the government without major statements critical of its positions. That is why Clinton's statement was so formulated.

The American families had mixed reactions. According to a Reuters report of July 21, 1998, one of the relatives who took part in the conference call with Albright and Berger, Rosemary Wolf of northern Virginia, said the reaction from relatives was mixed: "Some thought it might be a good idea, others believed it was an attempt that was bound to fail. Many of us feel that this is a betrayal. It won't bring justice closer but it might give the impression our policy has failed. ...It's almost 10 years now and enforcing the sanctions has become difficult so we have to find more positive ways to find a solution." She said Albright and Berger did not seem to have high hopes that a Scottish court could really sit in the Netherlands: "I had the impression they are not convinced this is workable and would result in a fair trial. Their attorneys aren't sure of that yet." Another family representative, the most hawkish among them, Susan Cohen, said it was "a black day" for her family. "They have lied to the US so I don't see why I should believe anything they say. ...This idea opens a Pandora's box and they just want to dump the sanctions. They have lost. Qadhafi has won. This is a collapse, a total reversal of everything they have stood for."

On the other hand, other victims' families expressed hope. "Overall, I was favorable," said Paul Hudson of Albany, New York. "We wrote to the president last year and asked for an international trial and we were glad to see that's moving forward. The majority of the group, including myself, feels strongly that this is an excellent suggestion, that it is time that we moved on because world opinion has shifted a little bit to Qadhafi," added Jack Schultz of Ridgefield, Connecticut.

Schultz, chairman of a group called Victims of Pan Am Flight 103, said some opponents were implacable: "There were two or three women who I think would object to anything." One U.S. official, refusing to be identified, said, "These women have nothing else to do. They keep calling and talking. That is all it takes for the government to consider them public opinion."

For the first time, however, U.S. officials were willing to talk about different positions among the families. That was taboo prior to that day. It seemed the U.S. government was showing its own commitment to the new process by trying to play that difference. The White House spokesman, Michael McCurry, was clear in saying during his daily briefing that same day: "The wishes of the families are that there is no unanimity of viewpoints in the family members. Each of them, you know, has got different ways of looking at this. And for some time, there have been differing points of view on how we ought to proceed at this point. It's been 10 years since this awful tragedy, and we are interested in trying and bringing to justice those responsible."

While American victims' families expressed different views, based on the aforementioned statements, the British families were more receptive. Dr. Swire asked: "What do Britain and America have to lose by agreeing to a neutral country trial, except perhaps a smidgen of national pride? Are not justice and truth more important than that?" But in his comment on the story, the substance of which he had lobbied for, Swire said it was time to break the impasse. "Of course, I would be delighted if the *Guardian* report is true. Common sense dictates that something has to be done." Later that day (July 21) he told the BBC, "I'd be over the moon because this is something we've been pressing for a number of years."

Libya kept quiet. The only official reaction was off the record; reporters who asked for comments were told, "This is a media story. Once we have anything official we will react." In London, that calculated silence was considered another expression of seriousness on the part of Libya, while Washington, though unwilling to acknowledge it, could not but notice.

The Scottish lawyer hired by the Libyans as a member of the defense team, Alistair Duff, was the only person who presented what could be close to a Libyan reaction. He said: "Experience teaches us not to believe everything we read in the papers but certainly, if this is correct, it's a major step forward and it's a step forward which my clients, I know, will welcome," he told BBC radio on the 21st.

After a few days of media hype, the issue went to the back burner. Many officials on both sides of the Atlantic could breathe again. Had Libya built publicly on the leaked story, its official reaction could have affected what was coming. Had the public reaction in the United States and the United Kingdom been as negative as very few American families described it, there might not have been an official announcement. All in all, it seemed the evolution in the American and British position would work. Everybody went back to a waiting mode, though not for long.

On July 29, 1998, the International Relations Committee of the United States House of Representatives held a scheduled hearing on "developments in the Middle East," during which Indyk reconfirmed the fact that a review of policy had taken place in order to prepare the House for an upcoming official position. In his presentation, Indyk said:

> As the tenth anniversary of the bombing of Pan Am 103 approaches in December of this year, we have also been preoccupied in recent months with the question of how to bring to justice the Libyan terrorists responsible. We are discussing with the United Kingdom and the Netherlands the possibility of conducting a trial of the two suspects in a Scottish court in the Netherlands. I should emphasize that the president has made no decision on this and will not consider the matter until we are satisfied that the large number of complex legal issues have been sorted out. I want to be very clear on one point, however. The United Nations Security Council resolutions call for the suspects to be tried in an American or Scottish court. We are exploring the establishment of a Scottish court in a third country venue. A Scottish court means a panel of Scottish judges, applying Scottish legal procedures and Scottish rules of evidence. It does not mean a World Court proceeding and it does not mean an international panel of judges. Our bottom line remains simple: we seek justice for the 189 American victims of Pan Am 103 and their families. Any arrangements agreed to will have to lead to this objective or demonstrate clearly to the world that Qadhafi has no intention of ever delivering the suspects, thereby helping to strengthen the United Nations sanctions against Libya.
>
> For far too long the victims and family members of the Pan Am 103 bombing have been denied justice. Libya, under the dictator Muammar Qadhafi, has refused to deliver for trial before American or Scottish courts, the two suspects in the case. After ten years, we are no closer to getting the accused into an American or Scottish courtroom. The possibility we are now examining is simply this: moving a Scottish court and Scottish law to another country, probably the Netherlands. We are discussing the possibility, and seeking to resolve the legal complexities. Until we do so, no decision will be made to proceed with this idea.
>
> Our bottom line is the same: there will be justice or there will be UN-mandated sanctions. We have told the representatives of other countries that, if we decide to proceed with this approach, it is non-negotiable on

a take-it-or-leave-it basis. We have told those who have urged flexibility on United States that they will have the obligation to urge Libya to accept this offer. And if Qadhafi demonstrates that he has been bluffing all along when he promised the Arab League to deliver the suspects to a Scottish court in a third country, we will expect them to help enforce and strengthen sanctions.

This was the first official American indication of the change of position. Indyk was clear that it would be a Scottish court held in the Netherlands, not an international panel. This was meant to calm some of the victims' families' criticisms that the administration had sold them out. It was also meant to address some worries of the lawmakers most interested in this issue, notably Senator Kennedy.

Another intention of this announcement was to lay the groundwork with the mediating countries on two aspects: no negotiations and the calling of Libya's bluff. If Libya did not hand over, these countries were not only to give support and halt any breach of sanctions but also to ask for stronger sanctions. It was, in a way, a carrot-and-stick policy.

For the following month, the change in the U.S.-U.K. position was all but officially announced. Officials in both countries were patiently awaiting the final arrangements in the formation of a new Dutch government. As the government was formed, there had to be another waiting period for the Dutch government to hold its first official meeting. Cook was personally following that arrangement and keeping the United States informed.

13

The United Kingdom's Announcement ... and a New Anxiety

Finally, on August 24, 1998, the new Dutch government was to meet. Cook was on the phone eagerly awaiting a call from Amsterdam confirming the government's official adoption of an agreement between the two countries. However, another procedural action had to be awaited: the British Queen still had to sign an "Order in Council" allowing a Scottish court to be held in another country. That order was finally signed in a dramatic manner: On September 16, while at the waiting lounge at Heathrow airport, Queen Elizabeth signed the order to allow the execution, two days later, of an official British-Dutch treaty for a Scottish court to sit in the Netherlands.

Robin Cook could not wait any longer. Standing alongside the Lord Advocate of Scotland, Andrew Hardie, barely one hour after that signature, Cook announced the "United Kingdom initiative." He said, "Throughout seven long years, Libya has repeatedly stated that it would accept a trial before a Scottish Court sitting in a third country. Omar Muntasser, Foreign Minister of Libya, said in January in a letter to the President of the Security Council that Libya ... accepted the proposal of the Arab States that the two suspects should be tried by a court in a neutral country and ... that they should be tried at The Hague by Scottish judges and in accordance with Scottish law."

Cook went on to refer to the open "meeting of the Security Council debate as recently as March where the Libyan Foreign Minister said that concerns about Scotland by the lawyers for the 2 suspects relate solely 'to the venue and have nothing to do with the judges or the law.' Those statements, made only this year, put to rest the claim that Libya has always demanded a trial before international judges. Both statements made clear that Libya would accept a trial before Scottish judges."

As for the legal details of the announcement, Cook said, "The only point at which the court will differ from the standard application of Scottish legal procedures is that it will not be a trial by jury, as it is not practical to require the attendance of 15 ordinary citizens for what may be many months of a trial in a foreign country."

Cook also promised a suspension of the sanctions if Libya complied, as called for in the original resolutions. "As soon as they are handed over for trial," Cook said, "we will support action in the Security Council to suspend the international sanctions against Libya. Until that happens these sanctions will remain in force and if Libya should refuse to surrender the 2 suspects, international support for the sanctions will be redoubled."

In Washington press briefings on August 24, Madeleine Albright was more forceful in her presentation of the agreement and clearer in saying it was aimed at "calling Libya's bluff." What Cook considered a result of sanctions, Albright acknowledged was a result of the fact that "sanctions have not altered Libyan intransigence."

Albright confirmed the original plan was not American but "has been suggested to the United States as a way to call the Libyan Government's bluff and to bring the fugitives into court at long last." She also mentioned that "after consultations with The Netherlands, we have concluded that such a trial is, indeed, possible. ...We note that Libya has repeatedly stated its readiness to deliver the suspects for trial by a Scottish court sitting in a third country. The Arab League, the Organization of African Unity, the Organization of the Islamic Conference and the Non-Aligned Movement have endorsed this approach. We now challenge Libya to turn promises into deeds. The suspects should be surrendered for trial promptly. We call upon the members of organizations that have endorsed this approach to urge Libya to end its ten years of evasion now."

Another element in Albright's statement was expressive of the pressure the United States had to face in order to make such a move, for despite the clear fact that the United States and the United Kingdom had to back off from their stagnant position, they had to insist this was "our own initiative," meaning they would have to make their own conditions—conditions that might have backfired had they been implemented to the letter and not left for internal public consumption. "Let me be clear," Albright said. "The plan the US and the UK are putting forward is a 'take-it-or-leave-it' proposition. It is not subject to negotiation or change, nor should it be subject to additional foot-dragging or delay. We are ready to begin such a trial as soon as Libya turns over the suspects. We expect—and the families deserve—an immediate answer."

Two different versions of the move were presented. One was intended to somehow provoke Libya to reject the change so that sanctions could go back on track. That was the American presentation, especially when taken in a wider context connected to what Albright had said three days earlier with regards to talks about military attacks against Libya.[1] The other was the United Kingdom's, which was doubtful about whether Libya really intended to hand over the two suspects but showed more willingness, diplomatically at least, to try to open the doors for the handover, easing Libya's hard feelings on this issue.

Statements made by Albright and Cook during the following days and weeks confirmed the previous assessment, which turned out to be Libya's assessment, leading the Libyans to distinguish between the British and American positions: welcoming the first while feeling concerned and doubtful about the intentions of the latter.

Libya received the new U.S.-U.K. position with calculated silence. The details were not so clear, leading to escalating worries on the part of Tripoli. Meanwhile, Dorda, who had awaited official word in New York throughout the long hot days of the summer, was in Cuba on an official visit, asking its leader, Fidel Castro, to fly to Tripoli on his way to the Non-Aligned summit in South Africa. The Libyan ambassador was to visit some other South American countries before heading to South Africa. He cut his trip short and went back to New York to follow the details and the immediate efforts the United States and the United Kingdom were pushing for: They wanted the UN Security Council to adopt the proposal in a resolution, making it harder for Libya to reject.

On the same day as the announcements in London and Washington, both countries' representatives sent a letter to the UN Secretary General which included the details of the agreement between them, and that between them and the Netherlands.[2] The cover letter included certain elements and demands:

> —In the interest of resolving this situation in a way which will allow justice to be done, our Governments are prepared, as an exceptional measure, to arrange for the two accused to be tried before a Scottish

court sitting in the Netherlands. After close consultation with the Government of the Kingdom of the Netherlands, we are pleased to confirm that the Government of the Netherlands has agreed to facilitate arrangements for such a court. It would be a Scottish court and would follow normal Scots law and procedure in every respect, except for the replacement of the jury by a panel of three Scottish High Court judges. The Scottish rules of evidence and procedure, and all the guarantees of fair trial provided by the law of Scotland, would apply. Arrangements would be made for international observers to attend the trial.

—The two accused will have safe passage from the Libyan Arab Jamahiriya to the Netherlands for the purpose of the trial. While they are in the Netherlands for the purpose of the trial, we shall not seek their transfer to any jurisdiction other than the Scottish court sitting in the Netherlands. If found guilty, the two accused will serve their sentence in the United Kingdom. If acquitted, or in the event of the prosecution being discontinued by any process of law preventing any further trial under Scots law, the two accused will have safe passage back to the Libyan Arab Jamahiriya. Should other offenses committed prior to arrival in the Netherlands come to light during the course of the trial, neither of the two accused nor any other person attending the court, including witnesses, will be liable for arrest for such offenses while in the Netherlands for the purpose of the trial.

—The two accused will enjoy the protection afforded by Scottish law. They will be able to choose Scottish solicitors and advocates to represent them at all stages of the proceedings. The proceedings will be interpreted into Arabic in the same way as a trial held in Scotland. The accused will be given proper medical attention. If they wish, they can be visited in custody by the international observers. The trial would, of course, be held in public, adequate provision being made for the media.

—Our two Governments are prepared to support a further Security Council resolution for the purposes of the initiative which would also suspend sanctions upon the appearance of the two accused in the Netherlands for the purpose of trial before the Scottish court and which would require all States to cooperate to that end. Once that resolution is adopted, the Government of the United Kingdom will legislate to enable a Scottish court to hold a trial in the Netherlands.

—This initiative represents a sincere attempt by the Governments of the United Kingdom and the United States to resolve this issue, and is an approach which has recently been endorsed by others, including the Organization of African Unity, the League of Arab States, the Movement of Non-Aligned States and the Organization of the Islamic Conference. We are only willing to proceed in this exceptional way on the basis of the terms set out in the present letter and its annexes, and provided that the Libyan Arab Jamahiriya cooperates fully by:

(a) Ensuring the timely appearance of the two accused in the Netherlands for trial before the Scottish court;

(b) Ensuring the production of evidence, including the presence of witnesses before the court;

(c) Complying fully with all the requirements of the Security Council resolutions.

—We trust that the Libyan Arab Jamahiriya will respond promptly, positively and unequivocally by ensuring the timely appearance of the two accused in the Netherlands for trial before the Scottish court. If it does not do so, our two Governments reserve the right to propose further sanctions at the time of the next Security Council review. They also reserve the right to withdraw this initiative.

—We have the honor to request that you convey the text of the present letter and its annexes to the Government of the Libyan Arab Jamahiriya. We would be grateful if you would agree to give the Libyan Arab Jamahiriya any assistance it might require with the physical arrangements for the transfer of the two accused directly to the Netherlands.

Within an hour of receipt by the office of the Secretary General of these documents, they were delivered to the Libyan Mission in New York. The following day, the United States and the United Kingdom moved to the Security Council and presented an already prepared draft resolution, asking for its adoption. It contained strong language including the "intention to consider additional measures if the two accused have not arrived or appeared for trial promptly." The Libyans were totally surprised at the swiftness of the American and British move at the UN Security Council and became worried that it was a plot to enlist support among the council members and around the world in order to force stronger sanctions—and within a time frame aimed at preventing the adoption by the NAM summit of a resolution similar to that adopted by the OAU summit. The swiftness of the move was more important to Libya than the contents, since they had no more than hours to study the substance of the new positions and documents that took about eight months of discussions, starting with the original idea and ending with the official proposal. Did the United States and the United Kingdom seek to achieve a solution, or was this a diplomatic ploy to turn the tables against Libya's progress with the international organizations, since such advances would definitely move to the UN within months? Libya asked that question while the United States and the United Kingdom were putting pressure on the Security Council to adopt their draft.

While the United States wanted to begin by setting a deadline for Libya to hand over the suspects, the United Kingdom managed to keep the timing vague, knowing in advance Libya would need some time to digest the proposals and its allies would not like a threatening deadline that would not give them time to further convince the Libyans to agree. This vagueness, mentioned in the draft as "promptly," became instrumental in the following weeks, leading to major efforts by President Mandela, Prince Bandar and others to formulate the guarantees Libya demanded before handing over the two suspects. Patience by the British proved useful while American haste could have caused the whole process to falter. That same day, Libya sent an official letter to the president of the UN Security Council.[3] In the letter, Libya requested "that a decision on the draft resolution presented to the Security Council be postponed until Libya's judicial authorities have completed their study of the documents it received and until the Secretary-General of the United Nations has played the role entrusted to him, in order to arrive at practical solutions that can be applied by the different parties, thereby ensuring that the two suspects appear in court in a neutral third country as soon as possible."

The United States reaction to this Libyan response came from the White House, considering it "not a response, as far as we're concerned. This proposal accords with what they have said they would agree to in the past, and we see no reason for delay on Libya's part. ...This proposal is non-negotiable and mandatory. Libya must comply promptly. Libyan study of the proposal is no reason to delay passage of this resolution in the Security Council."[4] The State Department spokesman said, "We don't believe there is anything to study—let me make that clear—and certainly nothing to negotiate. This proposal has been the subject of discussion for many years with Libya and its supporters having agreed in its favor for over five years. We expect Libya to respond promptly, positively and unequivocally. I think that there is little room for maneuver on Libya's part."

"And if they don't accept," the briefer, James Foley, was asked, "What happens?" Foley answered by leaving some room for debate, if not negotiations: "I'm not going to foreshadow what we might or might not do; we have a menu of options. ...We believe that, in calling Libya's bluff, the American-British proposal is compatible with the previous Arab suggestions which Libya has accepted. What we hoped would happen has happened, in fact; that various international bodies and nations that had supported the idea and obtained Libya's concurrence to the idea earlier that a Scottish trial be held in the Hague, have now stood up and endorsed this proposal and stated that Libya must accept the proposal. And so it would really be very difficult to fathom a Libyan refusal simply to comply with this offer. I don't want to foreshadow what we might or might not do. I think certainly if Libya does not follow through on what they've previously said they would accept, then Libya's international isolation will, I think, increase overnight and we will be in a much stronger position to pursue strong measures against Libya."[5]

Once again, it seemed the United States was pushing Libya to reject and not move toward a trial. The threatening language of the reaction was contributing further to Libya's suspicion of a hidden agenda: that one intention of the proposal was to prevent the Non-Aligned summit from adopting resolutions similar to that of the OAU; that another was to stop the African leaders from continuously breaking sanctions, especially come September, the month the OAU summit had identified as a deadline for the Security Council to take some measures to suspend or lift the sanctions, accepting one of the three proposals of the regional organizations. It is noteworthy here that the American threats of further sanctions (i.e., an oil ban) were not, once again, received positively by the Europeans, who made sure their "economic experts" publicly revealed their disagreement with such a move.

Libya's official response to the U.S.-U.K. revised position was issued in a statement by the foreign ministry on August 26, 1998. The statement said that Libya, "while announcing it accepts the evolution in the position of the United States and Great Britain governments it had called for previously, reaffirms the necessity of ending the sanctions that had been imposed on Libya ... [and] hopes that the Governments of the United Kingdom and the United States of America seriously want to finally settle this issue, and do so honestly and not out of necessity. The whole world can be sure of this if the procedure is free of any conditions through which the United Kingdom and United States Governments might obstruct the trial's progress. The Foreign Ministry wishes to reiterate that it will give positive consideration to the proposed measure and accord it all due importance and care."[6] It seems some mediators, namely Mandela and Bandar, had called the Libyan leader and urged him to accept the proposal immediately, with promises to work on the details. "There should not be any justification for the US and the UK to put more pressure, alienating the United States from you," some of the callers told Qadhafi.

Notably, Libya's worries were translated into that statement without giving a clear "yes" or "no." It accepted only to deal with the proposal. Clear-cut acceptance had not yet been issued.

Britain's language, however, was totally different from that of the United States. Cook issued a statement (dated 24 August, 1998), which read:

> I welcome this Libyan statement which looks like a positive development. We shall need to study exactly what the Libyans have said, and to ensure that they are not setting any conditions on their acceptance. The terms of the United Kingdom/United States initiative are set out clearly in the texts which the Libyans now have. We now look for an unequivocal acceptance of those terms. In due course we expect them to convey a formal response through the United Nations Secretary-General's Office, the channel through which this initiative has been conveyed to them.

On the morning of August 27, 1998, Cook appeared on BBC-TV to give another response to Libya's statements. It seemed that his staff had studied Libya's response and that Mandela had called London asking for a positive reaction. Cook was ready to talk about the details. This is how the interview went:

> INTERVIEWER: Foreign Secretary, is this an acceptance from Libya?
>
> FOREIGN SECRETARY: It is welcome as far as it goes, indeed one might say this is the most positive response we have yet had from Libya in the 7 years since the warrants were issued. But it does not get us to the end of the road. We are not going to have a clear understanding that the proposal is accepted until the two suspects are handed over for trial and that has to be what we now work for. But this, as an opening statement from Libya, is welcome and does give us a basis on which we can now encourage the Secretary-General of the United Nations to make the arrangements for the hand-over. It will be difficult for the government of Libya now to roll back from the very clear statement they have made that what we have offered is what they themselves were seeking— a trial under Scottish law with Scottish judges but in a third country.
>
> INTERVIEWER: When you say hand-over, they could be handed over to Dutch jurisdiction?
>
> FOREIGN SECRETARY: Since the trial would take place within the Netherlands, they would in the first instance have to be handed over to the government of the Netherlands. We would then apply for the extradition of the two suspects to a Scottish court sitting within the Netherlands, in other words not for extradition to Scotland but extradition to the Scottish court within the Netherlands. So in the first instance, yes, they are surrendered to the Dutch authorities.
>
> INTERVIEWER: And would we then lift sanctions?
>
> FOREIGN SECRETARY: We have said that we would support action in the Security Council to suspend sanctions the moment the two accused are surrendered to the Dutch authorities.
>
> INTERVIEWER: If that doesn't happen, then where do we go?
>
> FOREIGN SECRETARY: At the moment I think it would be unwise for us to speculate about failure, but the clear message that we are giving to the government of Libya is that you want the lifting of sanctions— indeed the raising of sanctions has become the number one priority, obsession, of Libyan foreign policy—we also want to make sure a trial takes place and that justice is seen to be done. There is one very simple way in which both those objectives can be met and can be met fairly speedily, and that is for you to surrender the two accused for trial. If Libya fails to do that then sanctions will remain in place and will remain in place with even greater international support than at present because Libya will be seen to demand a way out of the problem which it was not itself prepared to take when it was offered.

INTERVIEWER: But you are reasonably confident this morning?

FOREIGN SECRETARY: I am encouraged by a statement which has most certainly not ruled out the offer we have made, which has regarded it as positive, which has repeated the fact that, historically, the Libyans have said that they would accept such an offer, which I think makes it difficult for them to find a way out of. I very much hope that the Libyans will now proceed to what is the next stage, and the only stage at which we can then be confident that the trial will take place; namely, to hand over the two accused.

The Security Council, meanwhile, was willing to accept the U.S.-U.K. pressure to adopt the resolution immediately. Any delay, the two feared, might force some alterations of their proposal. They wanted to make sure it would stand as it was, while the United Kingdom emphasized it was willing to give the Libyans clarifications to any questions they might have, without negotiating the proposal itself.

That same day, the Security Council adopted the proposal in Resolution 1192. The United States and the United Kingdom insisted that it be adopted unanimously, thus they worked extensively with China and Russia and some of the Non-Aligned members to make some amendments, though cosmetic, to their original draft. They refused Chinese and Russian demands that the resolution not be adopted under Chapter VII of the charter. The Americans, however, continued their negative tone.

Minutes before the meeting was held, Peter Burleigh, Deputy U.S. Permanent Representative to the United Nations, said, "I do not claim I can explain Libya's intentions. I read two statements they issued in the past few days and I found vague and complicated words I could not understand, while not finding they clearly accepted the American-British initiative. It seems they accept a change in the American-British position. There is no change; there is a proposal I wish they will accept. This is my reading and, if they accept, I wish they would announce their acceptance in the Council's meeting."

Burleigh's and other American statements led Dorda to issue a statement of his own. He said, "One point needs to be reconfirmed. The two countries aim at the following through their maneuver:

"1. The defusing of the Ouagadougou (OAU) resolutions;

2. To precede the expected resolutions of the Non-Aligned Summit;

3. To keep sanctions imposed on Libya;

4. To isolate Libya from the international community which supported us through its regional organizations;

5. To return this issue to square one."

Libya was not yet convinced of the sincerity of the two countries. What added to their fears was the willingness of most of the supporters to accept the new evolution in the West at face value. Furthermore, the resolution included some new time demands of Libya:

> That the Libyan Government shall ensure that any evidence or witnesses in Libya are, upon the request of the court, promptly made available at the court in the Netherlands for the purpose of the trial;
>
> Decides further that, on the arrival of the two accused in the Netherlands, the Government of the Netherlands shall detain the two accused, pending their transfer for the purpose of trial before the court;
>
> Expresses its intention to consider additional measures if the two accused have not arrived or appeared for trial promptly.[7]

These, and the fact that this resolution was adopted swiftly, created new fears in the Libyan minds, pushing them further toward requiring their guarantees.

Many questions were presented regarding the conditions contained in Resolution 1192, mainly those in the last paragraph. What does "promptly" mean? Is it a month, two months? Who are the witnesses to be called? Will Qadhafi have to testify? Or some other senior officials? Where is this going to stop?

With the adoption of this resolution, which included a decision that sanctions "shall be suspended immediately if the Secretary-General reports to the Council that the two accused have arrived in the Netherlands for the purpose of trial before the court" and the pressure exerted on Libya's supporters, it became extremely hard for the Libyans to maintain those supporters' positions against the United States and the United Kingdom. A new stage was set, and Libya had to play by new ground rules despite the absence of the guarantees it had always sought. Those guarantees would become the cornerstone of their diplomatic efforts.

U.S. officials were not expecting any Libyan compliance. All they expected was a Libyan refusal, leading to its alienation. The Libyans, it seems, read the U.S. position accurately. They were not as confused with the British position, for London had mixed feelings but was able to overcome negative expectations. Britain sincerely wanted to finish with this case and bring the two suspects to justice. Direct official and private communications between the British and the Libyans made it easier for Tripoli to read and understand London's position. This position would later prevail; all developments from then on concentrated on that aim. Libya, in return, stood to get some normalization in its relations with the West or lose what it had worked for the previous nine years.

Based on its own readings of the reasons for the announcement and the efforts of the mediators, Libya chose cautiously positive language for its reaction to the resolution. It would agree to deal with it, while not officially accepting it. That language, Libyans hoped, would give them more room to test the intentions of the Americans.

PART V

The Role of Prominent Personalities, and the Handover

14

Isolation Starts to Crumble

The long years of sanctions had contributed to the taming of Qadhafi. His personality was such that he could not contain his dreams within the borders of a country inhabited by no more than 5 million people. His books and his constant restructuring of the governmental system internally are expressions of his constant outlook for global leadership. His extraordinary ability in breaking the isolation that the West, especially the United States, tried to force upon him could be proof that he is a shrewd politician. Immediately after the Lockerbie campaign against Libya began, Qadhafi moved to normalize relations with all neighboring countries, especially those with whom Libya was not on such good terms. He then turned his country's attention to the African continent. He established personal relationships with most of its leaders in a way that made Tripoli a capital for Africa. Hardly a week passes without one or more African leader visiting. His traditional and improved state and personal relations with the major symbols of the continent, such as Mandela, helped break isolation, bringing about the opposite of what his enemies wanted—to challenge the West on this issue.

These efforts did not stop at Africa and its leaders. Qadhafi also succeeded in convincing the Europeans that trade and infrastructure contracts with Libya would provide them with billions of dollars and benefit both sides. Qadhafi's generosity helped that process, but that

159

quality was also exploited by some, within and outside the regime, claiming certain direct contacts in London and Paris. Yet some others misled the leader, calling it unrealistic to achieve international leadership through the publication and distribution of a dream book, as well as other theoretical philosophies, that colored the whole world green.

Regardless, Qadhafi managed the Lockerbie crisis in a way that transformed the role of most international organizations into one that defended or supported Libya's positions. That success has culminated in the mediation led by the Saudi crown prince through his unusually able ambassador to Washington, Prince Bandar, and by the historical African leader Nelson Mandela, who, among others Qadhafi met, were impressed by his abilities, especially that of taking note of the most minute details.

Through many of his writings, Qadhafi demonstrated that he could be a thinker, an intellectual or even a philosopher. He reads voraciously. He pays close attention to events and news. He accepts a differing opinion from his aides. His problem, however, is being caught between that great vision of the world engulfed in his "third international theory" (as compared to capitalism and communism) and his constant feeling of having to serve the regular man on the street. He expresses that gap on a daily basis through his writings, "The Green Book," then "Escape to Hell," and how he conducts his leadership—ranging between the often accurate analysis of the international scene and the more local insistence on providing Libyans free housing to an extent abused by many. His ability to become his country's leader at a very young age may have deprived him of the necessary experience, internally or internationally alike, through daily practices. That youthful leadership is one reason he feels now among the elders. He became the "dean of Arab leaders" although he does not consider himself a president but a leader and an adviser, providing his people the direction they always demand from him. This self-described status explains the many awkward bumps during the final stages of the solution process.

In short, what Qadhafi lacked in practice he made up for in theory. The great gap between theory and practice will never be bridged except through experience. That is how someone should understand Muammar Qadhafi and his leadership of his country, without, of course, undermining the most important element in a leader's mind while on top: not to lose power. Still, a huge difference exists between one leader and another in the way they use the instruments of government to stay in power. Qadhafi could never be Saddam Hussein, for example; he could make a mistake but would try to correct it most of the time, whereas Hussein would make a mistake leading to irreparable damage, then try to correct it—with more catastrophic results.

The 1986 aerial attack, followed by the constant harassment ending with the sanctions, left an effect on the Libyan leader. Did he learn his lesson, as the Reagan administration claimed, when it killed his daughter? If so, why were the sanctions the U.S. government felt necessary to contain Libya maintained without any real strategy for a change of policy?

Many other questions could be posed. Their answers, however, were never recorded in the strategies and studies drawn in the policy-making circles. The only real answers are with Qadhafi himself. The next few years may hint at what they are.

While the Western isolation of Qadhafi failed on the foreign policy front, it succeeded internally due to the opportunism of many in the administrative hierarchy, leading to neglect of the daily needs of the infrastructure, thereby destroying much of what the Libyan revolution had established in more than two decades. The infrastructure reached a stage of near total incapacitation. Garbage would be thrown on the streets of cities such as Tripoli and Benghazi, known previously for their organization and cleanliness, while sewage disposal systems reached a stage similar to that of the early days of their installation: not ready yet. A visitor might have wondered whether the country had just come out of a civil war. And that is nothing compared to the situation of the school systems, universities and hospitals, where the reversal in status is so obvious no one even holds a positive outlook. A Libyan would have to travel to other countries, mainly Tunis and Jordan, to get the most basic medical treatment. And with the devaluation of the Libyan dinar, from about a dollar for a dinar to about three and a half dinars to a dollar, the government faces higher, unrealistic costs for medical treatment for the Libyans than any rehabilitation of the medical system in any country could warrant.

Every single official, when asked about the neglect, would blame the Lockerbie problem, as if every one of them had a say in world affairs. Qadhafi knew the realities: that only he and a few of his aides were involved in this issue, while others were busy adding to their millions through corruption, bribes and commissions, expecting the fall of the regime at any time during the nineties. That explains why, after the solution was reached, the Libyan government moved to charging many of those Qadhafi called "beneficiaries of the Lockerbie crisis," but only after the situation had worsened to what amounted to a need for reconstruction.

An indirect justification of this situation, and possibly an explanation of Qadhafi's state of mind, was written by Qadhafi himself. He reminded all where he came from: the desert. "I am a poor, simple person. I have no royal blood; I am a bedouin. I have no doctorate; I do not even like physicians, because they are called 'doctors.' They could not innoculate me against sensitivity—I am very sensitive, unlike city people, who have been vaccinated from the days of the Romans until the Turks, and most recently under the Amelicans."[1] (Qadhafi says he uses this misspelling of "Americans" because he "do[es] not know the meaning of America," a country he claims was discovered by an Arab.)

Qadhafi did not miss the opportunity to dispel some of the blame levied upon him for the absence of real administration of the country's day to day business. He claims (no doubt truthfully, like most leaders) "no knowledge of sewage systems, plumbing or narrow water lines," noting that he "had hoped that this spring would relieve me of answering all of those requests." This inexperience, nevertheless, did not stop other leaders from asking and getting the right people to deliver on these basic necessities of any society.

Qadhafi speaks at length of the country he had to confront the most, out of attack or self-defense. That is the United States. "America is very powerful, has its agents and its military bases in areas of influence. It has the right to veto when it concerns the interests of Israel. It recently acquired a house at the head of the Nile Delta, where the river splits into the Rosetta and Damietta, and a buffalo farm surrounds the house.... It is Amelica, as Hajj Mujahid says; he is the son of my aunt Azza, daughter of my grandmother Ghanima, who is the sister of Countess Maria."[2]

It should well be noticeable here how Qadhafi talking indirectly about the wider family with a strong relationship common in the Middle East and Africa. He might have had to deal with appeasing many of this wider family while confronting that one party getting stronger and bigger. That might have led to some confusion of priorities.

Qadhafi impresses those he meets. He is able to note details. Prince Bandar, for example, said, "Negotiating with him is a tough task, but he forces you to respect him for he knows what he is talking about. He possesses an unusual ability for raising issues and details that might not be on your mind, only to discover how important they were after you discuss them. That is how he got American and British concessions that might not have been possible."[3]

Qadhafi was ready for the solution in the summer of 1998. The Africans were on his side, the Non-Aligned Movement moved closer, the United Kingdom showed signs, though limited, of a willingness to move ahead with public and private assurances that there was no hidden agenda.

The playing field became ready for Libya's new image to cultivate the fruits of its ten-year effort of restraint, with the announcement of the new position of the United States and the United Kingdom. A whole new game was at hand, but not before a slow disposal of the old one.

The first non–Lockerbie-related issue to be tackled then was to improve the poor relations with Italy. Because of its geographical proximity to Libya and its long history with the country, which included occupation and other types of extensive relations, Italy had always had a place in Libya's heart. Similarly, Libya itself has had a special place in Italy's heart. It is the closest country across the Mediterranean and has provided a beachhead for Italy's adventures in Africa. Thus, it was most important for both to realize historical changes and needs in order to write a new chapter in their relations, and Libya decided to consider Italy its foothold in Europe and the West.

Relations began to improve, this time on Libya's terms. Italian businesses were the first from the West to return to Libya. Italy's foreign minister was the first Western minister to visit Libya since the sanctions days. Its prime minister was the first head of state to visit Libya after sanctions were suspended. By then, the role Italy was playing was in assuring the Libyans that normalcy could be achieved and in strengthening the hands of the Libyan circles that called for such improvements.

Italian foreign minister Lamberto Dini had given Libya great political incentive for the improved relations. After the signing of the accord, he said that, in every meeting Italy's government had had with Libyan officials, it had repeated that Libya's complete reintegration into the international community required that it fully honor the obligations imposed by the UN over Lockerbie. And he added: "The evidence we have is that Libya has not been involved in acts of terrorism either directly or indirectly for some time."[4]

The most important achievement of Libya's efforts, however, was the apology Italy presented in 1999 for mischief during the long years of occupation. This apology strengthened the Libyans' conviction that the world had changed and that Italy could play the vital role it wanted. It set itself on the practical path toward the West and toward normalcy. It led as well to the first visit of a western leader to Libya after the Lockerbie incident, when Italian prime minister Massimo D'Alema visited Tripoli. Reuters reported that a delighted Qadhafi declared while receiving D'Alema, on 28 November 1999, "Libya will become Italy's bridge to Africa and Italy will be for Libya it's door into Europe."

A New Diplomacy at Hand: Mandela and Bandar

Throughout these developments, President Mandela was not keeping silent. He was preparing the ground for a forceful mediation although he did not specifically know on what basis. He was privately exploring that possibility while expressing his personal beliefs, which were always critical of U.S. policies on many issues. His statements were becoming increasingly fiery, especially those in response to U.S. criticism of his positions and efforts. The following exchange took place during the daily briefing of October 20, 1997, at the U.S. State Department:

QUESTION: In the relation to South Africa, what's the US response to comments made by the President over the weekend, which described America as an arrogant and racist country, in relation to your opposition to his forthcoming trip to Libya?

MR. RUBIN: I haven't seen that specific quote, fortunately. But let me say that we have the highest possible respect for the President. He's a historical figure. We have the warmest possible relations with the government of South Africa.

However, we believe that when you are a good friend, you are capable of expressing your opinion. In our opinion, at a time when Libya is under sanctions and is refusing to abide by the international community's demands on an issue so fundamental—terrorism—an issue that undermines the very core of the international system, the use of terror in flying international aircraft, that it is important not to send the wrong signals.

So our position has been that governments should have the lowest possible diplomatic contact with the government of Libya unless and until the government of Libya returns to the norm of international behavior by complying with the international community demands, including, obviously, turning over the suspects who were involved in such a dastardly deed.

We have the highest respect for President Mandela. Obviously, there is a difference in that point of view, and so we would be disappointed if there were a ratcheting up of the diplomatic contact with a government under sanctions.

QUESTION: Would you hope that he'd be pressing the case on the Lockerbie suspects?

MR. RUBIN: Well, if he does choose to go, we certainly would very much hope that one of the prime topics of any discussion with the government of Libya by any nation would be the importance of Libya complying with Security Council resolutions.

QUESTION: Does it take any sting out of the situation, given the fact that he is going overland and not by air?

MR. RUBIN: Absolutely. By air would be a violation of the sanctions, and we did not suggest, nor am I suggesting here, that we have any indication that the President would be violating sanctions. This isn't a question of violating sanctions. Let me repeat that, so there's no misunderstanding.

What it's a question of is what level of diplomatic contact one wants to have with a regime that is prepared to pursue such rogue behavior as supporting international terrorism or preventing these people from being brought to justice.

QUESTION: Yes. Basically, you say that he is a friend of the US.

MR. RUBIN: Yes.

QUESTION: But his remarks are that Americans are dull. As a friend, what is the limit of that friendship; what are the boundaries?

MR. RUBIN: Well, we don't find Americans dull. I haven't seen the specific transcript of his remarks, but you're reading a report of his remarks.

Washington's reaction to Mandela's statements was a little more forceful than London's. The British publicly neglected his endeavor, keeping away from any official reactions while hoping privately he would play a role to their liking in their upcoming effort. Britain was facing another lobbying effort by Mandela, and, though it was not immediately responsive, it left him room to maneuver. The British described him as being "stubborn" in following up with his effort. Mandela felt both political and moral obligations to work on this issue and help his friends. Libya had helped his movement, the People's National Congress (PNC), and his people extensively during the long years of apartheid. That help could not easily be forgotten, especially when it was one of the reasons the United States and the United Kingdom detested Libya. The West, in general, was not forcefully acting against the apartheid white regime in power. The Black Africans felt the West's opposition to apartheid was more verbal while the Libyans, among others, were actively helping the struggle.

The Labor Party positions against apartheid were always a little more advanced than those of the Conservative Party in England, leading to better relations with the PNC. Mandela and his movement knew that their relationship with the Labor Party was on much better footing than that with the Conservatives and that they could build on it. Blair was willing to accommodate Mandela, even if that accommodation consisted of nothing more than hearing him out.

One upcoming occasion provided a great opportunity for the African leader to raise the issue. At a crucial juncture of developments, the Commonwealth heads of government meeting (CHOGM) was scheduled to be held between October 24 and October 27, 1997, in Edinburgh, Scotland. Both Blair and Mandela wanted to use this occasion to their benefit in exploring the Libyan issue in a continuation of the path Mandela had started with the British government in July. Blair wanted to consult all attending African leaders to find out how far they would go in their breach of the sanctions, a breach that was reaching a point of challenge.

Blair faced African anger at the sanctions and the lack of flexibility in the U.S.-U.K. position. Many leaders refused his warnings about breaching the sanctions by traveling to Libya by air and informed him they would adopt a stronger resolution in the following summit in 1998.

On his way to Scotland, the South African president made a point of traveling first to Libya. However, he continued to show respect for the UN Security Council by refusing Libya's request to travel by air to Tripoli's airport. He went by land through Tunisia. When in Scotland, meeting with Blair and Cook bilaterally, Mandela found they were prepared for him. He was surprised to find the British government more flexible than he had expected. The discussion lasted around four hours. Each side came out impressed by the other's position. The United Kingdom was impressed by Mandela's argument about the necessity to find a new way forward, including the need to lift the sanctions, and Mandela was impressed by the United Kingdom's argument about UN Security Council resolutions. According to anonymous sources present at the meeting, Blair told Mandela specifically, "You, out of all people, should understand the importance of upholding the United Nations resolutions."

Mandela went back to Libya to meet Qadhafi. His message was that his friend should continue to respect the UN resolutions, but he also believed there was to be an imminent change in the British position. That was the first direct indication Libya had about the forthcoming change. No one, including the British leaders themselves, knew what type of change it would be. For Mandela, the argument transformed from a demand to immediately lift the sanctions to launching an effort to work within those resolutions to find a solution. A few days later, when the invitation to the UN, the OAU and the Arab League to send observers to Scotland was announced, Mandela and Qadhafi thought that would be it. They were disappointed. After extensive private contacts, Mandela was assured that would not be it and that work was still going on. He calmed down and convinced Qadhafi to do so as well. Still, the United Kingdom had one vital doubt: Would Libya hand over the two suspects to face trial if the United Kingdom accepted a third-country trial?

Then came the pressure President Clinton personally confronted. While facing the heat of his battle with the Republican congress, culminating in his impeachment, he intensified his foreign travels to enhance his image while away from the political heat of Washington. One of his runaway trips took him to Africa, where he visited five countries including South Africa. U.S. officials called this trip "historic," one encompassing more stops and longer stays in the black continent than any conducted by a previous U.S. president.

Two incidents during that trip had a direct effect on the developments toward a solution of the Lockerbie case.

During his stop in Uganda, Clinton expressed concern about solving the problems of that region of Africa: the Great Lakes. He managed to hold a summit on March 25, 1998, with the presidents of Uganda, Kenya, Rwanda, Tanzania, the Democratic Republic of Congo (formerly Zaire) and Ethiopia. Most of the attending African presidents were considered terrorists by the United States when they were still "movements."

Many of the attending leaders discussed the Libyan issue with Clinton. Those who raised the issue first talked about the need for a solution based on compromise, noting the forthcoming African summit, in which they would adopt some form of sanction-lifting resolution. The American president reiterated the need to respect the UN resolutions and cease air travel to Libya. As conflicting as those positions were, they showed the United States that the African-Libyan offensive was not about to stop.

The second incident, which proved more important a few months later, took place during the South African leg of the trip. Prince Bandar was in the country and managed to talk with both the American and South African presidents in a private meeting. The main idea discussed was that sanctions had become a negative label, damaging the United States and its allies in the Arab world and Africa. Understanding that sanctions on Iraq were based on strategic threats and considerations, the sanctions on Libya had outlasted their necessity. A lifting of them would send a message in answer to the accusations in the Arab world that it was the only part of the world always targeted, the new weapon being: sanctions. What contributed strongly to this belief was the daily confrontations intensifying between the United States and Iraq. Only weeks had passed since an extensive campaign of bombardment was launched by U.S. and British airplanes against an Iraq determined to refuse to implement Security Council resolutions. Daily raids were continuing but with much less public and media attention. Iraq had succeeded, however, in gaining the support of some Arab street masses against the Western campaign, with some even calling it a "crusaders," campaign.

The Africans were not that far from that belief although their considerations were different. For them, the United States was treating them with a level of arrogance they could not easily tolerate anymore. And since the Libyans had always supported many of them, they were expected to show support in their moment of need.

The long discussion in South Africa strengthened British efforts aimed at rethinking the common American-British position. This discussion had a definite effect on Clinton.

The two self-appointed mediators were not conventional in their dealings, especially with one side unwilling to fully accept efforts. They had to be creative. New channels of diplomacy had to be developed, and an effort toward conformation of positions had to overcome many negative tendencies. That effort was a little shaky prior to the official announcements in Washington and London. By the time the announcements were made and the Security Council had adopted its position, the process had found legs to stand on. The mediators found what they were looking for: a clear framework of positions. Mandela and Bandar, among others, moved to convince Libya of the necessity of the handover, while persuading the British and the Americans of the need to provide Libya with the guarantees it was seeking. Libya needed to be convinced of the seriousness of the two countries in their endeavor to achieve the holding of the trial, nothing more.

For that to be achieved, all parties had to explore new ways and venues. Therefore, one could ask: How is diplomacy conducted? Is there a norm that cannot be changed? Can it be creative?

Answers to these questions might theoretically be easy. In reality, however, the gap between interpretations of diplomacy in the West and those in the third world is very wide.

Secret diplomacy has always been a tool for governments and leaders. Another one is direct personal contacts between leaders, bypassing the institutions assigned the given task. In both situations those institutions would be involved only in providing their respective leaders with some advice, although the leader might not fully accept it. The importance of such contacts would overwhelm differences that might not be workable, or agreeable, on lower levels. Still, assistants and ministers would be involved in that they are an integral part of the government and are trusted for their secrecy.

In the third world, for most diplomatic contacts to succeed, they should remain within a closed circle. It is common for some contacts to take place without the knowledge of high-ranking government officials, resulting in their alienation. Leaders consider such "back channels" much more vital for success since they might fear the "ambitions" of others within the country. And since everything that goes on in this world is related to a "conspiracy," this type of diplomacy could be called "conspiratorial diplomacy"—with a positive meaning.

Therefore, a contact between ministers of foreign affairs would be considered a privilege, showing the importance of a relationship. This is understood on both sides. The normalcy of relations necessitates, however, that these meetings be an occasion to discuss important issues, even if they remain secret. Whole governments become involved, one way or another, on a "need to know" basis. That is standard conduct. But a meeting between a minister of the country and the secretary of the minister of another is also normal conduct for achieving results in secretive societies and governments, although a major misunderstanding could erupt as a result of such meetings, since one party could consider them nothing but lip service while another could think this back channel had achieved a result an official meeting could not.

This background is necessary to understand why the United States and the United Kingdom were hesitant about any role to be played by Prince Bandar and Mandela's chef-de-cabinet, Jakes Gerwell. They were afraid the secret missions conducted by the two, with Mandela conducting a fatherly guiding role, would lead to understandings not fully acceptable to them. A word said by the two emissaries in private might leave a certain impression not intended by the American and British officials, who preferred official diplomacy through Annan or other Libyan officials.

Unintentionally, the contacts broke into five camps. The mediators worked on different levels: Mandela worked mainly in London; Bandar worked mainly on Washington, though both had some type of contact with all; both also worked on Qadhafi; and Annan became the mailman carrying official written messages among the parties. After the announcement of the handover, the Secretary General himself said that, when he visited with Qadhafi, he came to the conclusion that no solution would have been achieved without the mediators.

Based on that confusing multiplicity of efforts, personalities had to actually effect this new multidiplomacy. In New York, a different relationship had developed between the Libyan and British ambassadors, especially since they never ceased the exchange of official contacts, unlike the situation between the Libyans and the Americans.

In July 1997, when the new British ambassador to the UN took up his new appointment, not many thought this would extensively contribute to dialogue erasing full mistrust, replacing it with a willingness to accept the other's arguments. This new ambassador, Sir Jeremy Greenstock, was an Arabic speaker with extensive expertise in the Arab world. His previous post was foreign office political director. To the surprise of both Dorda and Greenstock, a very good working relationship developed between the two, leading to many private meetings and exchanges of views. Some of the meetings took place outside the framework of official positions, but, all in all, they helped considerably in achieving a solution on the practical field of UN work and an official channel.

Greenstock's professionalism was a major component in formulating details of work between the United States and the United Kingdom at the UN and in Washington. The Americans were facing a hard time getting congressional approval for the appointment of Richard Holbrook as the new UN ambassador, succeeding Richardson, who went on to become the Secretary of Energy. The U.S. mission was left with its senior career diplomat, Peter Burleigh, to lead the extensive political work they faced in New York. Burleigh, himself an "Arabist" who had extensive experience in the Middle East, was in charge of the Iraq desk at the U.S. State Department prior to his appointment as a deputy permanent representative at the UN. He had worked in the early nineties on the Libyan file during the meetings the three countries—the United States, United Kingdom and France—had held in preparation for imposing sanctions. His French counterpart at the time was Alain Dejammet, who had himself become France's representative at the UN.

Despite Burleigh's extreme politeness and diplomatic experience, he lacked the political personality that characterized most U.S. representatives at the UN. He was seen by some in Washington as ineffective on major issues that required exposure and toughness. He fumbled in one meeting of the council on Iraq, leading the United States to call back military airplanes on their way to bomb the Iraqis toward the end of 1997. The United States decided to conduct its major work for the UN directly between its Undersecretary for Political Affairs, Thomas Pickering, and Greenstock. Pickering, who had been a U.S. representative at the UN when sanctions were imposed, was himself a career diplomat and one of only five in his country to have the permanent title of ambassador. His personality is forceful and decisive. Albright brought him out of retirement to appoint him to a job that would give him practical control of the day-to-day running of the department. He made many contacts from Washington directly with Greenstock, giving the latter one very important privilege: the ability to whisper into the ears of Washington. That helped in the advancement toward a solution on the Lockerbie issue, as well as many others.

Dorda showed flexibility on the personal level, leading to a better ability to achieve results for his country. One instance came when Princess Diana died on August 31, 1997, in a car accident in Paris. Tripoli issued some statements accusing the British intelligence of causing the accident. British officials responded with the cancellation of an address that was supposed to be delivered to a British-Libyan business group by an official of the foreign office, John Shepard. However, in New York, Dorda telephoned his British counterpart to present his condolences. London understood the internal considerations that necessitate certain rhetorical statements while staying the course on the important issues. No harm was done.

With these different personalities and efforts, the whole process became clearly complicated and interwoven. It was not conducted according to any norm of diplomacy or to the understandings of both the traditional diplomacy of the West or the "conspiratorial" diplomacy of the third world. It was a strange combination of all that was known to work in the modern world. Simply put, major efforts were exhausted in order to achieve a solution at any price. A combination of perseverance, assurances and reassurances had to take place in order to convince all parties of the solution, especially Libya and the United States.

15

A Solution Is Near

During the early postannouncement days, it became clear that a long process was at hand. It was to be a process built on trust. Some of the steps taken by all parties had to be considered "confidence-building measures." Those steps and measures helped convince the parties of each other's seriousness at different stages and by different means.

Bandar, building on his still-secret meetings in South Africa, began his own search for the tangibles of a role he could play. The prince is practically self-made, due to complications within the Saudi royal family. He is a man who learned the hard way how to get things done. His successes were mostly due to his personal ability. He had been a man of secret missions for a long period of time. Prior to being his country's ambassador to the United States, a post he has been holding for around twenty years now, Bandar was his country's military attaché in the American capital. Throughout that period, he managed to weave a complicated network of personal relations that ranged between intelligence officials and major advisors to presidents and to presidents themselves. During the years of the Bush administration, he had special clearance to enter the White House just like any high-ranking American official. Although his relations with the Clinton administration never rose to that level, he managed to maintain a special working relationship with many officials which kept him extremely effective on his preferred path of secret missions in many areas in the world.

Other than his publicly announced justification for his and his country's role, no one knows yet what exactly triggered such a mission. The Saudis, including Bandar, insist the effort was launched as part of their constant efforts to aid fellow Arabs. In both public statements and private meetings, Saudi Crown Prince Abdullah Ibin Abdul Aziz Al Saud and Bandar repeatedly assured Qadaffi they were on his side.

Only the future may confirm the incentive, but one thing is certain: This is one more success story for this unusual prince. It was the success of an effort avoided by many other leaders or dignitaries, for it required courage and an ability to delve into the dangers of ambiguities on the part of the Americans and fears on the part of the Libyans. For almost ten years, no one had dared undertake such a mission. The mere fact that Bandar took it upon himself to swim against the currents, despite the political changes that later curbed his drive, should be an example followed by many such officials.

Whatever his motivation and however unconventional his methods, Bandar proved critically important. He saw momentum building toward a solution and jumped in. He began secret trips to Libya, exploring its need to put this issue to rest before there could be any signs of possible future change and success. The United States was afraid he might have offered much more than he could deliver, despite the fact that whatever he delivered was enough to convince Qadhafi and the Americans as they put on the final touches. That possibly mutual fear might, in fact, explain some of the hesitations Qadhafi faced in the late stages of the solution process, when some terms he expected did not materialize.

While Bandar was exploring the details, Libya began its own process to flesh out the seriousness of the United States and the United Kingdom. The guarantees were the only item left on a diminishing agenda. The trial in a third country was accepted. Libya's allies began feeling uneasy with the delays, calling for the finalization of the process in order to get the sanctions lifted. That feeling contributed to Libya's fears of further losses of support from the international community.

As a result of the mediation and with ideas and suggestions floating all around, the Libyans were under the impression that a certain deal would be arranged: An agreement would be announced in South Africa and signed in Saudi Arabia and under the auspices of the Saudi king and the South African president, by the foreign ministers of the United States, the United Kingdom, Libya, South Africa and the host, the Saudi foreign minister, with some UN representation. Such a ceremony would give Libya both a confirmation of the sincerity of the United States and the United Kingdom, as relayed by Bandar and Mandela, as well as the international umbrella and guarantees provided by the observer status of the not-so-directly concerned countries. Whether Libya misunderstood or the mediators misinterpreted the U.S. and U.K. positions, no one seems to be able to confirm. Regardless, it was the main concern of the Libyan leadership to test the sincerity of the evolution in the Western position and the willingness to satisfy Libya's wish to end all hostilities among the three countries. In short, this was a barometer for the future, directly affecting the type of guarantees Libya needed.

Libyan Requests for Clarification

While the mediators were trying to bridge the gap between the positions of the parties, Libya looked to its allies to support its demands and guarantees. It managed one more show of support from the regional organizations. Once again, a flood of letters from these organizations were sent to the UN Security Council reconfirming their "total solidarity and support for the legitimate Libyan demands":

> (a) That an agreement be reached by all the parties guaranteeing no surrender, no transfer and no transport of the two suspects to either the US or the UK for any reason whatsoever; and, in case of their conviction, that they serve their term in either the Netherlands or the Libyan Arab Jamahiriya;
> (b) That an agreement be reached by all parties limiting, clarifying and specifying the witnesses needed from the Libyan Arab Jamahiriya;
> (c) That an agreement be reached by all parties guaranteeing the right of the suspects—legal, religious, personal, social—during all the phases of the trial, as well as their safety and security during their travel to and from the Netherlands and during their stay there;
> (d) That the beginning of the trial must be the end of this dispute, for the Libyan Arab Jamahiriya has already responded to all the demands of the Security Council. The sanctions should be lifted upon the appearance of the two suspects before the trial.[1]

These demands/guarantees were translated differently on both shores of the Atlantic. The United States considered them nothing but a new Libyan maneuver to divert attention from the main request: the handover of the two suspects. It also considered them a new tactic to reject the handover. It considered what was presented in its documents on the new position as inclusive enough of all details Libya was asking about. No further discussions should take place, the United States repeated. They wanted to move swiftly to impose further sanctions, thinking the stage was set to ensure the support of those who had previously refused any strengthening of the sanctions. It was clear that the United States had already prepared a draft resolution on further sanctions. The new draft was never presented to the council officially, though some ideas were discussed privately with close allies.

With a guessing game being played by everybody, Prince Bandar and Gerwell began a new round of secret missions to Libya. Although the mediators went on numerous trips there, many were made prior to the announcement, laying the groundwork for the difficult task. The first trip substantially related to the process of dealing with the new American and British position was conducted the day after Libya celebrated the twenty-ninth anniversary of the revolution in September 1998. The main task of the two visitors was to try to convince Qadhafi of the sincerity of the American and British proposal.

Leaving the idea of the direct meetings aside, the British reading of Libya's demands was in line with its expectations. The British officials were prepared for further clarifications although they thought they had already answered many of the Libyan concerns in the text of the agreement presented to them. If Libya needed more clarifications or possibly assurances, the British were willing to provide them through the UN Secretary General. They were not willing yet to indulge in direct negotiations because they were not yet sure of the sincerity of Libya's intentions. The British pressed the Americans to do the same, then both informed the UN Secretary General of their readiness to provide any answers and clarifications the Libyans wanted. The Netherlands did so as well.

A further analysis, mainly by the British, of Libyan demands proved the following: They represented two levels of worry. The first was purely legal. Libya seemed to have some logical questions on certain legal issues and details. The Americans and the British thought many of the answers were already provided in the initiative; still they concluded it would not hurt to provide further clarifications. The second level was political; the Libyans seemed to fear the existence of a secret deal between the Americans, British and the Dutch, whereas the announced legality would be covered by a hidden agenda. The other outcome expected by the Libyans—the foreign ministers' meeting—would complement the outcome of public efforts at the UN.

Therefore, the aim, in the British view, was to convince the Libyans that no hidden agenda existed. The United States, on the other hand, was not as patient or understanding. While this legal process would leave them out of having to extensively deal with the really technical details of the legal issues (since this was to be a Scottish trial), it could not exclude them from the political process. And since the United Kingdom would not abandon its strategic ally, it would have to fully coordinate with its partner on both levels, legal and political. This process would later lead to the British hand-holding the Americans in order for both of them to walk a tightrope, making sure they would not fall into a pool of tough domestic lobbies objecting to the whole effort.

All parties to this process seemed to have started from different points and expected different results. For the United States and the United Kingdom, the foreign ministers' meeting in Saudi Arabia, or even in South Africa, was never on the table, especially as part of prehandover arrangements. It seemed that the offer made to Libya was not based on any acceptance by the Americans and the British. And although the Libyans kept waiting for this promise to materialize, suspending the process for almost six months while some hoped the others would change their minds, they had to settle for the guarantees provided through both venues.

Through the UN Secretary General, and based on much effort, public and private, legal meetings were arranged, to be attended by a team of Libyan lawyers headed by Kamel Hassan Al-Maghour, a prominent international lawyer with extensive experience representing his country. The team included two lawyers representing the government and two others representing the suspects as personal lawyers. The team would come to New York. The official justification, for the Westerners, would be that the talks were to deal with the legal office of the UN Secretary General. However, a legal team from both the United States and the United Kingdom would be in New York around the same time. Three exchanges of questions and answers would be presented in a go-between process in two different rounds, in October and in November. This legal process proved extremely useful, at the very least in the process of confidence building between two of the three parties. However, the United States kept claiming these positive signals would not mean anything until the hand over took place.

Washington was acting politically. It had built its whole process around a hand over. Nothing else seemed to satisfy the Americans. Even the hand over would not satisfy the Americans enough to deal politically with Libya. They were not able to accept the fact that the evolution in their position was based on their loss of the diplomatic battle. This was hard for them to accept. They had to show themselves that they were in control and were setting conditions by which the Libyans had to abide. That was translated initially into the answers they presented to the first set of Libyan questions.

The British saw the whole legal exchange differently. When they received the first set of Libyan questions from the UN legal counsel, they noticed seriousness on the part of the Libyans. The questions did not seem to be a ploy. They were written based on a deep understanding of the legal process, especially Scotland's. The Libyan lawyers had extensively studied that system and picked out what could be harmful to their clients and their case to inquire about. "Impressive," was the United Kingdom's assessment, but this was a legal process, and the United Kingdom could not be sure whether Libya would still hand over the two suspects once the clarification process was completed.

In the first round, the Libyans presented their questions in different sets to the United States, the United Kingdom, the Netherlands, France and in some instances to all of them. Each set contained specific elements regarding the roles of each party, starting with the handover and its technicalities, and ending with the political amplifications that would result from implementation of the demands of the Security Council.

The following is what the Libyans requested:

Request for Clarification Expressed by the Libyan Legal Team Regarding the Implementation of Security Council Resolution 1192 (1998)

Three matters of main concern

Would it be possible to ensure that despite the provisions of Article 29, paragraph 5 of the UK-Netherlands Agreement, the Agreement will not be amended to change its object and purpose to having a trial by a Scottish Court sitting in the Netherlands or to allow for the extradition of the two accused to the territory of either the US or the UK?

Would it be possible to ensure that given the provisions of Article 16, paragraph 2(b) of the UK-Netherlands Agreement, the accused will not be asked to consent to be transferred outside the Netherlands until the completion of the trial?

What are the legal grounds for the UK's insistence that, if the two accused are found guilty, the sentence will be served in Scotland and despite the provisions of article 16, paragraph 2(b) of the UK-Netherlands Agreement, would it be possible to arrange for the accused, if convicted, to serve their term in the Netherlands, Libya, or any other third acceptable country instead of the UK?

Clarifications sought from the Netherlands

Would it be possible for the lawyers of the accused to visit the location of the detention and the Court facilities in the Netherlands where the trial will be held?

At which airport will the plane with the accused land in the Netherlands?

What procedures will be followed upon the arrival of the accused in the Netherlands, in particular, in the light of the fact that they expect to be accompanied on the plane by at least one lawyer and one family member each, as well as a doctor and possibly by an observer from a human rights organization? Under what law will the accused be detained by the Dutch authorities? Will they be handcuffed upon their arrival?

Where will the accused be held in the Netherlands during their detention by the Dutch authorities and how will their safety be guaranteed? Will the accused be held in detention with other detainees or will they be in a separate detention facility?

What assurances could be obtained from the Dutch authorities that no authorities of a third country or other authorities, except for the Dutch authorities responsible for their detention, and members of the defense team, doctors and relatives, will have access to the accused during their detention by the Dutch authorities?

How long will the accused be detained by the Dutch authorities before they are transferred for purposes of the trial to the Scottish Court sitting in the Netherlands?

Will the Dutch authorities alert the media and allow it to be present at the airport?

Will the Dutch authorities undertake to issue multiple entry/exit visas to enable the members of the defense team of the accused to exit and re-enter the Netherlands as the need arises in their efforts to conduct an effective defense?

Will the Dutch authorities undertake to issue multiple entry/exit visas to a medical doctor accompanying the accused and to the family members of the accused who wish to attend the trial?

What protection will the lawyers of the accused and the documentation used by them enjoy in the Netherlands? Will their papers be protected from search and seizure? Will they enjoy the same protection as the Dutch lawyers have during court proceedings?

Will the Dutch authorities issue the necessary visas to all witnesses identified by the defense team?

Clarifications sought from the United Kingdom

When, approximately, will the Scottish Court be ready for the trial in the Netherlands?

When will the UK announce the appointment of the three judges of the Scottish Court sitting in the Netherlands and, in the meantime, can the lawyers of the accused be provided with the list of eligible judges from which the members of the Court will be appointed?

Given the provisions of Article 1, paragraph (j) of the UK-Netherlands Agreement, what arrangements could be made to allow the foreign lawyers, who are members of the accused's legal defense team, to participate in the defense of the accused in the Scottish court?

How frequently will relatives of the accused be allowed to visit them during the trial?

Will the British authorities within the framework of law provide the lawyers of the accused, including those who are not Scottish solicitors and advocates, with a reasonable opportunity to reproduce and/or examine the sealed materials when they are released?

Clarifications sought from the UK and the USA

Will the UK and the USA ensure that any evidence or witnesses in their territory or under their control are, upon the request of the Scottish Court, made available at the Netherlands in accordance with their respective laws?

Will the UK and the USA undertake to issue visas to the lawyers of the accused so that they could have access to witnesses and documents in their territory or under their control identified by the Prosecution or the Defense if they are not available in the Netherlands?

Clarifications sought from the UK, the USA and France

Since the French judicial authorities have stated their satisfaction with regard to the bombing of UTA 772 (S/1997/858), will the measures set forth in Security Council resolutions 748 (1992) and 883 (1993) be immediately suspended upon the arrival of the two accused in the Netherlands as provided for in paragraph 8 of Security Council resolution 1192 (1998)?

The first answers from the Netherlands led to a setback.[2] The Dutch responded to these questions with typical law enforcement answers. The Libyans were surprised. They challenged those answers by insisting there was no law in the Netherlands that would cover such a situation, including whether to handcuff the suspects, and similar technicalities. The Libyan legal team returned the Dutch answers in their entirety to the UN legal office, rejecting their contents. The Dutch reviewed the answers and came back later with a second set that showed they would be more flexible and accommodating in treating this case differently from the way they would any typical criminal case in their country. The Libyans accepted the new set and later described the Dutch authorities' treatment of the suspects, when they arrived, as "full of respect."[3]

The United States, the United Kingdom and France came back with a simple answer to the last question: Yes, sanctions would immediately be suspended upon the arrival of the accused.[4] But other answers from the first two countries required further clarification. That second set of questions was a breaking point for London and Washington to some extent; they showed further Libyan sincerity and professionalism in dealing with the legal aspects.

After a few indirect meetings and indirect contacts arranged by the UN's legal adviser, Hans Corell, the Libyan team returned to Libya to discuss what they had received. New sets of follow-up questions were prepared and presented to the UN in early November, during the second round. The answers of the three came back shortly.[5] The Libyans felt they needed further guarantees with regard to some issues they had not received satisfactory answers on. Corell informed the Libyans those issues would have to be answered by the UN Secretary General since they were "political." The UN Secretary General informed Dorda that he had to work on them personally. Annan felt he would need to visit Libya to discuss these issues. That meant he wanted to discuss them with Qadhafi personally when it became clear that the whole legal process was satisfied and the political process had to be reenergized.

The most important points considered legal and agreed upon were these:

—Specifications of details concerning the rights of the accused while in custody, and regarding technicalities on how they would be arrested and treated, such as rights of visitation, eating habits and religious practices;

—Guarantees that no American or British authorities (meaning intelligence agents other than those of the court and through the lawyers) would be allowed to interrogate the two suspects while in custody with the Dutch or British authorities;

—Guarantees the two would not be transferred to any other country, or to the custody of any other authority, unless proven guilty and have to serve their sentence in Scotland;

—The court, or authorities, would not ask Libya to enforce the appearance of any further witnesses. The Lord Advocate and the Defense team could ask for any witness to appear, but the countries where such witnesses resided would not force that appearance if any witness chose not to appear. That was the case the Americans presented when Libya asked if the defense could summon someone living in the US or in the UK, and Libya answered the same if the witness summoned lived in Libya;

—No further accusations would be raised against Libyans other than those concerning the two suspects;

—No new cases or issues would be raised and connected to the current case;

—Full cooperation by the American and British legal authorities with the defense team.

The points considered political were the following:

—Where would the two suspects be held if convicted?

—After their suspension, would there be an official lifting of the sanctions within the ninety-day period provided in the original resolutions as the period during which Libya's cooperation would be confirmed; and how would that be with regards to the compensation?

—What type of relations would Libya have with the US and the UK post-solution?

For Libya, a whole legal process was transferred from Scotland to the Netherlands. That meant if the two were convicted, their imprisonment would be where they were tried or in Libya. The United Kingdom presented its answers from a different perspective: The location of the court would be under Scottish jurisdiction. Camp van Zeist was offered for the trial only, and Scotland could not set up a prison in another country. Legally and technically, that was out of the question.

The two other elements required political engagement. Here, the parties were talking about the practical normalization of relations with Libya. The United States was not politically ready to even begin a process. Its answers would be negative, while the United Kingdom was more receptive to ideas. There was a strong belief that what Qadhafi wanted was an international umbrella for the solution: Who would protect Libya if the United States and the United Kingdom reneged on any of their promises? Who would cover Libya's responsiveness?

To satisfy these worries, the United States and the United Kingdom had to accept some mediation. But who? The mediators in place or someone else?

Already worried about Bandar's negotiating tactics, the Americans and the British turned to exploring what the UN Secretary General would be able to do. That was not an easy task, for they were worried about Annan's tendencies to drift away from their guidelines. Washington and London had a tough choice to make. The only choice they could make was to insist that any official diplomacy, meaning contact, had to be made by the UN Secretary General. But Annan had disappointed them earlier that year when he overplayed a mission to Iraq that had delayed a military attack by the United States and the United Kingdom. Hoping he had learned his lesson, they felt that by choosing him, putting the office above the person, Annan would save them the embarrassment of having to make political deals that might drift away from the Security Council resolutions. Still, the United States and the United Kingdom were getting nervous about any endeavor similar to that with Iraq. Annan could possibly promise more than they wanted him to, and the fact that he was so secretive about his plans to visit Libya made them worry even more.

Exploring how far the UN Secretary General would commit them to what they might not agree to, the United States and the United Kingdom, especially the former, noted that the Security Council resolutions demanded nothing of them, other than suspending the sanctions when the two suspects were handed over and lifting them three months thereafter. The lifting, however, was connected to many conditions that could not be implemented. Even the Americans would never be able to satisfy these conditions within the three-month time frame set therein. The United States would be let off the hook if it kept threatening the use of veto against the formal lifting of sanctions. So any mediation by the office of the Secretary General would be much more limited in scope than any other possible mediation.

Annan, on the other hand, began his own exploratory process. He had privately talked about a possible visit to Libya on many occasions. The opportunity provided itself when he was arranging for a mission to North Africa, where he was to undertake an effort of mediation between Algeria and Morocco regarding the Western Sahara. That tour was scheduled for the second week of November. Still, Annan did not give a definitive date for a visit, especially since he could not get a commitment from Qadhafi to meet him. Another condition raised by the Americans was that he should, at the very least, get a commitment on a date for the surrender of the two suspects, if not take them out on his plane.

In early November, Dorda headed to Libya in order to arrange the meeting and the rest of the details once a date for the visit was officially set. Libya's main concern was that Annan get a commitment from the United States and the United Kingdom for sanctions to be lifted within the time frame set by the Security Council resolutions. Libya wanted Annan to have that written commitment without having necessarily to hand it over to them. That commitment would make the political atmosphere created by the Mandela-Bandar channel mediation more official, and exchanges to finalize the details of the imprisonment of the two suspects could resume, with a more assured outlook toward a positive outcome.

While in Morocco, the continuing escalation of the Iraq problem was reaching the stage of a possible military strike by the United States and the United Kingdom. The inspectors of UNSCOM, the commission established by the UN Security Council to destroy Iraq's weapons of mass destruction, were ordered out of the country. Annan faced many U.S. accusations about the integrity of the agreement he had reached with Saddam, with the latter reneging on it less than nine months after its signing. How could he be trusted to find a final solution to the Lockerbie problem while losing credibility on the Iraqi issue? That concern was shared by Libya as well, for it was beginning to ask whether it could trust any commitments given by Annan if he could not deliver the American and British assurances to abide by them. That distrust would later give his trip to Libya a different perspective, especially after the two countries had launched their military strikes against Iraq.

Because of the developments in Iraq, Annan cut short his visit to North Africa and went back to New York. While working on the Iraqi file, he kept working on his possible visit to Libya. Two weeks later, he managed to resume his tour of North Africa. Dorda went back to his country and stayed in touch with Annan, wherever he was, discussing the previous conditions they had both raised. Finally, while in Algeria, the Secretary General officially announced he would visit Tripoli on December 8. It was then that the United States and the United Kingdom were formally informed of this visit. They managed to pass him only a simple message: Stick to the Security Council resolutions. He knew what they meant, for he could not afford another embarrassment.

Between Algeria and Libya, Annan had a scheduled visit to Tunisia that included a day of rest. While there, his contacts with Dorda continued. The Libyan official assured the Secretary General that Qadhafi would receive him, despite many public statements to the contrary. The visit was finally set to take place but to last only a few hours. It would not include a sleepover in Libya, Annan claiming he had to go on to the United Arab Emirates (UAE) where the summit of the Gulf Cooperation Council (GCC) was to be held in celebration of the tenth anniversary of its establishment and where he would meet Crown Prince Abdullah to discuss this issue.

On the morning of December 8, Annan's plane landed at Tripoli airport. Qadhafi, however, was not in the capital or in Sirt, where he was spending much of his time. That was his way of preventing any pressure to meet with the Secretary General, for he was almost fully relying on Bandar and Mandela, since Annan was not bringing any commitments from the United States and the United Kingdom. While Annan was meeting the foreign minister and other officials, Dorda and some of his colleagues were pressing Qadhafi and his immediate office to meet with Annan. Reluctantly, the Libyan leader agreed, and Annan was driven through the Libyan desert to the meeting.

Qadhafi received Annan very seriously and did not give him the usual warm welcome. In his own mind, the Libyan leader had noted that the UN Secretary General had prevented a military attack against Iraq in February but could not hold that ground for long. He knew how the United States had turned against him. He thought he should not fall into the trap of promising something to someone who could not deliver. Thus, he lectured the UN Secretary General about the world, Africa and the UN. He also mentioned that the efforts of Mandela and Bandar were under way, leaving him with an impression Annan would reveal only after the handover.

Annan left Libya convinced that the efforts of the two other mediators, and not his, were the ones that might deliver the solution. In September, Bandar had given him an idea of what he was trying to do. Annan was in contact with Mandela as well. This meeting with the Libyan leader would only confirm what the UN Secretary General was suspicious of.

Publicly, it was not until April 5, only hours after the handover, that Annan acknowledged the mediators' vital role in convincing Qadhafi of the solution. He presented that aspect diplomatically, trying to claim some responsibility for their involvement. At a press conference at the UN Annan said: "After my discussions with [Qadhafi], it became clear that President Mandela and the Government of Saudi Arabia could play a role, and I asked them to work with me on this. And so they have worked in support of my efforts, and I think we have to be aware of that, in these sort of protracted issues, one doesn't go in and expect a quick resolution, but you prepare it and work on it gradually. And I am happy that we are there now."

Annan had left Libya empty handed. He qualified that later, in the same press conference, saying he had asked Saudi Crown Prince Abdullah and President Mandela, two days after that visit, to officially help him. That request was made at the GCC summit. Qadhafi seemed intent on preferring their mediation to his. The official UN stamp was needed later by the United States and the United Kingdom. All Annan could do then was wait for the next appropriate moment for his intervention.

While en route to the UAE, Annan telephoned Albright and Cook. He informed them of the meeting, giving very few details. The only substance he provided was that the process was moving ahead but it needed more time to materialize. He asked them to be patient. There was nothing else they could do.

The United States was facing time pressure. The tenth anniversary of the Lockerbie incident was coming up. Clinton wanted some substantial progress to report to the families when he addressed them on that occasion. Since Libya was not about to announce a handover, the United States needed to show its own pressure. Officials made some threatening statements, claiming they were losing patience with Libya. Libya was responding with statements of its own, accusing the United States of intransigence on the guarantees it was demanding. The United Kingdom was showing uneasy patience. Clinton had to address the memorial held for the tenth anniversary with calculated words of patience:

> You know better than anyone else it is beyond your power to alter the past. There is no such thing as perfect justice. No trial or penalty or elimination of the facts can compensate you for the profound loss you have suffered. But as long as we can bring those responsible before the bar of justice and have a real trial, you have a right—and society has a need—to see that done. ...Since then, the Libyan leader, Mr. Qadhafi, has given the US mixed signals. We believe there is still some possibility he will accept your offer. That would be the best outcome, for it would mean that finally there would be a trial. But let me be absolutely clear to all of you: Our policy is not to trust Mr. Qadhafi's claims, it is to test them. This is a take-it or leave-it offer. We will not negotiate its terms. If the suspects are convicted, they will serve their time in Scotland. And if the suspects are not turned over by the time of the next sanctions review, we will work with the United Nations, with our allies and friends, to seek yet stronger measures against Libya. In doing so, we will count on the support of all nations that counseled the US to make this proposal in the first place. If the proposal fails, all should make clear that the responsibility falls on Mr. Qadhafi alone.[6]

Despite their insistence that the United States would not negotiate, Clinton's aides had already given the Libyans certain guarantees, while some others were still being discussed by the mediators. Political concessions were given later and implemented, such as a face-to-face meeting with the Libyans. The two demands they refused were the final official lifting of sanctions and the location of the prison if the two suspects were convicted.

Solutions

The issue of imprisonment of the two suspects, if convicted, was the easiest to solve, although it was important to Tripoli. The issue was solved with the promise of establishing consular relations with the United Kingdom whereby Libya would post a consulate in Scotland to monitor the situation of the convicted, who would be imprisoned under full supervision of UN observers. The UN flag would be raised at that location. This was one major concession by the British since any consular relations would practically mean reestablishing diplomatic relations between the two countries. Libya accepted.

Technically, however, it took a lot of maneuvering by all parties to get both the solution to this point and the other remaining guarantees demanded by the Libyans. Qadhafi, personally, was not yet fully convinced, through the legal guarantees, that the United States would not reach out beyond the two suspects. He felt some other political maneuver by the Americans could override the commitment that the lawyers got. He needed political guarantees.

Bandar was set for another mission to Libya by the end of 1998, resulting from the lack of progress following the inconclusive end of the legal meetings and the clarifications received. This was the first time he acted with the prior knowledge of the Americans and the British. His previous trips were not officially communicated to them although he had some informal communications.

One issue bothered them all. For the first time, Bandar was to fly into Tripoli airport. They did not want him to do so. He was insistent. The United States and the United Kingdom hurried to fix some type of a label on the trip. They did not want any official business conducted outside the framework of the UN. It was arranged to have the Secretary General's office send a request to the sanctions committee asking permission for Bandar's plane to fly into Libya, with the justification that he and Gerwell were carrying a mandate to further Annan's efforts with Libya and conveying messages from Crown Prince Abdullah and President Mandela. The messages formulated general positions aimed at giving Bandar's trip some official status, while insisting it should definitely not be seen that he was carrying messages from the United States and the United Kingdom.

The South African letter was as follows:

> It is our great honor to convey to you our warmest fraternal greetings and to extend our good wishes to yourself, your family and the people of Libya during this holy month of Ramadan. You are in this time constantly in our thoughts as a fraternal people, just as we think of the entire people of the Maghreb and the Middle-East. It is our fond and sincere wish that lasting peace shall at last be found for our brothers and sisters who in so many cases suffered so long and so much, not only in those regions but all over our continent and in the world. We pray together with you, My Brother Leader, that this last year before we enter into the new century may see us mobilizing the efforts of leaders across the world to work for peaceful and just settlements to the various conflicts which are still plaguing the lives of too many of our people across the globe.
>
> We are very mindful and appreciative, My Brother Leader, of your own concern for assisting in bringing peace, stability and progress to our continent. Your various meetings with other leaders from the continent to address some of the major conflicts, bear testimony to that concern. It has been our privilege to interact with you on some of those issues and we must take this opportunity of again thanking you for your understanding and cooperation. We are very grateful for your understanding of South Africa's position borne out of your own experience that inclusive negotiations between erstwhile enemies were the only way of leading our country out of long and destructive conflict. We know, My Brother Leader, that with regards to, for example, the Democratic Republic of the Congo, you share our view that a process towards an inclusive political settlement is what is ultimately needed in that situation.
>
> My Brother Leader, we write to you on this occasion particularly to raise once more the matter about which we have been exchanging ideas in our personal meetings, telephonic discussions and through our personal envoys; we refer to the matter of Lockerbie.
>
> Since our last discussion, Brother Leader, and following your kind meeting with our personal envoy, Professor Jakes Gerwel, we consulted with the Secretary-General of the United Nations Organization and had the opportunity of speaking to His Royal Highness, Crown Prince Abdulla bin Abdulaziz Al-Saud, as well as His Royal Highness Prince Bandar bin Sultan, who together with Professor Gerwel represented the Crown Prince and myself in the efforts to resolve the Lockerbie matter.
>
> My Brother Leader, it is our considered view that the time has come for us to finally move this matter towards a resolution. The Crown Prince and ourselves have brought our energies to bear on this matter in an attempt to have the UK and the US agree after a decade to have the trial of the suspects held in a neutral country. The envoys of the

Crown Prince and ourselves have represented your viewpoints regarding aspects of the eventual agreement between the governments of the UK and the Netherlands to those governments and to the Secretary-General of the United Nations. The Crown Prince and myself, personally and through our envoys, have implored the Secretary-General to involve himself in the clarification of those matters in the agreement which might still have stood in the way of a resolution of this longstanding dispute.

It is against this background, My Brother Leader, that I, together with His Royal Highness the Crown Prince, now wish to appeal to you to accept the Secretary-General's proposals put to yourself, and subsequently explained to the Crown Prince and myself, and to concretely progress by having the suspects delivered to the Netherlands in terms of the agreement. The Crown Prince and I, on behalf of the peoples and governments of our respective countries, can assure you, My Brother Leader, that we shall vigilantly watch over the rest of the process to ensure that the spirit and letter of the agreement are abided with. Our personal envoys with whom you have developed personal relationships, My Brother Leader, shall be at your disposal to ensure our continued and consistent personal involvement.

The time, My Brother Leader, has arrived for our continent to seek to liberate itself from all the constraints on our development. The decade-long restrictions on Libya and its people have not only constrained our friendly brothers and sisters in Libya but have represented a barrier to the development of that region and our common continent in which you, Brother Leader, have such an important role to play. We need now to progress also with regards to a resolution of the Lockerbie matter, and the proposals of the Secretary-General provide a basis for such progress, we believe.

We forward this letter to you as speedily as is possible, but shall strive to have our personal envoy Professor Jakes Gerwel, hopefully together with His Royal Highness Prince Bandar, deliver this letter and that from His Royal Highness the Crown Prince to you personally. We thank you, Brother Leader, for once more receiving them on our behalf.

Please remain assured, My Brother Leader, of our highest consideration."[7]

The Saudi letter read:

May peace and the blessings and mercy of God be upon you.

At the beginning of the holy month of Ramadan, I have the pleasure to convey to you every good wish and my heartfelt hope that the Almighty will bless this month for all of us in the Arab Islamic nation.

You are well aware of the Kingdom of Saudi Arabia's concern that a solution be found to the issue of the sanctions posed on the Libyan Arab Jamahiriya that will both satisfy you and protect the interests of the Government and people of your country, while at the same time leading to the goal to which we all aspire, namely, the irreversible lifting of those sanctions. Saudi Arabia has therefore gone to great lengths, with your full knowledge, in its mediation efforts with the Governments of the US of America and the UK. These efforts have been coordinated with the sustained endeavors made by our friend His Excellency President Nelson Mandela and the timely follow-up of Mr. Kofi Annan, Secretary-General of the United Nations.

After intensive discussions with His Excellency President Mandela and Mr. Annan at the recent Gulf Cooperation Council summit held in Abu Dhabi, and pursuant to the discussions held with officials of the UK and the US, we wish to advise you to accept the proposals made by the Secretary-General, which we agree represent the ideal solution to the issue.

Saudi Arabia will continue its indefatigable support for the position of the Libyan Arab Jamahiriya and will make every possible effort to ensure that a just solution is found that is satisfactory to yourself above all, and which will lead to the desired results. We are, furthermore, confident that the Secretary-General will continue to use all his good offices and make every effort to obtain the best possible results, which we hope to see as soon as possible.

May peace and the blessings of God be upon you.[8]

The text of the two letters combined the strict demands of the United States and the United Kingdom to confirm that any final solution be reached through the UN Secretary General, not through the mediators. It was a position developed upon the forceful imposition of those mediators of their efforts as the only possible track for any eventual resolution of this conflict.

The two governments were also trying to send a more important message to Qadhafi: Bandar and Mandela do not speak on our behalf; anything they communicate as an American-British position is not authorized by the United States and the United Kingdom.

Drafts of the two letters were presented to Washington and London. The contents were not rejected as such, although some minor changes were requested. When that work was completed, the sanctions committee gave permission. That was on December 27, 1998.

Annan was tracked down while on vacation. He sent the letter to the sanctions committee of the council, with an attachment: a request from Bandar to travel to Libya. Annan's letter to the president of the committee said:

It has come to my knowledge that on 30 December 1998 a waiver from the prohibition on flights to the Libyan Arab Jamahiriya instituted by the Security Council in its resolution 748 (1992), was submitted to the Committee chaired by you, in order to enable emissaries of His Excellency Mr. Nelson Mandela, President of South Africa, and His Royal Highness Crown Prince Abdullah bin Abdulaziz of Saudi Arabia, to fly to the Libyan Arab Jamahiriya and deliver messages in support of my own efforts with regard to the implementation of the relevant resolutions of the Security Council.

I welcome this expression of support for my personal efforts by President Mandela and Crown Prince Abdullah bin Abdulaziz. It is my sincere hope that their messages will help convince the Libyan leadership to heed my call for compliance with the resolutions of the Security Council without further delay and without preconditions.

Bandar's letter explained:

On behalf of the Kingdom of Saudi Arabia and the Republic of South Africa and as a follow-up to the conversation I had with the Secretary General of the United Nations regarding the Lockerbie situation, I am kindly requesting the permission of the Security Council Committee, established pursuant to Resolution 748 (1992), to travel directly to Tripoli and Sirt, Libya.

After submitting the technical details of the flight, airplane and passengers, Bandar concluded:

This mission is in support of the Secretary-General's initiative to president Qadhafi where we will deliver two letters from our respective governments pursuant to his effort.

Bandar succeeded in making his mission official with the involvement of the United States and the United Kingdom approving the trip, despite their previous positions. They could not categorically reject his proposals anymore. They had to deal with them. Officially or not, Bandar became "the" mediator to be reckoned with.

On New Year's Eve, the holy month of Ramadan began. Usually, this is a month during which even the most important business is placed on the back burner in the Muslim world. Libya is no exception. That led to expectations that there would be no handover until after the end of that month, if at all. Qadhafi, however, felt the process should go on. He needed a solution based on the guarantees he was requesting. He continued to manage the issue while fasting. He received Bandar and Gerwell and discussed further details with them.

16

The Dénouement

The Libyan decision to hand over the two suspects was made on February 9, 1999. The actual official announcement was made on March 19. Two specific issues remained to be sorted out in the interim: Libya's receipt of an official document from the UN certifying what had been agreed upon privately through the mediators and the discussions of the legal teams, and the preparation of the internal situation in Libya for a "proper" decision on the handover.

While on yet another secret visit to Libya in early February, Bandar and Gerwell had to discuss the remaining details of the guarantees Libya requested. Other issues discussed were political confirmations of what was presented to the legal team, especially with regard to limiting the trial to the Lockerbie case and to the two named suspects. Those verbal political guarantees were reaffirmed through Bandar and Gerwell. The other elements were a little more complicated. The United States was not yet ready to accept a formal lifting of the sanctions; to the contrary, it had reaffirmed its listing of Libya as a sponsor of terrorism. Libya had to be convinced that the listing was procedural since relations between the two countries had not improved and since the lobbies opposed to Libya were still operating their campaign against Tripoli. The mediators assured Libya, however, that the solution to the Lockerbie issue would pave the way and that they would assist in the improvement of those relations. The faster evolution in the British position (establishing diplomatic relations) would play as another factor in convincing the Americans to change while assuring the Libyans of the new attitudes in the West. The United States would be isolated if it did not move. Still, some type of gesture by Washington had to be shown. After much pressure, Washington agreed to hold, under the UN auspices, a direct meeting with the Libyans which could be considered a launchpad for further improving relations. That proved enough to convince Qadhafi on that aspect.

Based on the understandings, Qadhafi wrote Mandela, the "Historic African Hero," on February 9, informing him of his conditional decision. In that letter, Qadhafi said:

> As a result of the praiseworthy efforts of yourself and the leaders of Saudi Arabia, and to crown the exhausting shuttle journeys made by your high representatives Prince Bandar and Professor Jakes, and the role of Mr. Kofi Annan and his aides, we achieved an obstacle-free basis, free of roadblocks that were on the road, to solve the issues that were under discussion including the lifting of the sanctions, the place of trial and the place to implement the final ruling when it is issued in condemnation. It seems the parties concerned with your continuing efforts acknowledged the goodwill of each other and the sincerity in solving this problem, for which the credit goes to you and to my brothers the leaders of Saudi Arabia. There remains only the formulation of the solution in its legal and final form binding to all parties, without reliance on verbal or bilateral undertakings, because, my dear brother president, the case had been made subject to resolutions of the Security Council, therefore it has to be solved the same way."[1]

A similar letter was sent to the Saudi leaders.

The three elements mentioned in that letter were more psychological than actually legal or political. Qadhafi could not understand why a former U.S. military base had to be chosen for the court to sit in. He feared that choice implied a possible attempt by the Americans to kidnap the two Libyans when held there, if not while en route to the Netherlands. The issue of imprisonment was still connected to the previous fears. The lifting of the sanctions was also an important issue since the Libyans consider their official existence is enough of a burden, making them like a watchdog ready to jump at sudden movement.

The substance of that letter was communicated to Annan. Bandar visited him in New York, and they discussed what type of response Libya would get in return. Annan began consultations with the U.S. and the U.K. representatives in New York. He faced some problems dealing with the U.S. representative, who seemed not suited for such an important commitment. Pickering had to come to New York to meet the UN Secretary General and discuss the details with him.

The letter in response from Annan had two elements in it: the legal discussions conducted in late 1998 and the political promises delivered verbally by the mediators. Annan was described by the Americans as being sympathetic to Mandela's and Bandar's efforts. They were extremely cautious, for they felt they did not know exactly what the mediators had promised. The only thing they could agree to be included in Annan's response would be what had been agreed upon in the legal discussions. In other words, no further guarantees were to be provided.

The United States was afraid any response from Annan might contain language that could be interpreted differently from the American position. That language, the Americans feared, was already included in the agreements reached between the legal teams and was more related to British concerns than theirs. The Americans wanted language saying that the Libyan regime would not be undermined and that the trial would be limited to matters pertaining specifically to the Lockerbie case. They were not agreeing to anything, they stressed, that would permit Tripoli to bar full disclosure of who and what was involved in the bombing. They were trying to balance flexibility with conditionality.

On February 17, 1999, after further consultations and discussions on the substance with the United States and Britain, Annan prepared a letter addressed to Qadhafi in which he says, "In pursuance of the understanding reached with the envoys, I attach a document setting forth the relevant details thereof."[2] Annan went on to confirm that "after reviewing this document, the governments of the UK and the US have confirmed to me that they share the understanding reflected therein." Annan was warned by one concerned diplomat that his letter would raise concerns with the Libyan leader. It was clear, however, Annan was not ready, or allowed, to move beyond what he had already presented, for he did not take the notes of this diplomat into consideration. The letter was sent.

That letter angered Qadhafi. Not only did it ignore certain understandings he had reached with Bandar and Mandela; it also contained a veiled threat. In the letter, Annan referred to the review of sanctions due to be held by the Security Council on February 26. "It would be most helpful," Annan said, "if the practical agreements already agreed upon between the Libyan legal team and my own legal counsel could be set in motion before that date." In this sentence, the UN Secretary General actually said the agreement was between Libya and the UN, not between Libya and the United States and the United Kingdom. Furthermore, a veiled threat was directed at Qadhafi by setting a date for a handover. The Libyan leader also felt betrayed.

Barely two days later, Libya's foreign minister, not Qadhafi, responded to Annan's letter. His essential message was that the Secretary General had no business communicating with the leader of the revolution. He had to communicate with the foreign minister. Then, Muntasser went on to reject the date set while reflecting that other understandings were missing from that letter, most importantly those regarding consular relations with Britain and other arrangements on the issue of imprisonment. He also addressed the issue of the necessity to lift the sanctions without the need for suspension and asked for the Secretary General's "personal intervention to help settle these issues to the satisfaction" of Libya and for "a decision that will be binding on all parties."[3] The Libyan demands remained the same as those in the letters to Mandela and the Saudis. Annan had not satisfied any of them.

The Americans misread this response and thought, once again, that Qadhafi was backing off from his agreements. They did not believe in the necessity of providing Libya with the international umbrella he sought. The review in the Security Council was coming up. They set themselves to move for strengthening the sanctions against Libya, considering that letter a refusal of the agreements. As usual, the British were more understanding. They had come to believe in the sincerity of the Libyans in this process and the need for the Americans to do the same.

With this atmosphere threatening the whole process, Blair, Mandela and Bandar were on the phone discussing how to overcome this obstacle. The three were working the Americans as well, as was Cook. The United States and the United Kingdom agreed that Annan should send a response to Libya, answering its concerns.

In this response, Annan referred once again to the Security Council resolutions which "request me to report to the Council on the compliance of the Libyan Arab Jamahiriya with the remaining provisions of the resolutions. Should my report conclude that the Libyan Arab Jamahiriya has complied in every possible way with these provisions, I would expect that the Council would adopt a favorable decision with respect to the lifting of the sanctions."[4]

Then Annan moved to the second issue:

> It continues to be my firmly held view that the arrangements described in the third, fourth and fifth paragraphs of the annex to my letter of February 17, 1999 would provide comprehensive and adequate guarantees for the well-being of the accused during their period of incarceration, should they be found guilty. As indicated in the annex, these arrangements would be subject to discussions with the United Nations. I stand ready personally to see to it that such discussions result in the best possible arrangements for the United Nations monitoring. With regard to your reference to a Libyan Consulate, I am informed that the British authorities are ready to give a favorable consideration to this matter and to discuss it directly with the Libyan authorities.

In his last paragraph, Annan practically closed the door on any further discussions on the whole process. He said clearly:

> It is my assessment that we have now reached the point where a further postponement of the implementation of resolution 1192 (1998) could serve no useful purpose and could not be justified. It would be my expectation, therefore, that in light of the additional clarifications set out in this letter, the Libyan side will now be in a position to indicate a firm date for the transfer.

The issue of imprisonment was practically solved. The consular relations Britain promised Libya through Annan were accompanied by a private promise through diplomatic circles. The United Kingdom would quickly move to sort out the remaining issues between the two countries in preparation for reestablishment of full diplomatic relations. That was an extremely important assurance the Libyans received, helping them in turn to accept less from the Americans.

Annan's letter, however, failed to discuss any possible meetings with the Americans, an issue left to be discussed by the mediators. Whatever the UN Secretary General was dealing with had to be limited to what the Americans would officially agree to. The meeting with the Libyans was not something they would easily accept; it had to stay within political, not diplomatic, circles. It was communicated verbally to the UN Secretary General, through him to the Libyans and through the mediators as well.

The issue of direct concern, diplomatically, was to satisfy the U.S. need for tools of defense against the internal domestic lobbies. That was what was communicated to Annan, and that was what he was authorized to translate into language he would communicate on paper. It was the fact that the review of the council, coming up the next day, with the flare the United States would attach to it. The Americans would not budge. They needed to show resolve. They could not follow the British, who understood that this file had to be closed. No further guarantees were possible.

As for the formal lifting of the sanctions, the United States was in a difficult position. They would accept only the suspension, spreading in diplomatic circles that, if there were a need for them to once again impose, that would not be possible with the situation existing in the world and the UN Security Council. And to show their resolve, internally, the Americans kept threatening the use of their veto at the council if they were pushed to vote on the formal lifting of sanctions. That was the only way they could balance the pressure of internal lobbies and international obligations.

Libya was finally having to face the moment of truth. Whatever commitments it would get, in addition to what was in those letters, would be only verbal and up to the United States to abide by. The only element left was to convince the Libyan leader of the sincerity of what he already had.

With Washington raising the stakes once again, London felt the process was about to fall apart. It was beginning to sense the solution was near, with doubts, of course, although those doubts were lessening. The United Kingdom understood that Libya and the United States were distrustful of each other and in desperate need of help. They seemed like two children jumping into a swimming pool for the first time. Someone had to hold their hands and help them swim, possibly teach them how to swim together.

At this stage, London thought that, first of all, it was necessary to get through this review in the Security Council without endangering the process. The diplomats at the United Nations watched as the United States representative went into the meeting threatening a time limit: Thirty days should be enough for Libya to hand over the suspects. If it did not by then, further sanctions would automatically be imposed. The United Kingdom did not agree on the time limit although it accommodated the United States on the issue of uneasiness with the long delay in Libya's decision. The other council members refused to set the time limit the United States asked for. Still, Burleigh walked out of the meeting and claimed that the council had agreed to give Libya thirty days to hand over the two, or else. All other ambassadors refuted that statement, but the news wires had already carried the story. The Libyan leader was furious once again. He felt as if that statement by the United States was the real response to his foreign minister's letter to Annan. Libya launched its own campaign, rejecting that threat.

If Libya had at all intended to hand over the two suspects at any specific date, that date would certainly now have to be after the thirty days the United States set. However, there was no chance that Libya would abide by such a threat. If the Americans were pushing for a hand over, that would not be the way to do it. If they were pushing Libya for a full rebellion against the process, Libya would not oblige them either. The United States would not be able to outmaneuver a process that had surpassed all the maneuvers of the decade between the two countries. Libya turned to fine-tune the remaining guarantees it requested, knowing full well that a few days would be sufficient for that effort and for a final decision to be made. A handover would not take place until the period of threat had expired. Libya would make that final concession only on its own terms.

On March 1, after a few contacts with the United States and the United Kingdom, Mandela and Crown Prince Abdullah telephoned

Qadhafi, imploring him to restrain himself and assuring him that everything was still going according to plans. The reports from New York were indicating that the American statements were nothing serious and intended mainly for public consumption. Libya agreed to remain calm, but any implementation of the agreements would not be within their time frame. That was fine with all, as long as it would take place in the end.

Crown Prince Abdullah, who himself called Qadhafi on many occasions to help solve some issue, was critical in these final days. He phoned the Libyan leader repeatedly and sent some messages, the most important of which came after Annan's last letter, along with a letter from Mandela, to provide Libya with the guarantees the United States could not provide through Annan in any written form. Qadhafi was not able to accept verbal assurances from enemies or friends alike. He had to await written guarantees which were presented to him. The letters provided him the international safety net he sought.

The most important element in the two letters was that a meeting between American and Libyan diplomats would be held under the UN auspices. The Saudis and Mandela convinced the Libyan leader that this would be a first step toward normalization and that he had to be patient. They understood the problems Washington faced on this issue. They spoke to him in a language reserved for warm friends and brothers, assuring him that they would not agree to anything likely to be a danger to Libya.

Internal Preparations in Libya

Internally, Qadhafi was preparing his people for the final phase. The General People's Congress, theoretically the highest authority in Libya's complicated system of governing, had to be the party making the final decision. It was impossible for Qadhafi to claim for years that he held no official status in the executive system, then come out with such a major decision by himself. Many statements were issued to that effect, especially when Annan was to visit him and after the letter of February 17 from the Secretary General. Stories in Libya's national news agency, JANA, surfaced during that period, saying the Libyan leader could not make such a decision, for he held no official post. That was the public gesture of anger he used when wanting to rebuff someone, keeping quiet when he felt receptive of someone else.

Preparation of the internal front went on for months. It had begun with the early stages of the process when voices would rise during the local and national congresses, demanding guarantees prior to handing over the two suspects. Another national congress was to be held in March. It would provide the best opportunity to have it declare its acquiescence to the leader's recommendation that the two be handed over. Qadhafi invited Mandela and Bandar to that meeting in order to serve as witnesses to what he would announce and what the congress would decide. Their presence would further confirm to the conferees that international guarantees were provided and a handover would definitely not be a surrender.

Qadhafi knows his country very well. He knows the tribal and national complications of its society. He prepared for a special kind of address with the presence of Mandela and Bandar at his side. They would second his recommendations theoretically, since they did not have a role in the congress. He managed it perfectly.

In the general congress, Qadhafi had to explain many pros and cons of Libya's situation. One of the latter was the debate on the case at the ICJ, of which he said, "The court is now studying the case; after a few months or a few years, the court will issue a verdict and may say, 'These people must be tried in America, or in Britain or in Libya, and the verdict of the court must be accepted.'"[5]

He went on discussing, in his own words, what had led to the latest stage, beginning with the ICJ resolution, expressing his regret that "this did not come from the Arab League, the Arab Maghreb Union or the OIC. Here, the Arab Maghreb [Union] should have rejected the resolution (of the UNSC) from the outset. Now it has been proved invalid. I wish they had rejected it, said it was invalid and supported the ruling of the International Court [of Justice], but they did not do it."

As for the mediators, Qadhafi said:

> We thanked them and said that they were welcome because we trusted them. We had Mandela who we knew played a significant role since the beginning. He said we would not abandon Libya and we would not forget the kindness of Libya when he was in jail and when his people were struggling and were denied their right to freedom. Mandela said at the time (that) Libya stood by us and the time would come when we return the favor and stand by it. ...They both trust the two sides; they intend to resolve the Lockerbie case and get rid of it. They are serious, and President Mandela said to me: I am confident in the talks between me and Blair who is my friend—The British President [sic] and President Mandela are close friends—and, before you expose the matter to the Libyan people, please—I know that the Libyan people have the power to decide and the last word—we cannot leave it with the Libyan people; this is a diplomatic issue which we can resolve.

Calling what was reached "a compromising and face-saving solution for all the parties," Qadhafi turned the responsibility once again to the mediators:

> In reality, I trust our brothers in Saudi Arabia and the other Arab countries; I trust President Mandela who has involved himself personally in the case. He spoke to me over the phone several times; last night we had a long talk over the phone. Mandela is an historic hero of Africa, an international leader, and one has to respect his mediation and role; one should not cast doubt on them. If we cast doubt on a personality like Mandela, which other personality then would be worthy of trust? This is reality. When a state like Saudi Arabia or South Africa gets involved in a mediation like this, one has to think well that they are not ordinary states. They are respectable states which carry weight in the world, in their respective regional areas. The brothers are asking us to accept, and there is no problem.

Qadhafi had to justify the handover. The best way to do it was to repeat Libya's compliments of the Scottish legal system with some touches of his revolutionary vision:

> Scotland is not Britain; it is an island struggling to secede from Britain. It is bound to secede one day. I wish it was an independent state, not belonging to Britain. There would not have been a problem then; from the first day we would have accepted a trial there. But it is still part of Britain, a divisible part of Britain, a part that may be divided, because Scotland is not England. Regarding Scottish law, no one can cast doubt on its fairness, but anyone can cast doubt on an American court. The jurors, the cowboys. I would cast doubt on the fairness of an American court because the intelligence service interferes in it, and there may be a great deal of pressure on it. The Zionist lobby may also interfere in it; it is bad and we do not trust it. But British justice, generally, and especially the Scottish law, which is different from British law, and the Scots have no enmity against Libya. Quite the contrary, Scots feel sympathy to Libyans because they are both persecuted. Here I meant that a Scottish judge has no hatred for Libyans. We have heard the statements made by the Lockerbie victims association, headed by Dr. [Jim] Swire, who is also a Scot, and his fellow members. In their statements they have supported Libya. They have thanked Libya for being flexible and positive. They also said Libya should not be provoked. They were the first to protest against the deadline. They even told them that Libya would certainly reject such a deadline. They told them: You knew very well Qadhafi's reaction when he was faced with deadlines in the past, he just told you to sod off. So why are you giving him another deadline? Do you mean that you do not want a trial or what?
> What I wanted to say here is that there is no doubt whatsoever about the fairness of a Scottish court because it will not be under pressure from intelligence services, nor will it be under the government's influence. The British government is not going to interfere in it; it will

never bring pressure to bear on it. This court will not have a jury, it will be held outside Britain, in the Netherlands, and therefore [pauses] I told them guilty or not guilty is not the issue here; this is a lawyer's problem. Our concern has always been about the means to resolve this problem. Guilty or not guilty is a legal matter which will be determined at a court of law. And it is not our problem whether [the two accused] had blown up [the plane] or not; this will [be] determined by the court. As far as we are concerned, we only want to deal with the political side of this case. I wanted to say here that I prefer to see the two accused tried by a Scottish court rather than a Dutch court. Because the court is in Holland, we could have asked for a Dutch court. To be honest with you, we can never guarantee that a Dutch court is going to be fairer than a Scottish one. I mean, a Scottish court, either in Scotland itself or anywhere else, will undoubtedly be a fair one. It will not find them guilty if they are not guilty and it will not find them innocent if they are not innocent. As far as we are concerned, it is not our problem whether they are going to be found guilty or not, this is purely a legal matter. Therefore, as far as the court and its laws are concerned, there is no worry on our part, nor is there fear on our part.

17

The Handover

On March 19, 1999, Mandela addressed the congress and uttered long-awaited words:

> It is with great admiration for the Libyan people that I can today announce to the world that Libya has decided to write to the UN Secretary-General to give a firm date for the handing over for the trial in the Netherlands of the two Libyan nationals. The leader has entrusted to me the choice of the precise date. The Jamahiriya agrees to ensure that the two suspects would be available to the UN Secretary-General to take custody of on, or before, the 6th of April, 1999, for their appearance before the court.

Mandela would later add some drama to his announcement. Waving a paper in his hand, he said:

> I have the letter which the Libyan authorities have written to the Secretary-General and I am confident that the Secretary-General will pardon me for publicizing the content of a communication to him before he receives it. We do so because the writing of this letter has taken great courage and self sacrifice from the part of Libya. And because King Fahd, Prince Abdullah and I take responsibility for our part in the decision. We therefore want you and the world to know that we and Saudi Arabia put our honor before you as a guarantee of the good faith of the leadership of the UK and the US as well.

On a personal note, Mandela referred to personal appreciation for his friend, saying:

> When I eventually retire to the peace of the village of my birth, the memories of your friendship will enrich my days. And I shall be happy in the knowledge that there are good men and women in leadership positions all over our continent and in the world—men and women of a generation that will lead us into the next century in pursuit of a better life for all humanity.

Qadhafi was ready. He could not refuse such personal appreciation and assurances from the South African and Saudi leaders. "When Mandela and King Fahd asked me to let it into their hands, it would not be responsible for me to set conditions," the Libyan leader informed his people, to the liking of Mandela and Prince Bandar, who immediately stood and embraced him.

Such an announcement should have been more than welcomed in Washington and London. But, as usual, the former was skeptical while the latter looked for ways to confirm the announcement and the commitment. An official at the State Department in Washington said, "There's a lot of skepticism. The test is when these guys turn up in the Netherlands for the trial."

Why the 6th of April? Many asked at the UN and around the world. The answer was simple. Two reasons: First of all, any deadlines set by the United States had to be passed over. The hand over should not be considered obedience to the Americans. The second reason related to a Muslim holiday that was to occur a few days after the American deadline elapsed. The accused should be allowed to celebrate with their families, not in prison. Therefore, after hearing hints of those reasons from the Libyan leader, Mandela chose the date he announced.

The waiting turned now to the letter from Libya officially informing the Secretary General of that decision. This wait was not long. Hours after the announcement, the letter reached the UN, finalizing the official segment of the decision-making process.

That letter, signed by Libya's foreign minister, contained the following:

> The Jamahiriya agrees to ensure that the two suspects would be available for the Secretary General of the United Nations to take custody of them on or before 6 April 1999 for their appearance before the Court. This is based on the following agreed points:
>
> 1. A Scottish court shall be convened in the Netherlands for the purpose of trying the two suspects in accordance with Scottish law and based on the agreement reached between the legal experts of the United

Nations and Libya, and with the presence of international observers appointed by the Secretary General of the United Nations, and also in consultation with the Republic of South Africa and the Kingdom of Saudi Arabia.

2. The suspects if convicted will serve their prison sentence in Scotland under UN supervision and with assured access to a Libyan Consulate to be established in Scotland in accordance with the arrangements reached with the British Government.

3. The sanctions imposed on the Jamahiriya will be frozen immediately upon the arrival of the two suspects in the Netherlands. The sanctions will be lifted upon submission of the Secretary-General's Report to the Security Council within 90 days stating that the Jamahiri has complied with the Security Council's resolutions.[1]

The third point of the agreement included in the Libyan letter seemed to be more of what Libya expected than what the Americans would agree to. A diplomatic battle would be fought when the ninety-day period elapsed in order for Libya to achieve the formal lifting of the sanctions, only to be faced with threats of a veto by the United States.

The Libyan letter, however, did not fail to lay the burden of moral guarantees for the implementation of the agreement on the mediators. Including their private promises and guarantees in this letter would give them some international prestige in that they would be considered part of the overall agreement with the UN. That was something Libya needed for self-assurance that what Mandela and Bandar had promised was not isolated from the rest of the official documentation.

The same letter would try to satisfy the remaining demands of the council for the lifting of the sanctions. They were as follows:

1. The Jamahiriya, as it has stated before on numerous occasions, opposes all forms of terrorism and condemns all acts of such heinous criminality. As you know the Jamahiriya itself is victim of such terrorist acts which no religious, human or international laws, could condone.

2. The Jamahiriya pledges co-operation within the framework of Libyan laws and legislation with the investigation, the procedures and the trial.

3. The Jamahiriya reiterates what it had previously declared regarding compensation in the event of the two suspects being found guilty by the court and a final verdict being reached.

For Libya, these assurances should have been sufficient for the UN to begin work on sending a delegation to Libya to confirm the nonexistence of terrorist camps in the country. The cooperation with the trial and commitment to compensation would answer the other concerns. Still, the United States objected to the first element and considered that time alone would decide whether the other two would be implemented. This "time" was not yet defined because of America's domestic complications. That did not stop the Americans, however, from announcing certain pleasure at Libya's position regarding terrorism and its role in Africa.

For three days, diplomats battled over Libya's request for some type of official confirmation by the council of Libya's move. Upon insistence by the Libyans, the council issued a statement, distributed as an official document on March 23, welcoming the letter of March 19. The Security Council members, in that same statement, "looked forward to the implementation of that hand-over in accordance with the agreed arrangements and, taking into account also the information provided by the French authorities regarding UTA 772, to the immediate suspension of sanctions with a view to lifting them as soon as circumstances permit, in accordance with relevant Security Council resolutions." Now, all had to wait for that April Monday set by the Libyans.

The wait was hard. The date Libya set coincided with the Easter weekend of 1999. Officials in the West were worried about their long weekend while still wondering whether Libya would actually hand over Megrahi and Fhima. They still feared a last-minute change of mind. That fear in itself showed their continuing inability to understand a country such as Libya and a leader such as Qadhafi. They were not able to understand what the Libyans had been repeating as a slogan that became like a bible: "There is no turning back. All goes forward from here on." No matter at what stage of the solution process they were asked, they repeated their belief. The Westerners would not even believe private comments from personalities such as Prince Bandar, who said Qadhafi is one of two Arab leaders that gives you the hardest time negotiating but, once they make a promise or a decision, they always deliver. Qadhafi, barring unforseen developments, was not about to change his mind.

At last, these officials, some with surprise, were able to breathe easier. It was on the afternoon of April 5. For the previous two days, officials from many countries had been going to Libya, by land still, for this occasion. Bandar was there. Corell was there. The two suspects were there. All met in the lounge of the long-deserted Tripoli airport. They finally boarded the Italian plane provided by the UN. Hans Corell, representing the UN Secretary General, officially declared he had the accused in his custody. Four hours later, all walked down from the plane in the Netherlands. The accused walked toward a few Dutch policemen. They got into police cars and were transferred to the site of their imprisonment at Camp van Zeist. They were handed over to the Scottish police and read their rights. All was reported to all concerned: Tripoli, Washington, London and, most important, the UN.

Sanctions Suspended, But Not Lifted

In midmorning, New York time, Kofi Annan walked into the briefing room at the UN headquarters and officially announced that all had gone according to schedule. He declared it was automatic now that sanctions would be suspended; there was no need for any action by the UN Security Council. He would later send a letter to the president of the council in which he informed him that "all the necessary assistance has been provided to the Libyan Government and that today, 5 April 1999, the two accused have safely arrived in the Netherlands on board a United Nations aircraft. During the flight, the two accused were accompanied by my representative, Mr. Hans Corell, the Legal Counsel, who has been in charge of the operation. After the aircraft landed at 9:45 a.m., New York time, at Valkenburg airport in the Netherlands, the two accused were detained by the Dutch authorities ... pending their transfer for the purpose of trial before the Scottish court sitting in the Netherlands."[2]

In the same letter, Annan refers once again to the French confirmation of Libya's cooperation with the UTA investigation. Annan concluded that Libya had fully implemented the demands of the council in return for which sanctions would have to be suspended. Minutes later, the president of the council made a statement to the press expressing the fact that sanctions had been officially suspended immediately after the council received the report. Nine months of diplomatic negotiations and seven years of diplomatic battle proved fruitful for Libya.

Libya insisted, however, that a resolution be adopted. The council members did not agree since such a resolution was practically adopted in 1192. All that was needed was the report of the Secretary General on the actual hand over.

Despite all the verbal statements and assurances Libya received regarding the suspension of sanctions, it needed an official document confirming that fact. This insistence was expressive of another conflict of perceptions between the West, where complicated readings and interpretations could be sufficient confirmation, and the third world, where only documented papers are considered official. Three days later, the Security Council obliged the Libyans and issued a presidential statement, officially documented, in which it "notes that, with the letter of the Secretary-General of 5 April 1999, the conditions set forth in paragraph 8 of resolution 1192 (1998) for the immediate suspension of the measures set forth in resolutions 748 (1992) and 883 (1993) have been fulfilled. In this regard, the Council recalls that, in accordance with resolution 1192 (1998), the measures set forth in resolutions 748 (1992) and 883 (1993) were immediately suspended upon receipt of the letter of the Secretary-General on 5 April 1999 at 1400 Eastern Standard Time. This development was immediately acknowledged through a statement of the President of the Security Council to the press on 5 April 1999 following consultations of the whole (Press Release SC/6662)."[3]

Although this statement would close one chapter of Libya's demands, another battle was still at hand: the promise to officially lift sanctions within three months. But the Libyans would get a different lift, further isolating the U.S. opposition to the formal UN Security Council lifting of sanctions. On April 5, the presidency of the European Union remarked that the handover of the two Libyans brought about the "suspension of the US and European Union Lockerbie related sanctions against the Libyan Arab Jamahiriya. The European Union expressed its conviction that the arrangements made for the Scottish court sitting in the Netherlands would guarantee a fair trial for the accused. It stressed that full compliance with the stipulations of all relevant Security Council resolutions would enable the Libyan Arab Jamahiriya to regain its position as a full member of the international community in the near future. The European Union felt that the suspension and, in due course, the lifting of the sanctions against the Libyan Arab Jamahiriya would open up new perspectives for the social and economic development of the country."[4] The Europeans officially lifted their sanctions within weeks.

During the three long months until the council's action was supposed to take place, another major development had to take place: the meeting of the American and Libyan officials at the UN. Annan had many scheduled trips and the parties were busy tackling another issue: Kosovo.

While the lifting of the sanctions was still facing the threat of a U.S. veto, the long-awaited first meeting between the American and Libyan officials took place on June 11. Annan, Greenstock, Burleigh and Dorda were present, along with some of their aides. It was held in a meeting room adjacent to the Secretary General's office. The official pretext was to discuss the remaining demands of the council for the lifting of the sanctions.

In reality, the meeting was supposed to serve one purpose: to break the ice between the parties. The atmosphere was extremely formal. Any further action was to be taken privately, if at all. All present repeated their positions formally. No outcome was reached.

As for the official lifting of the sanctions, the United States kept refusing any such action, repeating the official demands: End and renounce support for terrorism; pay appropriate compensation; cooperate with the investigation and the trial and acknowledge responsibility for the actions of the Libyan officials. These demands again seemed political. Many of them were already included in the letter of March 19. Libya was once again asked to accept responsibility prior to the trial. It was asked to pay compensation before the two Libyans were convicted.

The American demands were explained in details in a paper handed to the Libyans. It detailed the demands as follows:

(I.a.) *Terrorism*

Requirement: "Libya (must) commit itself concretely and definitively to cease all forms of terrorist action and all assistance to terrorist groups. Libya must promptly, by concrete actions, prove its renunciation of terrorism." This requirement is contained in the joint US/UK/French demand and was incorporated directly into UNSCR 748 as a demand of the Council.

Meeting the Requirement: Libya should:

> (a) Commit definitively to cease all forms of terrorist action and terminate all assistance to terrorist groups. This commitment should be made directly by Col. Qadhafi;
>
> (b) End all support for the Abu Nidal Organization, Fatah-The Intifada, the PFLP-GC, the Abu Sayyaf Group and the Kurdistan Workers' Party (PKK);
>
> (c) Provide counter-terrorism information of interest to the US, such as information of Egyptian and Algerian Extremist Groups, Lebanese and Gulf Hezbollah Groups, Iran and Sudan; and
>
> (d) Take clear steps to become party to the International Counter-Terrorism Conventions.

(I.b.) *Accept Responsibility*

Requirement: "Accept responsibility for the actions of Libyan officials." This is contained in the US/UK demand.

Meeting the Requirement: Libya should provide, in writing, a clear statement that Libya accepts responsibility for the actions of its officials.

(I.c.) *Cooperate with the Investigation*

Requirement: "Disclose all it knows of this crime, including the names of all those responsible, and allow full access to all witnesses, documents and other material evidence, including all the remaining timers." This is part of the joint US/UK demand. In addition, UNSCR 1192 provides that "The Libyan Government shall ensure that any evidence of witnesses in Libya are, upon the request of the court, promptly made available at the court in the Netherlands for the purposes of the trial."

Meeting the Requirement: It is exceedingly unlikely that this requirement can be satisfied in advance of the trial, because it contemplates Libyan cooperation with requests made by the Scottish court—requests which will likely occur during the trial and, necessarily, long after the S-G issues his 90-day report. It may be possible to make a determination on this issue prior to conclusion of the trial, depending on Libya's response to requests made through the court by the Scottish prosecutors, and on the pace and course of the trial itself. Recalling Libya's failure to cooperate with investigations in the past—as noted in UNSCR 731, OP2—the US expects Libya to meet a high standard in this regard and reserves the right to make its own assessment in this matter.

(I.d) *Compensation*

Requirement: "Pay appropriate compensation." This is a joint US/UK demand set forth in S/23308.

Meeting the Requirement: Libya should pay appropriate compensation. The US encourages Libya to meet with legal counsel for the Pan Am 103 families to discuss settlement.

The British ambassador presented similar demands with regard to cooperation with the trial but did not discuss the ninety-day issue in the conditional/impossible-to-implement presentation of the Americans. Britain had been pressing Washington to close that file, as it did. The Americans could not accept any further losses; they had to stick to unrealistic demands. The Security Council resolutions had called for the ninety-day period to implement those demands in order for sanctions to be lifted. The United States was well aware, as presented in its document, that no one could prove cooperation with a trial within three months when the trial would not even begin for seven months. Annan himself asked Peter Burleigh just who had proposed the three-month period, and why. The U.S. representative had no answer. He could not say his current boss, Pickering, while ambassador in New York, had written the draft resolution at a time when no one could question the Americans, not even the Americans themselves. This was one piece of mischief all had to live with.

The British demands were presented in a paper prepared by the Crown Office in Edinburgh as early as May 6, 1999, and titled "Libyan Co-Operation with the Scottish Judicial Authorities." After a recap of previous resolutions and events, the paper says:

> 7. Libya thus requires to co-operate with the Scottish judicial authorities in the following ways:

On receipt of a Letter of Request issued by the competent prosecuting authority in Scotland, i.e., the Lord Advocate or by the competent judicial authority, i.e., the High Court of Justiciary, the Libyan Government will ensure promptly and in accordance with the time-scale described in the Letter of Request, or, in the case of any request where there is no indication of a specific time-scale, within fourteen days of receipt of the Letter of Request, that

(a) any documentary or real evidence requested is made available to the relevant Scottish authorities, whether in Scotland, the Netherlands or Libya, as described in the Letter of request;

(b) arrangements are made for any interviews which may be requested with individuals and that such arrangements are communicated to the relevant Scottish authorities;

(c) any enquiries which the Libyan authorities may be required to carry out, are carried out and the results communicated to the relevant Scottish authorities;

(d) any witness whose attendance may be required at the court in the Netherlands for the purpose of the trial is duly cited and appropriate arrangements are made for their attendance at the premises of the Scottish Court in the Netherlands, subject to payment or reimbursement of traveling and subsistence expenses of the witness by the party to the proceedings who has requested the attendance of the witness.

8. Any evidence provided in response to a letter of Request will not, without the consent of the appropriate authority in Libya, be used for any purpose other than the Lockerbie criminal investigation and criminal proceedings arising out of it.

9. Any witness entering the Netherlands and attending at the premises of the Scottish Court in the Netherlands for the purpose of the trial shall not be prosecuted, detained or subjected to any other restriction of his or personal liberty, by the authorities of the Netherlands or the Scottish authorities in respect of acts or convictions prior to his or her entry into the territory of the Netherlands, but that immunity shall cease on the departure of the witness from the territory of the Netherlands, or following the elapse of 15 days from the date when his or her presence at the trial is no longer required and during which he or she has had the opportunity to leave the Netherlands and has not done so or, having left it, has returned, unless such return is for the purposes of the trial. Furthermore, such a witness shall not be subjected by the authorities of the Netherlands to any measure which may affect the free and independent exercise of his or her functions.[5]

In other words, the British demands were sidestepping the politicalization of the process from then on. It had become a legal process and all demands were related to that process only. What the Americans kept referring to as "US/UK demands" were more American demands from that point on.

When the time came for a Security Council resolution to formally lift the sanctions, the United States repeated its demands in public, while claiming in private: Do not put us in an awkward situation. Sanctions are practically lifted. Realistically, no one can reimpose them. We are having a hard enough time with our internal situation; do not make the United States veto a resolution to that effect.

The Secretary General was considerate enough. On June 30, he presented the report requested by the Security Council regarding Libya's implementation short of confirming full compliance by Libya of all demands despite his presentation of that full implementation of the demands, considering, indirectly, the remaining elements were impossible to implement prior to the conclusion of the trial.[6]

The first point of that report concerned French demands. Annan refers to "a 12 April 1999 statement by Libyan Prime Minister Mohammed Al-Mangush in which he confirmed that his country would respect its commitment to France." Furthermore, Annan refers to "the legal discussions held in October and November 1998 in which legal issues related to the implementation of Security Council resolution 1192 were resolved to the satisfaction of all those concerned, with the assistance, inter alia, of the Government of France." He further notes that he had "subsequently been informed by the French authorities that the requests they had made, on the whole, have been satisfied."

As for the demands on Libya's cooperation with the trial and payment of compensation, Annan considered that they

> could only be undertaken by the Libyan Arab Jamahiriya during and following the conclusion of the trial of the two persons charged with the bombing of Pan Am Flight 103 by the Scottish court sitting in the Netherlands, and the trial has been postponed. It appears that, under the circumstances, Libyan Arab Jamahiriya may only be expected to provide assurances of its commitment to comply with those requirements, particularly as it regards access to witnesses, relevant documents and other material evidence. It is worth noting, in this regard, that paragraph 2 of resolution 1192 provides that all States shall cooperate to that end and that, in particular, the Libyan Government shall ensure that any evidence or witness in the Libyan Arab Jamahiriya are, upon the request of the court promptly made available at the court sitting in the Netherlands for the purpose of the trial. For that reason. I am not in a position to provide any factual information on that country's compliance with the relevant requirements. However, I would like to point out that the Libyan authorities have, indeed, provided assurances that they will cooperate with the Scottish court. Such assurances, on behalf of the Libyan authorities, were given to the United Nations Legal Counsel, Mr. Hans Corell, by Mr. Kamel Hassan Maghour, the head of the Libyan legal team, during their discussions in October and November 1998. The Libyan Arab Jamahiriya reconfirmed these assurances in a

letter addressed to me by Mr. Omar Mustafa Muntasser, the Secretary of the General People's Committee for Foreign Liaison and International Cooperation of the Libyan Arab Jamahiriya, dated 19 March 1999 (S/1999/311). According to that letter, the Libyan Arab Jamahiriya "undertakes to cooperate with the investigation and the proceedings within the limits permitted by the law and the legislation in force in the Great Socialist People's Libyan Arab Jamahiriya."

Annan made sure he referred to many previous Libyan statements confirming readiness to pay compensation if the accused were proven guilty, although he considered any discussion of that aspect "premature."

Clearly, Annan was under tremendous pressure from the United States not to consider Libya in full compliance. He could not find any better language to consider the American demands as political obstacles to full normalization of the international community's relations with Libya. He hoped that further meetings, similar to those held in June or directly between the two countries, would create better understanding, leading to better relations between America and Libya. Little did he know that he would be left out of further deliberation.

PART VI

The Scottish Court in the Netherlands

18

The Lockerbie Trial and Appeal

The United Kingdom and the
Kingdom of the Netherlands Treaty

It is most unusual for a trial using Scottish Laws, precedents and practice to be held outside of Scotland (i.e., a criminal trial held in a third country). The Hague in the Netherlands is the seat of the International Court of Justice and was suggested on previous occasions as a venue for such a trial. The Netherlands venue has a long history in international law, and the peace and tranquility provided there ensure due deliberation and justice. Therefore, international criminal law can only grow with the Lockerbie trial experience. First, as a result of the changed political circumstances, a treaty was negotiated and executed on September 18, 1998, between the United Kingdom and the Kingdom of the Netherlands, which provided, inter alia, the following:

The Netherlands, as the host country, was to "make available adequate premises for the trial" and "detention of the accused for the purposes of the trial, and, in the event of their conviction pending their transfer to the UK," all "in accordance with Scots law and practice" (Article 3).

"The premises of the Scottish Court shall be inviolable," Article 5, and "the competent authorities of The Netherlands shall have full responsibility for the external security of the Scottish Court ... to ensure that the tranquility of the Scottish Court is not disturbed" (Article 7).

"The Scottish Court shall be entitled to display its emblem and workings, as well as the appropriate flag, on its premises" (Article 13).

"The judges and officials of the Scottish Court, the Registrar, the Lord Advocate and the Procurator Fiscal, shall enjoy the privileges, immunities and facilities accorded to diplomatic agents in accordance with the Vienna Convention" (Article 14).

"The solicitors and advocates of the accused shall not be subjected by the host country to any measure which may affect the free and independent exercise of their functions under Scots law ... in particular ... inviolability in respect of all documents relating to the exercise of their functions as solicitors or advocate of the accused" (Article 15).

"After the accused are transferred to the Scottish Court, they may only be transferred to the UK for a 'trial by a jury in Scotland' with their written agreement confirmed in person to the High Court of the Justiciary in the presence of any counsel instructed by them" or "for the purpose of serving a custodial sentence imposed by a Scottish Court following the conviction of the accused" (Article 16).

"The Treaty provides for International Observers, permitting their "entry into the territory of The Netherlands for the sole purpose of attending the trial" and "they shall not be subject by the Host Country to any measure which may affect the free and independent exercise of their functions" (Article 18).

"All costs and expenses relating to the establishment and sitting of the Scottish Court and incurred by the Host Country "shall be borne by the Government of the UK" (Article 24).

The UN Appointment of International Observers

UN Secretary General Kofi A. Annan advised the Security Council by letter that he had appointed five international observers to attend the trial in Camp van Zeist. They were Mrs. Hired Ade-Balogun, representing the Organization of African Unity and the Non-Aligned Movement; Mr. M. H. Boerenboom, representing the European Commission; Dr. Nabil Elaraby, representing the League of Arab States (later elected as a judge in the International Court of Justice, starting in 2001); and Dr. Hans Koechler, president, and Robert W. Thabit, permanent representative of the International Progress Organization (IPO) to the UN.

The IPO is a nongovernmental organization founded in 1972, based in Vienna, and enjoys consultative status with ECOSOC of the UN. IPO is interested and active in resolving international disputes affecting human rights internationally and establishing a new and just international economic order.

The Scottish Court Facilities and Administration at Camp Van Zeist

The site selected for the Scottish Court was an old American-Dutch air force base at Camp van Zeist in the province of Utrecht, the Netherlands.

Zeist is a small village, a sprawling suburb of private middle-class homes set in a largely wooded area. While it is accessible to main highways passing through Utrecht, it has a certain bucolic air filled with peace and tranquility. It was a setting conducive to clear thinking for the prosecutors, defense counsel and the judges, who, ultimately, had the weighty task of deciding all the legal issues as well as determining whether the crown had met the burden of proof beyond a reasonable doubt, required for a conviction or, if insufficient, the acquittal of each of the accused.

The site includes the courthouse, prison, media center, restaurant facilities and parking lots, as well as accommodations for police and prison officers. The courthouse has ancillary offices and rooms for judges, prosecution and defense lawyers, witnesses, the police, administrative staff and the international observers. There are special lounge facilities, in this case, for the families of the victims and the accused. The entrance has extensive individual search facilities and security. The site was patrolled by Scottish policemen wearing bulletproof vests, armed with automatic weapons and side arms, around the clock. The exterior of Camp van Zeist is under the protection of the Netherlands police force, although their presence was not noticeable.

The prison is in a former medical facility, initially constructed as a nuclear, biological and chemical shelter, recently converted to a modern prison facility.

The costs of construction were about 12 million English pounds. The operating costs through the trial were estimated at 50 million English pounds. The average monthly running costs of Camp van Zeist are between 2 and 3 million English pounds. The United States had contributed 4.77 million English pounds and incurred other expenses in connection with its Office for Victims of Crime (OVC) program.

The court facilities are high tech in all respects. The court has a highly sophisticated visual control center that is better than the facilities developed for the International Criminal Tribunal for the former Yugoslavia (ICTY) in the Hague. There are six cameras running at all times and an audio visual director. The director rarely shows defendants except as may be necessary (i.e., if a witness is asked to identify a defendant).

There were more than eighteen hundred exhibits and twenty-seven thousand pages of documentation stored on video discs. This video display system has saved innumerable days in court for all concerned.

If a witness is in a witness protection program, a metal screen can be rolled up to block the public's view of the witness. The video picture as well as the voice of the witness is distorted. However, the judges, lawyers, defendants and the UN-nominated international observers on the other side of the screen however can see and hear the witness testify.

Despite all of the technological advances implemented, the official record of the proceedings are the written transcripts. There was to be no retained record of a video tape of the Lockerbie trial. And since the transcripts of the trial were about ten thousand pages by the end of the trial, that would be ample proof that the old systems are still viable.

The courtroom has video monitors for each judge, each lawyer, the defendants, the witnesses and the international observers, as well as six large monitors in the public gallery that display the exhibits or the person who is addressing the court.

In order to keep pace with the demands of the victims' families who couldn't spend time in the Netherlands, the proceedings were sent by delayed encrypted transmission to two sites in the United States—New York and Washington, D.C.—where families of victims could follow the proceedings live, as well as to Dumfries and London for British family members.

On most days of the trial that international observers attended court, there were fifteen to twenty people sitting in the main gallery, most of whom were family members of the victims. Also in attendance were the family members of the accused, sitting on the left side of the gallery, the side where the accused sit in the dock. In addition to the gallery, which could seat two hundred, there was an overflow auditorium for members of the public and a separate media center for the press, which covered the trial extensively.

Although it is a three-bench court, there were four senior judges sitting. The fourth judge had been sitting with the other judges for the purpose of discussion but was not to vote unless one of the other judges was unable to act because of illness or disability.

The court could make one of three possible findings:

guilty
not guilty
not proven

Both not guilty and not proven have the same result; the accused would be free to leave the court and the Netherlands. The verdict would be announced in court, and a written judgment setting out the reasons would be issued. If found guilty, the accused would serve any custodial sentence in Scotland and could not be extradited to the United States or any other country to face other Lockerbie-related charges in accordance with the treaty. The burden of proof would be on the prosecution, and they must prove the case beyond a reasonable doubt with corroborated evidence on all essential elements of the crime.

The Judges and the Attorneys for the Prosecution and the Accused

The four judges were Lord Sutherland (Presiding Judge) Ranald Iain Sutherland; Lord Coulsfield John Taylor Cameron; Lord Maclean Ranald Norman Munro Maclean; Lord John Alastair Cameron Abernethy.

The attorneys for the Crown (prosecution) were Lord Advocate, Colin Boyd, QC; Advocate Depute, Alastair Campbell, QC; Advocate Depute, Alan D. Turnbull, QC; John A. Dunn, Principal Depute.

Solicitors: Jonathan Lake; Morag Armstrong; Brian Murtagh, US Department of Justice; Dana Biehl, US Department of Justice.

The attachment of two attorneys from the U.S. Department of Justice was a most unusual arrangement. Although they did not speak in court, they were active making and passing notes to the crown counsel, and probably even more active behind the scenes. There is no doubt that the high loss of American lives in the Pan Am 103 bombing was reason enough for their inclusion in the prosecution's team, but it was still very unusual in a criminal trial under a foreign legal system.

The first accused was: Abdelbaset Al-Megrahi.

The attorneys for the First Accused were: Counsel: William Taylor, QC; David Burns, QC; John Beckett. Solicitors: Alistair Duff; Alex Prentice.

The second accused was: Al Amin Khalifa Fhimah.

The attorneys for the Second Accused were: Counsel: Richard Keen, QC; Jack Davidson, QC; Murdo McLeod. Solicitors: McGrigor Donald; Eddie Mackechnie; Gavin Walker; Andrea Summers and the combined team for both accused: Libyan Legal Consortium: Kamel Maghur; Mohammed Crewi; Bassim Tulti, translator; Alan Jenkins.

A queen's counsel was the mark of an advocate's seniority after about thirteen years of service; advocates are recommended for approval by the senior judge and appointed by the queen or monarch. They are also practitioners and appointed by the crown for a particular case or a particular term. Campbell confirmed that the crown advocates are bound by Scots law, cases and practice to ensure a fair trial, and they were ever mindful that this case was important and would be reviewed for some time to come. It is worth noting that the advocates were the ones who appeared and spoke in courts, while the solicitors did everything else (including research for the advocates) except speak in court. While both Richard Keen and William Taylor were very thorough in stating their opinions and motions or "submissions" to the court, they were always polite and referred to the prosecution as "my learned friend." The crown was equally polite. Both the crown and the defense always showed a great deal of respect to the court and demurred to the court's decisions.

A Meeting with the Defendants and Counsel

The governor of HM Prison Zeist, Ian Bannatyne, has been involved with prisons in Scotland since 1974.

This experience was unique for Bannatyne. Not only did he have to operate outside his own country, but he also had to provide superior prison quarters in this instance. This prison had to be unlike any previous one. It had to hold two prisoners and treat them according to a treaty between two countries. Thus, a nurse was on duty for medical care, the food supply included "halal" meat (required for Muslims) "that was safe and secure," the prisoners had an exercise yard that had light and air and was a good size, and the prisoners had a changing room where they put on their national clothing before going to court. They were locked in when the guards were eating and at night, moved from the prison to the courthouse under guard and in an armored car, and, while in the courthouse, there was a guard for each defendant. The governor described the prisoners as very cooperative.

The prisoners were also able to have visits from family members and met regularly with their attorneys, without much constraint.

When the international observers met with the prisoners in October 2000 for over an hour in an open area adjacent to their cells, they were warm and friendly and acted as if they were in their own home. They offered fruit drinks and Turkish coffee.

Megrahi spoke more of the political and diplomatic atmosphere surrounding the whole Lockerbie issue. He explained that he understood that the sanctions would be lifted against Libya within ninety days if they surrendered. The sanctions were only suspended, which was a great disappointment. The United States, however, did not suspend its unilateral sanctions imposed on Libya, claiming that Libya had not complied with every element of the UN resolutions. UN sanctions were not expected to be lifted until at least the end of the trial, the appeal and apparently not before compensation was paid to the victims' families.

In connection with the actual indictment, the two defendants, in a private meeting with all of the international observers, proclaimed their innocence, and both said all they wanted was a fair trial. They said they had both studied in the United States and had nothing against America or Americans. They said the differences between the United States and Libya and the misunderstandings that result from differences in Western and Middle Eastern cultures, societies and religions should not affect their right to a fair trial.

They complained about the translations from English to Arabic, specifying one translation in June, two in August and one each in September and October. Thabit noticed firsthand, on October 10, 2000 that, while the questions to a witness were translated, the answers weren't. He brought this to the attention of an assistant to the registrar and it was immediately corrected.

These complaints were later discussed with Gordon Beaton, the court registrar, who acknowledged that in the first several weeks of the trial there had been a considerable problem with translations, but it had improved greatly. They appointed a committee of three academics, who reviewed a sample of the tapes of the trial. If the translation was inadequate, they ordered a written translation of the entire session. They reviewed the translations in August and reviewed the intervening sessions again in late October 2000.

The two defendants also expressed concern that their case was receiving special treatment, and they felt the Scottish law and rules should be applied in this case as well. They pointed to the decision of the judges to have Fhimah's diary, which had been taken from his office desk drawer without his permission, "to be admissible" nonetheless because "the public interest in the prosecution of crime has to be given due weight" and that "what occurred can properly be regarded as excusable."

They also complained of the deficiencies in the labels on some exhibits, which their attorneys fully and quickly pointed out during their cross-examination of the crown's witnesses, although the court did not prevent the admissibility of the exhibits.

Highlights from the Trial

The crown examined 270 witnesses and submitted over 280 exhibits of the more than 1,800 available. While the defense had listed about 30 and 70 witnesses, for Megrahi and Fhimah respectively, the defense called only one or two witnesses after the crown had rested the prosecution's case.

Under Scots law and practice, the crown has the public interest for justice and the duty to provide the defense with anything that raises doubts of the prosecution's case and anything that can benefit the defense must be disclosed to the defense.

The crown and the defense agreed on two memos of "uncontroversial evidence" covering various types of radar and recordings concerning the Pan Am 103 flight on December 21, 1988, the list of those killed as a result of the bombing, and the passports of the two accused, provided by them. In addition, there were many joint minutes covering a variety of items of evidence that were accepted by the defense and did not need to be proven in court. These agreements were said to have shortened the court proceedings considerably.

Several written opinions were issued during the proceedings and reflect the thoroughness with which the crown and the defense approached every issue in the trial. The points were argued at length, with appropriate citations after a great deal of research from both sides. The judges were also involved, asking questions of counsel and generally asking both sides whether they had anything more to add, in order to give each side every opportunity to make its point before ruling. A ruling came after the judges conferred in an off-the-record discussion with the chief judge.

There were several crucial witnesses for the prosecution of this case which merit close review.

The first is Abdul Majid Giaka, a Libyan who visited the American Embassy in Malta on August 11, 1988 and agreed to be a double agent. Giaka was an employee of Libyan Arab Airlines (LAA) in Malta and knew Fhimah, who was for some time the station manager for Libyan Arab Airlines in Malta until he resigned in September 1988. Giaka was considered the crown's star witness.

Giaka met American agents ten times including December 20, 1988, before the Lockerbie bombing. The United States paid Giaka $13,000 in 1989; $20,000 in 1990; $26,000 in 1991; and $26,000 in 1992. Giaka received a total of $324,000 by October 1994. In 1991, Giaka was placed in the witness protection program after being interviewed by the FBI aboard the USNS Butte, which was twenty-seven miles off Malta's coast.

Cross-examination of Giaka was withering on a number of issues in an effort to destroy Giaka's credibility. Giaka's finances were inquired into at length, demonstrating his intention to improve himself financially at the expense of the U.S. government as a paid informer and his probable status as a small-time smuggler increasing his income. On a salary of $1,200 per month, Giaka had accumulated $30,000 and asked his U.S. contact person to help arrange another $30,000 loan from the United States to help him set up a business in Malta.

He was being threatened by his U.S. contacts to come up with something or he would be dumped. After that threat, Giaka reported to his contacts that a brown Samsonite suitcase had been brought into Luqa International Airport in Malta by Megrahi with Fhimah. He said they left the airport with the bag without going through customs. There was never any mention of a brown suitcase, Samsonite or otherwise, in the CIA cables. Giaka also induced his contact person to pay for two surgical procedures to his arm, costing about $10,000, which prevented him from serving in Libya's army.

Another point made by William Taylor, Megrahi's counsel, was that, when pressed for some useful information Giaka told his contact person of seeing a cache of eight kilos of orange-colored explosives (TNT) in LAA's office, under Fhimah's control. Taylor and Richard Keen continuously called Giaka a liar. When pressed, Giaka often reverted to the time-worn excuse "I can't remember" because of the long passage of time.

The crown said that some twenty-five CIA cables were all the cables they had regarding Mr. Giaka. The cables were presented to the defense, broadly edited. On being pressed by the defense, with support from the judges, portions of the redactions, which were claimed to be based on U.S. National Security or protection of sources and intelligence-gathering techniques, were removed and revealed no sensitive material or much that was really relevant to the defense's case. Subsequently, some thirty-five additional CIA cables were presented. The additional cables were definitely relevant to the defense's case and made available to the defense. The defense's cross-examination of Giaka was withering, but he remained defiant and confirmed what he had testified to earlier.

One of the CIA cables reported: "If Giaka is not able to demonstrate sustained and defined access to information of intelligence value by January of 1990, the CIA will cease all salary and financial support until such access can be proven again. ...The CIA officer will therefore advise Giaka at the 4th of September meeting that he is on trial status until the 1st of January 1990."

While the court pressed the crown regarding the CIA cables and some other issues, they were passive regarding other issues, such as a statement made by Giaka claiming that Colonel Qadhafi was a Mason. When the defense requested proof of that claim, Giaka confirmed that he had made the statement but refused to disclose the name of the Libyan who had told him that, in order to protect him. The court agreed that he need not divulge the name of the individual, leading to many questions regarding the even-handedness.

The cross-examinations by Taylor and Keen continued for the better part of three days, challenging the witness's credibility—the principal aim of defense counsel—as they covered his activities from high school through his being taken to the United States by a Department of Justice representative. The discrepancy between the material in the CIA cables and Giaka's testimony in the Scottish court was attributed either to the interpreter or Giaka's loss of memory of events ten or more years prior. After many discrepancies were disclosed by Taylor and Keen, Giaka insisted that he "had always told the truth."

Another significant witness for the crown was Edwin Bollier. Bollier is the "BO" of MEBO AG, the Swiss manufacturer of the MST-13 timer used to detonate the bomb on Pan Am 103 contained in a Toshiba RT SF 16 cassette recorder. MEBO had supplied such timers to the Libyan army and the STASI (Staatssicherheit) of East Germany. Megrahi, the first accused, was known to Bollier as he was involved in buying electronic equipment for Libya from MEBO. Allen Feraday, former head of the Defense Evaluation Research Agency (DERA), confirmed that "there can be no doubt that the fragment of circuit board originated from a circuit board with a MEBO brand MST-13 timer." Erwin Meister (the "ME" in MEBO), a partner in the firm, also testified that he recognized Megrahi, with whom he had had business dealings in Zurich and Libya before the Lockerbie bombing.

After studying the fragment with a magnifying glass, Bollier testified: "They have been modified. I swear they have been modified." But he did acknowledge that they came from an MST-13 circuit board. He admitted that circuit boards could have come from timers sold by MEBO to either Libya or East Germany or even that "it could be counterfeit."

The defense pressed Bollier and Meister as to the possibility that MST-13s sold to the STASI might have gotten into the hands of Palestinian terrorists, including the PFLP-GC, with whom the STASI had contacts. They also raised doubt about Bollier's credibility.

Fhimah was station manager for Libyan Arab Airlines in Malta until September 1988, when he left LAA. After he left, he formed Med Tours Services, Ltd., with Vincent Vassallo, a Maltese citizen, and opened an office in Mosta, Malta. Megrahi was Fhimah's superior in charge of security for Libyan Arab Airlines. He was a member of the Libyan intelligence service, the JSO, and also traveled with Libyan passports under the names of Ahmed Khalifa Abdusamad and Nasser Ahmed Salam. Vincent Vasallo was another important witness. It was Vasallo who, without Fhimah's consent, had turned over Fhimah's diary to Scottish and U.S. Department of Justice investigators. The diary contained a reminder to pick up "LAA Tags."

The clothing determined to be in the suitcase that contained the bomb was allegedly bought at Mary's House, a clothes shop in Sliema, Malta. Anthony Gauci is one of the owners of Mary's House. Gauci testified that the purchaser "resembled Qadhafi, 6-foot tall, Arab-looking, about 50 years of age and heavy body." Megrahi was less than six feet tall and, while Arab-looking, was about 34 and slim at the time.

The prosecution claimed the clothing was bought on December 7, 1988. The defense's position was that the clothing was bought on the November 23, 1988, by a Palestinian. That Palestinian was believed by the defense to be Abu Talb, an active member of the Palestine Peoples Struggle Front (PPSF) (an Egyptian organization) who was convicted of terrorist attacks in Denmark and is now serving a life sentence in Sweden. Abu Talb had connections with the PFLP-GC, a Palestinian organization originally suspected in the Lockerbie bombing, and had been in Malta in October and November 1988.

In previous interviews, Gauci was shown photos of possible suspects on many occasions, including Megrahi's photo. He said that he was "not exactly the man I saw in the shop." When he was shown Abu Talb's photo he said, "Yes, he resembles him a lot." Abu Talb, brought in as a witness, denied any connection with the Pan Am 103 bombing.

There is also the additional factor of the umbrella found with the clothes in the suitcase containing the bomb. On December 7, 1988, when the crown claims Megrahi purchased the clothing, it was not raining, according to a Maltese weatherman called by the defense. However, on November 23, 1988, when the defense claims the clothing was purchased, it was raining.

D. C. McInnes, a police officer involved in the identification of debris from Pan Am 103, acknowledged on cross-examination that the sheer volume of wreckage, plus erratic labeling, resulted in expert guesswork to locate evidence and date its discovery retroactively. For weeks following the disaster, trucks filled with wreckage arrived at a warehouse, where an initial reconstruction of the plane was made. Not every individual piece was labeled by the police, who had conducted "fingertip line searches" over vast stretches of open farm and countryside, and some paper labels were rained on and destroyed. The detective agreed that it was now "utterly impossible" to reconstruct where, when and by whom individual pieces of evidence had been found. The defense naturally raised serious questions regarding the labeling and the chain of custody of the evidence gathered and the difficulty in securing the crime scene.

The crown and the defense went into detail on the "Autumn Leaves" investigation that took place in Germany in an effort to determine whether any Palestinian elements in East Germany might have been involved. However, there was nothing of significance that the lengthy investigations revealed.

An Arab-American of Lebanese origin, Khaled Jaafar, was also a possible suspect as the carrier of the bomb. Jaafar was one of the victims of the bombing. However, in the course of reviewing all the available evidence, it was clear that his suitcase did not contain the bomb.

After the conclusion of the crown's case, the counsel for the second accused, Fhimah, made a submission or motion that the crown had made a "no case" to answer. At that stage of the proceeding, the court considered whether there was a sufficient quantity of evidence to sustain a guilty verdict. (The quality of the evidence is not considered at this stage.) The court rejected the submission but made comments and raised questions on the crown's case. The judges could take into consideration the inferences which had to be drawn from the evidence as most probable, not simply those which favored the prosecution.

On January 15, 2001, the crown formally withdrew charges 1 and 3 and amended charge 2 of the indictment and removed the charges of conspiracy against Fhimah, accusing both defendants of the murder of the 270 people in the Lockerbie bombing.

After the prosecution rested, the defense was hoping to receive the Goben document from the government of Syria, which purportedly showed that the Palestinian Front for the Liberation of Palestine, General Command (PFLP-GC), may have been responsible for the Pan Am 103 Lockerbie bombing. Unfortunately for the defense, Syria rejected the request, and no documents were ever delivered to the defense or to the court.

When both sides rested after final arguments were presented and the case finally went to the court for its consideration and decision, the burden of proof which had to be met by the prosecution was proof of guilt "beyond reasonable doubt."

Burden of Proof and the Verdict

The Scottish court deliberated a very substantial crime: the premeditated murder of all the passengers and crew on Pan Am 103 and eleven civilians on the ground who were killed in Lockerbie, Scotland. A total of 270 lives were taken in a horrible tragedy, and only two individuals (Libyans) were charged. Someone had to pay for this crime, regardless of whether the proof presented met the legal requirement of proof beyond reasonable doubt. The families of the victims needed closure, and the confrontation between the United States and the United Kingdom and Libya also required closure. A conviction of even one of the two charged would be sufficient to bring an end to the Pan Am 103 Lockerbie bombing.

It is significant too that the Libyans required that the case be tried as a nonjury case, believing that they could not get a fair hearing if the jury were made up of fifteen Scots men and women who had suffered eleven deaths in Scotland, just as they believed a jury trial in the United States or the United Kingdom would be equally impossible to be fair. While a jury is inherently more emotional than judges, a trial before judges also has its handicaps. Judges are more experienced in assessing the credibility of witnesses and in weighing all the evidence to determine whether there is reasonable doubt about the guilt of the accused.

The prosecution's case was founded on purely circumstantial evidence, albeit an extensive record of more than 270 witnesses and over 280 exhibits. The witness Giaka, a Libyan-turned-U.S. informer, whose principal motivation was financial gain and U.S. residency, was found by the judges to lack credibility. However, the testimonies of Edwin Bollier, an agent for the timer's manufacturer and Anthony Gauci, the shopkeeper who sold the clothes found in the suitcase which contained the bomb, were sufficient for the judges to find Megrahi guilty and Fhimah not guilty.

The Decision

After twelve days of review by the four judges, the three-bench court appeared in open court on January 31, 2001, at 11:00 A.M. to deliver its verdict. The courtroom was packed. The auditorium was also overflowing. The press had arrived from all over the world with cameras ready, but only a few were allowed in the courtroom on a pool basis. The media center had a live TV monitor, and over one hundred from the media followed the proceeding.

A hush enveloped the courtroom as the four judges entered, and everyone rose out of respect for the court. After the clerk called the case, he asked the judges whether they had reached a verdict. Lord Sutherland said: "We have." The clerk asked for the verdict for the first accused, Abdelbaset Al-Megrahi. Lord Sutherland said: "Guilty." The court made certain deletions to the indictment. The judge was asked whether the verdict was unanimous or by a majority. Lord Sutherland answered: "Unanimous."

The only disturbance in the gallery, which had remained calm, was by an elderly father of one of the victims, Dr. James Swire, who lost consciousness briefly and was carried from the gallery.

The clerk followed the same routine with the second accused, Al

Amin Khalifa Fhimah, who was found not guilty. Again, the verdict was unanimous. Lord Sutherland advised Fhimah, "You are now discharged and are free to go," to be followed by Mr. Keen, his counsel and associates.

Next, Lord Sutherland called on the Lord Advocate, who moved for the sentence of the accused, setting a dramatic stage for the rest of the proceedings. The lord advocate said the defendant was forty-nine, married with children, that he had been delivered to the Netherlands, arrested by the Scottish police and in custody since April 5, 1999. He went on to state that the names of those who died had been read in court, that each had left relatives, wives, husbands, parents and children. More than 400 parents lost a son or daughter, 46 parents lost their only child, 45 women were widowed, and 11 men lost their wives. More than 140 lost a parent, and 7 children lost both parents, and all who lost loved ones "are also victims of the Lockerbie bombing."

William Taylor, counsel for Al-Megrahi, said, "My client maintains his innocence and, therefore, there is nothing by way of mitigation," and, second, that the sentence should run from April 5, 1999.

The court recessed and returned to pronounce sentence at 2:00 P.M. on January 31, 2001.

Lord Sutherland declared: "The mandatory sentence for the crime of murder is imprisonment for life," to be backdated "to the 5th of April 1999." The judges took into consideration that he would be serving "this sentence in what is to you a foreign country. The period that we recommend is substantially less than it would otherwise have been. ... The appropriate recommendation ... is that a period of 20 years should elapse before you are considered for release. You will also be recommended for deportation at the end of the sentence."

Given all the facts and circumstances, that 270 people had lost their lives, the sentence, with a minimum term of twenty years before possible parole and deportation, was moderate in all respects.

The court handed down its written decision in eighty-two pages.

The written decision of the court demonstrates the difficulties the judges had with the evidence, although it did not prevent them from making the decision unanimous. The last paragraph of the written decision attests to the political considerations inherent in judging this case:

> We are aware that in relation to certain aspects of the case there are a number of uncertainties and qualifications. We are also aware that there is a danger that by selecting parts of the evidence which seem to fit together and ignoring parts which might not fit, it is possible to read into a mass of conflicting evidence a pattern or conclusion which is not really justified. However, having considered the whole evidence in the case, including the uncertainties and qualifications, and the submissions

of counsel, we are satisfied that the evidence as to the purchase of cloth-ing in Malta, the presence of that clothing in the primary suitcase, the transmission of an item of baggage from Malta to London, the identification of the first accused (albeit not absolute), his movements under a false name at or around the material time, and the other back-ground circumstances such as his association with Mr. Bollier and with members of the JSO or Libyan military who purchased MST-13 timers, does fit together to form a real and convincing pattern. There is noth-ing in the evidence which leaves us with any reasonable doubt as to the guilt of the first accused, and accordingly we find him guilty of the remaining charge in the Indictment as amended.

The verdicts returned were by a unanimous decision of the three judges of the Court.'

After the decision and a joyous reunion between Fhimah and his family, the defendant was escorted a day after the verdict to a Dutch airbase for a special nonstop UN flight in a Dutch Royal Air Force plane to Libya, where he was given a hero's welcome. Colonel Qadhafi, in wel-coming Fhimah, made a statement that Megrahi was equally innocent.

According to the treaty between the United Kingdom and the Netherlands, Megrahi would serve his sentence in a Scottish prison in Scotland.

The Appeal

The appeal was heard by the lord justice-general (Cullen) and Lords Kirkwood, Osborne, McFadyen and Nimmo Smith. The appellant, Al-Megrahi, was represented by Taylor, QC, and the crown by Lord Advo-cate Boyd, QC, and Advocate Depute Turnbull, QC.

The appeal was heard over a period of fourteen days from January 23 to February 14, 2002, in some 1,845 pages of hearing, before the decision was handed down a month later, on March 14, 2002. In less than one minute in open court, the lord justice proclaimed, "We have reached the conclusion that none of the grounds of appeal is well founded. The appeal will accordingly be refused."

The High Court of the Justiciary gave Counsel for the defendant more than enough time to present its position fully and for the crown to respond. The two-week public hearing took considerably longer than typical in a capital felony case under any legal system.

The appeal, inconceivably, did not include the pro-forma ground of insufficient evidence in law to convict Al-Megrahi. In addition, dur-ing the trial, the defense presented only a few of the 30 witnesses it had given notice it would call, which necessarily left the trial court with mainly the prosecution's case, the testimonies of 270 witnesses and 280 exhibits submitted to the court and an insignificant body of evidence to support a "not proved" decision or to reverse it on appeal.

The appeal presented a variety of issues: The evidence "was not of such character, quality or strength to enable a certain conclusion," "the trial court's treatment of evidence and defense submissions," "misinterpreted evidence," "failed to give adequate reasons," and that the trial court "failed to take proper account of, or have proper regard to, or give proper weight to, or gave insufficient weight to, certain evidence, factors or considerations."

The underlying ground of the appeal was that there had been "a miscarriage of justice," based on the trial court's failure "to give adequate reasons for its conclusions, including reasons of adequate clarity." The appeals court held, "It is our opinion this submission was misconceived. It is plain that reasons do not require to be detailed; that the trial court does not have to review every fact and argument on either side; and that reasons do not require to be given for every stage in the decision-making process."

This Lockerbie appeal will no doubt become a landmark decision on the limits of an appellate court's function:

The court said:

> Once evidence has been accepted by the trial court, it is for that court to determine what inference or inferences should be drawn from that evidence. If evidence is capable of giving rise to two or more possible inferences, it is for the trial court to decide whether an inference should be drawn and, if so, which inference. If, of course, the appeal court were satisfied that a particular inference drawn by the trial court was not a possible inference, in the sense that the drawing of such an inference was not open to the trial court on the evidence, that would be indicative of a misdirection and the appeal court would require to assess whether or not it had been material.

The appeals court then reviewed the trial court's decision (which had been set forth in 90 paragraphs in 82 pages) and the principal aspects of the case, pursuant to the principles of law it had set forth for an appeal, to determine whether to sustain the decision of the trial court. This detailed review required 309 paragraphs (in 164.5 pages of the decision) to bring to a close any doubt that the trial court's decision was defective in any material regard. While the case was decided on "circumstantial evidence," the appeals court found it was well supported by the evidence noted in the trial and appeals court's decisions.

There were no doubt criticisms and allegations that "political considerations" played a role in the appeals court decision. Doubt surrounded the identification of Al-Megrahi as the person who had bought the clothing. There was inconclusive evidence as to how the bag got on Pan Am 103 as unaccompanied baggage from Luqa Airport in Malta, despite evidence presented to the appeals court that security for the luggage had been breached before the luggage was actually loaded on the aircraft. Numerous other matters still raised doubts in the minds of many observers as to whether justice had been done in this matter. All of the international observers met with Al-Megrahi after the court recessed. Al-Megrahi continued to say that he was innocent of the crime for which Libya and its people had been punished by U.S. and U.N. sanctions.

While the UN's sanctions were suspended, U.S. sanctions will probably remain in effect until compensation has been paid.

Al-Megrahi's Postconviction Options

There is one possibility of appeal through the privy council of the United Kingdom, although it has very remote chances of even being available after the appeal court's unanimous decision. Perhaps appeal might be possible if Al-Megrahi threw himself on the mercy of the privy council and agreed to be questioned in depth and to testify under oath in support of his position that it was not he who purchased the clothing from Gauci's shop in Sliema, Malta. However, it is doubtful that his Libyan lawyers would agree to such a procedure, as it might be considered a threat to Libyan national security.

Another possibility is an appeal to the European Union's Human Rights Court in Strasbourg (i.e., that Al-Megrahi was deprived of his human rights to adequate defense counsel in the Lockerbie trial). Certainly, the conduct of the trial, including the defense's failure to use Edwin Bollier's letter, and the appeal left much to be desired in both courts from the defendant's perspective. Seif Al-Islam Qadhafi, Colonel Qadhafi's son, alluded to the inadequacy of Al-Megrahi's defense counsel in an interview on "Future Television" in Lebanon on November 2, 2002.

The final alternative is for Al-Megrahi to serve the remainder of his minimum term and then return to Libya and his family, a not very pleasant future for the next seventeen years plus.

Al-Megrahi's young wife broke into tears after Chief Judge Cullen read the decision. She left the court or was carried out by friends and relatives and became hysterical for some time after she left, no doubt contemplating life for her and their five young children without her husband.

Al-Megrahi was whisked to Scotland the evening after the decision, where he was installed in a special prison cell already prepared. It was earlier agreed by the United Kingdom and Libya that a Libyan consulate would be opened in Glasgow to permit the Libyan government to maintain contact with Al-Megrahi and to act as liaison with his family, who would be visiting him from time to time.

The families of the victims who were present, while not overly jubilant, were pleased that justice had been accomplished. They can probably look forward to a quickened pace of negotiating a settlement of their claims against Libya.

The Libyan government increased public security around the U.S. and U.K. embassies in Tripoli after announcement of the appeal's failure. A Libyan spokesman considered the failure of the appeal to be largely the result of political considerations and that the Scottish court system was flawed, being subject to political pressures.

Libya's Complaint Against American Aggression (the 1986 Bombing of Tripoli and Benghazi)

The Libyan government filed a civil complaint in the Tripoli (Libya) court of appeal in 1986 against the governments of the United States of America and the United Kingdom, as well as a number of individual American civil servants (John Poindexter, Oliver North, William Casey, Robert Oakley, Robert Gish, Frank Kalo former admiral of the Sixth Fleet], Jack Filch [fighter pilot, U.S. Defense Department] and Phil Eleston [armaments officer of the U.S. Air Force]. The action was served on the U.S. Department of State by the Libyan interests section of the embassy of the United Arab Emirates (Libya's diplomatic link to the United States in the absence of formal diplomatic relations between the two countries).

The allegations state that:

• 170 fighters attacked Libya on the morning of April 14, 1986, from bases in the United States and Britain and from aircraft carriers in the Mediterranean Sea. The raids injured innocent citizens and damaged the home of the leader of the revolution. Roads, utilities and telephone networks were destroyed. Forty-one Libyans were killed and 226 were injured, many seriously.

• That the aggression was in violation of international law and the UN Charter and was condemned by a resolution of the UN General Assembly on November 20, 1986, as well as a declaration of the conference of presidents of the Organization of African Unity on July 28–30, 1986; a political declaration adopted by the states of the Non-Aligned Movement conference on September 1–6, 1986; the final statement of the meeting of the Islamic Congress of Ministers of Foreign Affairs in New York October 3, 1986; and a declaration of the Arab Lawyers Conference in Damascus on July 19–22, 1989.

• That pursuant to Article 224 of the Libyan criminal procedures law as well as Article 166 of Libyan civil law, which provide that anyone who causes damages to a third party shall be obligated to compensate that party, as well as international law and numerous provisions of the Libyan penal code.

• That Libya has suffered the following monetary damages:

1. 20 million Libyan dinars (LDs) for each individual's death or a total of 820 million LDs.

2. 5 million LDs for each individual injured, for a total of 1 billion 130 million LDs.

3. Tripoli City:

    A. 13 million LDs for demolition and reconstruction of the home of the Leader of the Revolution.

    B. Destruction of public utilities including roads, water and sewer lines, electricity and telephone systems, trees, etc.: 12,999,000 LDs.

    C. Damages to the agricultural sector: 12,999,000 LDs.

4. Benghazi City:

    A. Destruction of Al Shura Elementary School, Arous Al-Janoub School, Zahrat Al-Madein School, Rehabilitation Center for the Handicapped, some public utilities and housing units: 2,990,873.602 LDs.

    B. Emergency expenses: 56,993.631 LDs.

5. Economic damages including negative impact on economic growth as well as its impact on material and human capabilities: 10 billion LDs.

6. Harm to the reputation, sovereignty and dignity of the Libyan people, in violation of international laws regarding State sovereignty; an aggression against innocent people and a sovereign State and member of the UN, it is considered "an act of organized terrorism," which targeted the life of the Leader of the Revolution estimates "moral" compensation of 20 billion LDs.

The alleged Libyan damages total approximately US Dollars 2,036,577,585.18 at current exchange rates.

Another significant question arises as to who will reimburse Libya for the human and economic losses suffered by its citizens and the country for the seven years of sanctions imposed by the UN and the United States. The U.S. sanctions are still in full force and will probably not be lifted until compensation is paid to the victims' families. Who will compensate the families of Libyan victims of America's bombing of Libya, including the death of Colonel Qadhafi's adopted daughter?

Can or will Libya bring suit in the International Court of Justice against the United States and the United Kingdom to recover the enormous economic damages it suffered during seven years of sanctions?

In addition, criminal indictments were issued against the people named earlier to appear in Tripoli criminal court to answer the charges filed against them for the criminal acts charged in connection with the same attacks. However, realistically and legally, since there is no extradition treaty between the two countries, it is doubtful that anything will come of these charges, except perhaps a trial in absentia. Judgments may be entered and at some point in time will be used to offset some of the U.S. and U.K. claims arising out of the Pan Am 103 case, which is proceeding in federal court on Long Island, New York.

19

Conclusions

Compensation for Lockerbie's Families

While the Lockerbie trial may be considered a closed chapter, the issue of compensations had to be settled before normal relations between the United States and the Great Socialist Peoples Libyan Arab Jamahariya are achieved. Numerous cases have been filed and are pending in the U.S. district court on Long Island against Libya for the Lockerbie bombing. These cases were originally placed on hold until the Lockerbie trial ended.

Indeed, compensation had become the most difficult obstacle for Libya. Payment of compensation was the reason the United States gave for not restoring diplomatic relations. And, although American representatives spoke on different occasions of many other conditions, many considered the noncompensation issue the primary one. Washington was under pressure from the victims' families and other lobbies not to let Libya off the hook. The Clinton administration began to set the stage for a solution to the bilateral issues when the multilateral sanctions were all but officially aborted by the international community. President Clinton himself had met Colonel Qadhafi at a diplomatic-social function in Africa, although he later ignored suggestions by the Libyan leader, focusing instead on the Israeli Palestinian conflict as the path to a Nobel peace prize, which he did not win.

By the time the Bush administration took office, the issue of Libya had become a burden for the United States on two levels: the political-diplomatic level, which had resulted in a measure of isolation of the United States in its stands regarding sanctions, and the economic level, which found United States oil and contracting companies complaining of the absence of relations with Libya. While continuing with the Clinton policy regarding sanctions, the Bush administration paid more attention to the pleas from the oil companies, especially since many of its officials were active in that sector. And since Libya's position had evolved, a political decision was made to help Libya move toward ending the remaining issues. Compensation was the cornerstone of U.S. demands.

The United States had started direct diplomatic meetings with Libya around the fall of 2000. It was not ready, however, for direct meetings without an umbrella. That umbrella was provided by the British government as well as Prince Bandar himself. Five meetings between Libyan, American and British officials were convened, all in England. The first two were during the last days of the Clinton years, and the others during the Bush years. But, in the second meeting, the U.S. representative informed his counterparts that Washington would be concentrating on the elections and that he would resign his post after that. All Libya could do was wait, again.

Meanwhile, Libya reverted to the maxim "There are no permanent friends, only permanent interests" and began to rely on its interests. It had to overlook what were considered obstacles to good relations with other countries for thirty years. It had to consider that its interests lay in a stable region and a stable oil market, without resorting to extreme measures, as it had in the seventies. It had to filter and strengthen its network of friends based on new realities: Most of its old friends were no longer revolutionaries; they were leaders that befriended the United States to some extent, yet helped Libya in its struggle. Libya must also consider its relations with the United States. No conflict should remain between the United States and Libya in the future; if it did, their friends would choose the superpower rather than an isolated friend.

Libya began to pay attention to another positive role it could play: It could help bring peace to the African continent. It succeeded in many instances, to Washington's liking, for Libya seemed now to possess most of the required qualities of a mediator. Those efforts were leading the West, including the United States, to recognize the vital role Libya could play in a continent where the Americans were having a hard time selling their policies and mediation. One such recognition was presented by Dr. Ray Takeyh, a senior fellow at the Washington Institute for Near East Policy, before the House International Relations Committee on July 22, 1999. Takeyh said:

The post-Lockerbie period has witnessed a continuation of Libya's pragmatic diplomacy. Qadhafi has emerged as one of the leading mediators of African crises. The colonel brokered the accord, leading to the departure of Chadian forces from the Congo and an apparent reconciliation between Kinshasa and Kampala. Qadhafi has also been instrumental in convincing the many internal factions in Congo to resume discussions with an eye toward some type of reconciliation. In the Horn of Africa, Libya has attempted to craft a settlement ending the conflict between Ethiopia and Eritrea. The critical questions is [*sic*] whether Qadhafi has abandoned his revolutionary radicalism and metamorphosized [*sic*] into a force for peace and stability.

Another view was more officially presented by Deputy Assistant Secretary of State Ronald Neumann on November 30, 2000. He noted that "the most significant changes in Libya's behavior has [*sic*] been its declining support for terrorism. Since April, Libya has taken a number of important steps to reduce its support for terrorist groups and activities." Neumann also said that "the US Government welcomes the Libyan support for the Palestinian Authority and views it as a strong symbol of Libyan willingness to support the peace process." These statements are expressive of the problems the United States faces, for all they really could do is acknowledge Libyan progress without being able to take part or contribute.

In practice, the United States showed some official willingness to improve its relations with Libya through two major decisions. The first was announced days after the actual handover and the suspension of sanctions. It issued a special permit to U.S. oil companies to send personnel to Libya to inspect their assets and look into possibilities of doing business in the country. The second, without much public notice, was a decision by the State Department easing, though not officially lifting, the ban on travel to Libya by American citizens. These two decisions, though minimal, would pave the road for better understanding and may prepare the ground for a seminormalization of relations between the two countries.

Many efforts by former U.S. officials were exhorted as soon as a solution was becoming feasible. Herman Cohen, who headed the State Department's African bureau during the Bush administration, said Qadhafi had assumed the role of peacemaker in Africa and also appeared to have abandoned his previous sponsorship of terrorist activities. "There have not been any terrorist acts attributable to Libya in a number of years," he told reporters after visiting Tripoli and meeting Qadhafi early in September 1999. Cohen went on to play a major role in organizing different sessions for a public dialogue between different sectors of both societies.

Another former official, Robert Pelletreau, formerly the U.S. ambassador to Tunisia during the early days of sanctions and an assistant Secretary of State for Near Eastern Affairs during the years of Bush (Sr.) and the early Clinton administration, offered his services to Libya to reestablish relations with American businesses and government. He frequently communicated with the Libyans and established personal working relationships with many top-level officials.

September 11: A Shock and a Helping Hand

As the appeal process was going on, a major incident took place in the United States that was to change the world and force new roles on everybody.

On September 11, 2001, a group linked to Islamic fundamentalist Osama Bin-Laden hijacked four airplanes and crashed two of them into the World Trade Center in New York, a third into the Pentagon in the Washington area, while the fourth crashed in Pennsylvania before it reached its destination. This incident was billed as the gravest terrorist action ever on U.S. land and the first attack against the U.S. since the Japanese attacked Pearl Harbor.

Feeling like a wounded lion, the United States had no room for justification for these attacks. Many countries around the world understood. Libya was among them. Statements of condemnation and offers of help issued from Tripoli and led the U.S. government to send letters of thanks, promising to resume direct contacts as soon as they sorted out their response to those attacks and expressing their intention to call on Libya if necessary. That led not only to the beginning of the solution of bilateral relations but also to cooperation between the security organizations of both countries. Libya had experienced similar attacks by Islamic fundamentalists, although not at the same level. Furthermore, when the United States issued a warrant to the Interpol, calling for the arrest of Bin-Laden, the memo acknowledged a similar Libyan request, indirectly admitting that both countries had the same goal this time.

On the political level, it became clear in direct meetings and other actions and pronouncements that Washington was looking for ways to justify its response to that level of terrorism. And since the response was directed at an Islamic and Arab organization, such justification needed to be two-faceted: Islamic and Arab nationalistic. Libya provided the latter for its history in defending Arab causes, and Lebanese Hezbollah provided the former for its Islamic credentials in fighting the Israeli occupation of South Lebanon. The latter effort did not materialize for many complicated reasons, mainly Israel's insistence on continuing the fight against Hezbollah, Iran and Syria.

It is noteworthy that when this process of solving the Lockerbie issue began as an effort to lift sanctions and as a reward to a country that abides by Security Council demands, in order to justify their continuation on another that never abided by such demands, such as Iraq, the hastening of the political process was due to the need to prove, once again, that the American offensive against terrorism was justified.

When the dust had settled and the United States had gone back to its normal daily business around the world, the Americans requested a meeting with the Libyans. Once again, England was the site. And, once again, the British were present in the official meetings. Again, Prince Bandar was present. His efforts were to help organize direct meetings between the Libyans and the Americans without any publicity. The Libyans needed to hear words of assurance from the Americans, so Bandar invited both delegations to a private dinner at his home in London.

In the official trilateral meeting, the U.S. representative, Assistant Secretary of State for Near Eastern Affairs William Burns, restated his government's welcome of Libya's positions regarding the events of September 11. He qualified his position with a "hope" that Libya would not help those under attack by the U.S. forces in Afghanistan. It must have been an effort to express certain worries within the administration about Libya's old ways. He heard nothing but confirmation that Libya was on board in this battle, although the Libyans still had some reservations about the inaction of the West, mainly the United States and the United Kingdom, against those Libyans opposed to the regime, aligned with the Islamists and still living in both countries. They did not receive any promises.

It became clear at that juncture that the issue of compensation was the only issue of value remaining on the table.

Earlier, in Libya, a long and hard debate was taking place. Should Libya pay compensation? Should it even agree to that principle while the trial and the appeal were taking place? And since both, at different junctures, were showing many defects in the crown's case, what would happen if both accused men were acquitted?

The Libyans were divided on this debate into many camps. Some were more legal and logical in their thoughts, while others were sentimental and logical as well.

The first group supported the idea of paying compensation or accepting the principle while awaiting the right time for action, based on two facts: that there will always be civil cases against Libya and the political winds were not in Libya's favor. The civil case, they explained, had a legal basis even if the two accused men were found not guilty.

And since both the Americans and the British, let alone the whole world, expected Libya to sort this out before full normalization of relations could take place, Libya should act on it. Some went so far as to calculate the monetary costs of the compensation, concluding that Libya could reimburse itself from its oil sector within a year or two. Perhaps it was best, they thought, just to turn the page and move on.

Those opposed to the payment talked a good deal about a simple question, asking the other group: How on earth can somebody acquitted in a criminal trial be forced to pay compensation? That was, of course, before the appeal was rejected.

Qadhafi, for his part, was noncommittal while leaning toward agreeing to the payment. But, once again, he raised detailed issues as to how such an act would close the files and whether the Americans and the British would raise other demands. He even looked at the situation from the perspective of the victim: My people suffered from an American and British attack. I have an airplane that was downed by the Israelis with many civilians aboard. Don't they all deserve compensation as well? Are American and British lives more valuable than Libyan or other lives?

Once the trial ended with what Libya considered a political decision, an appeal was launched and many in the West felt their position was much stronger in demanding compensation. The Libyans, looking also at the civil cases, had yet to be convinced of the validity of the argument.

At this juncture, Prince Bandar proposed another idea: Establish a fund that would be open for contributions from other governments and companies doing business in Libya and the region, with Libya providing the largest sum. Some originally thought the fund would compensate all victims of terrorism but, after September 11, that idea was put aside because of the obvious complications.

Another tripartite meeting was arranged in March 2002. Libya was not ready to make any commitments. Its delegation went to the meeting with one mission: to explore whether there would be any new demands and how far they could work with the United States and the United Kingdom on noncompensation issues. In both trilateral meetings and private dinners at Bandar's home, Burns reiterated that, once Libya sorted out the issue of compensation, the United States would quickly work with them on the other items on the multilateral agenda while setting the final stage for sorting out the bilateral issues, which were not much.

Burns went so far as to tell the Libyans that his country did not care what type of arrangement was involved as long as the compensations were paid, based on an agreement with the victims' families. The issues of Libya's acceptance of responsibility for the actions of its citizens and its renunciation of terrorism were a matter of linguistic importance for all who had no problem with the main substance such statements would communicate, despite the importance of certain words and sentences here and there.

At that juncture, those who argued against the payment of compensations turned their efforts toward arguing about the amounts that would be paid, how to pay them, and what diplomatic or political benefit would accrue to Libya in return. They tried to connect compensations to the lifting of U.S. national sanctions against Libya. They tried other arguments that only expressed their frustration at the fact that they had to pay those compensations. The ultimate solution would be a simple equation: Libya pays compensations and accepts minimal responsibility for the actions of one of its nationals in return for lifting UN sanctions and gradual normalization with the United States, including the lifting of U.S. sanctions. With Bandar's help, such an equation was worked out.

In August 2003 an agreement was reached whereby Libya was to pay $2.7 billion to settle all claims for the 270 people killed in the bombing of Pan Am 103, at $10 million for each family. The payments would be in three installments: $4 million when UN sanctions were lifted, $4 million when U.S. sanctions were lifted and $2 million when the U.S. state department removed Libya from the list of states sponsoring terrorism. This would satisfy one element of American and British demands and was negotiated directly between Libyan lawyers and the lawyers for the victims' families while officials from all three countries were negotiating the other elements.

Even after the compensation agreement was achieved, negotiators still faced obstacles in settling the question of responsibility. Some in Libya were still debating whether accepting responsibility would actually mean indicting Libya, its officials and leader in this act. They could not distinguish between criminal responsibility, not an issue here, and civil responsibility along with that of a state for its officials. The negotiating team, consisting of Azwai, Al-Obeidi, and Moussa Koussa, was convinced that some language could be worked out satisfying this issue. The U.S. and U.K. could not agree to sort out the Lockerbie problem without some sort of statement from the Libyans regarding responsibility; initially they tried to suggest language much more aggressive than the wording eventually presented in their letter to the Security Council in 1992, which was adopted in UNSC resolution 731.

After long months of negotiating directly and through the mediators, mainly Prince Bandar, all sides agreed on language regarding responsibility. The 15th of August, 2003, was the date all documents and announcements would be made official. The atmosphere was similar to that preceding the handover of the two suspects, though with much less fear. All were anxious again, but this time more of the anxiety was in Libya, which was waiting to finally reap the fruits of its long process of rehabilitating its relations with the international community.

A letter from Libya was delivered in the morning hours of the 15th to the president of the Security Council. In it, Libya listed its recent actions—"a sovereign State has facilitated the bringing to justice of the two suspects charged with the bombing of Pan Am 103 and accepts responsibility for the actions of its officials"—and cited its cooperation with Scottish authorities in the investigation and the agreement to pay compensation. The letter went on to list other elements of Libya's implementation of UNSC demands. It concludes, "The Libyan Arab Jamahiriya affirms it will have fullfilled all Security Council requirements relevant to the Lockerbie incident.... It trusts that the Council will agree. Therefore, the Libyan Arab Jamahiriya requests that in that event the Council immediately lift the measures set forth in its resolutions 748 (1992) and 883 (1993)."[1]

"Responsibility" was the magic word. The victims' families were already satisfied with the compensation agreement and eagerly awaiting the conclusion of that official side of the process to get their compensation. They were beginning to press their governments to find the appropriate language and solutions. More and more, the West was in favor of restoring normal relations with Libya without any major constraints, especially those of the UN sanctions. The U.S. was willing to move forward, albeit slowly and reluctantly. On one hand, the United States had some urgent considerations impelling it to agree to some movement; on the other hand, they did not wish to move too quickly, for reasons that might or might not have been related to the main issue, or to Libya at all.

Officially, Washington and London moved on that same day to accept Libya's letter and announce they would approve of the lifting of sanctions at the UNSC. The U.S., however, made sure it did not issue a completely positive statement. It had communicated as much to the Libyans during the negotiations, explaining that it needed time to change the mood and positions of some circles in Washington. Hence the announcement by Secretary Powell on August 15 came with no major surprises to Libya. Powell said:

> As the White House spokesman also announced today, Libya, in a letter to the UN Security Council, stated it accepts responsibility for the actions of its officials in the Pan Am 103 bombing, which exploded over Lockerbie, Scotland, December 21, 1988; and made arrangements to pay

compensation to the families of the victims in accordance with an agreement worked out directly between the families and Libya. Previously Libya transferred the two Libyan suspects charged in the bombing, one of whom, Abdel-Basset al-Megrahi, was convicted of murder and is now serving a life sentence.

In recognition of these steps, and to allow the families' settlement to go forward, the United States has notified the United Nations Security Council that, when the necessary sums have been deposited into the agreed escrow account, we will not oppose the lifting of the UN sanctions that were suspended in 1999.

The lifting of sanctions at the United Nations will not affect U.S. bilateral sanctions on Libya, which will remain in place. We remain deeply concerned about other aspects of Libya's behavior, including its poor human rights record and lack of democratic institutions; its destructive role in perpetuating regional conflicts in Africa; and, most troubling, its pursuit of weapons of mass destruction and their related delivery system. Libya also remains on the state sponsors of terrorism list, which carries its own sanctions. Libya must address the concerns underlying these bilateral measures. Libya must continue to take definitive action to assist in the fight against international terrorism.

The efforts undertaken by the U.S. government in connection with the bombing of Pan Am Flight 103 should serve to remind all who would engage in terrorist acts that the United States will always pursue justice and redress for its citizens. Combating the evil of terrorism remains a paramount commitment of the United States. We will not relent in that continuing struggle.

The U.S. and U.K., in a coordinated effort with the Libyans, similarly and instantly, sent their own letter to the president of the Council in which they said that their governments were "prepared to allow the lifting of sanctions."[2] The U.K. then moved to work the Security Council to take the appropriate measures while the U.S. sat back, accepting what was going on without any interference either way.

Then there came to the surface a surprising new obstacle. France suddenly raised an objection: It would veto the lifting of sanctions if Libya did not renegotiate the amount of compensations it had already paid and settled with the French families and victims of UTA flight 772. The French, it seemed, felt they were "low-balled" by the international norm of compensations, while the U.S. and U.K. families received very high amounts considered normal only in the U.S.

France claimed, as a justification for its position, that it had received promises from the Libyan leader's son, Seif Al-Islam, head of a philanthropic fund, to raise the compensation for the French families. Libya's foreign minister, Abdul Rahman Shalqam, rejected such promises in a meeting with French president Jacques Chirac. He told the French that

Seif Al-Islam held no official position in the Libyan government and, therefore, Libya could not be committed to his personal promises. If Seif Al-Islam wished to pay out of his own funds, it was up to him to do so, but that should not and did not hold the Libyan government to any commitments financially or politically. Qadhafi the leader seemed more willing to accommodate the position of the Foreign Minister than to hold to that of his son, though he tried to find a solution to this issue without creating too many precedents. Among the problems he was forced to juggle were newly raised claims by some in Germany asking for compensation for the victims of the LaBelle discotheque bombing, of which Libya was accused of bombing. It seemed the $10 million per family whetted the appetite of many around the world.

The U.S. and the U.K. intervened, with agitation at times, asking the French to move along. At one point, the U.K. created a precedent at the Security Council. It suggested, and got adopted, a resolution to set a date for the vote on the resolution for lifting sanctions. The intention was to get the French to make a choice: either accept the lifting, or face the world and possibly lose French economic interests in Libya. France obliged and finally accepted the lifting of UN sanctions on September 12, 2003. Its vote, however, left many questions as to what the future of its relations with Libya would be. France abstained, as did the U.S. (the result of the vote was 13 in favor and 2 abstentions). Libya had expected the U.S. abstention, since Washington's intentions had been communicated to them long before, during the negotiations in London.

The explanation of the vote by the U.S. representative during the Council meeting, along with Powell's statement a month prior, raised some fundamental issues as to whether the U.S. was at all willing to improve bilateral relations with Libya or was just negotiating public-relations positions aimed at making sure Libya would implement what was left of U.S. demands. Speaking for the United States, James Cunningham said his country's decision "must not be misconstrued by Libya or by the world community as tacit United States acceptance that the government of Libya has rehabilitated itself. The U.S. continues to have serious concerns about other aspects of Libyan behavior"—at which point he listed the same issues raised by Powell a few weeks earlier.

The U.K. representative, who was the president of the Council for that month, had a totally different expectation of the future. He said his country "looks forward to the full re-emergence of Libya into the international community."

With the international sanctions behind them, the Libyans eagerly sought to start the process of normalizing their relations with the U.S. Washington, in turn, was noncommital in public, sending different signals in private. Meanwhile, Libya felt it had discussed the bulk of its bilateral issues and considered those discussions "understandings" on how the two countries would move past the lifting of UN sanctions. But some observations might lead to different conclusions regarding the easiness of such a process.

By the time the Security Council lifted those sanctions, the United States had moved to occupy Iraq under the pretext of the existence of weapons of mass destruction in that country, a claim that in the months following the invasion could not be proved, creating a problem of credibility for the administration of George W. Bush and the United States as a whole. It was possible that the Bush administration, overwhelmed by so-called neo-conservatives, had its own unrevealed agenda. Rumors suggested that this group had a list of countries they intended to occupy after Iraq; if so, they were held back by resistance in Iraq and lack of a real post-occupation plan for reconstruction and rehabilitation of the country.

Among the countries on that rumored list was Libya. Some in Washington whispered that the administration, or its neo-conservative faction at the very least, was not on board for the lifting of UN sanctions and was not going to let U.S. sanctions be lifted, easily, if at all. The issue of Libya's possession of weapons of mass destruction (WMDs) was reemerging as a major bone of contention. As in the early days of preparation for the invasion of Iraq, this issue seemed to provide an easy excuse for U.S. action. By September 2003, however, the Bush administration was beginning to feel the heat of protests, both international and domestic, that the Iraq invasion was unjustified and ill conceived. Possibly this might lead to a better atmosphere in which the Libyans could sort out these accusations and prove the nonexistence of WMDs in Libya.

Some officials were of the view that there was no chance of any sanctions being lifted without serious Libyan actions on WMDs, although the original reason for the sanctions was Libyan support of terrorism and the U.S. now could certify that Libya was free of terrorists. Officials suggested privately that they might start offering the official lifting of passport and travel restrictions to Libya as a cost-free bargaining chip. These same officials noted that the neo-conservatives still had major support in Congress on this issue. The only pressure for further improvement would come from victims' families and oil companies. Those two lobbies have not fully moved as of this writing, but they may suddenly turn on the heat when they see a prolonged delay in action from Washington, especially when the U.S. oil companies could benefit from at least 650,000 barrels' daily production in Libya.

As for the Libyans, they have continued to move carefully after the lifting of UN sanctions. They have not made a lot of noises regarding the U.S. sanctions, leaving them to the bilateral negotiations. They feel confident they can deal with the U.S. accusations and rebuff them with material evidence. They are willing to receive European experts and officials to visit certain sites the U.S. claims are producing WMDs. They are ready to prove that their policies in Africa are helping to find peaceful solutions. In short, they are the new Libyans, changing their presentation while preserving principles of independence.

Postsanctions Libya

Reviewing the statements Qadhafi made in March 1999 and fully understanding them show that he is a leader who is aware of the necessity for dramatic change—of policy and practice alike. That change is not concerned so much with the immediate issue of the handover (since Libya's conditions for that event never changed from the outset) as it is with a major change in the country's direction. The revolutionary mindset was now being replaced by allowing a more realistic reading of the world's alliances and interests.

Internally, a new system had to be formalized.

The Libyan government cannot be ignorant of its internal needs, such as the rebuilding of its infrastructure and services systems. Mentalities have to change. Modernization, to whatever level possible, has to take over. Old methods have to cease. When a country such as Libya declares its shores on the Mediterranean a beachhead for its African brethren, it has to realize that it must transfer a vital commodity both ways, keeping many of their values for itself: It must develop a new kind of civility. The north exports to the south and the south exports to the north and should not pass over Libya without a benefit. Libya can be that permanent bridge—mentally, economically, politically and, most important, intellectually. It has the basic requirements: economic and intellectual wealth. What was lacking was the ability to integrate both. That is what Libya needed, and that is what its leadership was trying to do, while integrating, as well, its need for security with its ambitions of modernization. Therefore, Qadhafi has to learn how to manage water and sewage systems, without having to become an expert on them. He could find a way to balance both efforts. That would be the best way for translating his "third" theory into an implementable program of work internally and externally. Postsanctions' words and events signal Libya's willingness to jump into the waters of change.

This is a new beginning for a people that have many unfulfilled dreams. The dreams have to change in order for the fulfillment to be feasible. The challenge for Libya and its revolution is to start anew, on the basis of a state's vision, not on the fervor of its revolution. The success of the revolution was proven for about thirty years, and the success of the state has been proven as well in the past two years. The new experience has proved much more fruitful, as Libya is poised to play a more constructive role in the international arena.

Appendix: Documents

Regarding the Implementation of Security Council Resolution 1192 (1998)

   Annexes 2–9: Responses to Requests for Clarification

   16. Text of United States' and United Kingdom's Requirements for Libya to Meet Re: U.N. Security Council Resolution 748 of 1992, as presented in First Tri-Lateral Meeting, May 6, 1999

   17. Text of United Kingdom's Requests for Libya's Cooperation with Scottish Judicial Authorities, May 6, 1999.

   18. U.N. Document S/2003/818: Letter from the Libyan Jamahiriya to the U.N.

   19. U.N. Document S/2003/819: Letter from the Permanent Representatives of the United Kingdom and United States to the U.N.

   20. U.N. Document S/RES/1506 (2003): Resolution 1506.

1. Security Council Resolution 731 (1992), January 21, 1992

**UNITED
NATIONS**

S

Security Council

Distr.
GENERAL

S/RES/731 (1992)
21 January 1992

RESOLUTION 731 (1992)

Adopted by the Security Council at its 3033rd meeting,
on 21 January 1992

The Security Council,

Deeply disturbed by the world-wide persistence of acts of international terrorism in all its forms, including those in which States are directly or indirectly involved, which endanger or take innocent lives, have a deleterious effect on international relations and jeopardize the security of States,

Deeply concerned by all illegal activities directed against international civil aviation, and affirming the right of all States, in accordance with the Charter of the United Nations and relevant principles of international law, to protect their nationals from acts of international terrorism that constitute threats to international peace and security,

Reaffirming its resolution 286 (1970) of 9 September 1970, in which it called on States to take all possible legal steps to prevent any interference with international civil air travel,

Reaffirming also its resolution 635 (1989) of 14 June 1989, in which it condemned all acts of unlawful interference against the security of civil aviation and called upon all States to cooperate in devising and implementing measures to prevent all acts of terrorism, including those involving explosives,

Recalling the statement made on 30 December 1988 by the President of the Security Council on behalf of the members of the Council strongly condemning the destruction of Pan Am flight 103 and calling on all States to assist in the apprehension and prosecution of those responsible for this criminal act,

Deeply concerned over the results of investigations, which implicate officials of the Libyan Government and which are contained in Security Council documents that include the requests addressed to the Libyan authorities by

92-02490   4117Z (E)

/...

S/RES/731 (1992)
Page 2

France, 1/, 2/ the United Kingdom of Great Britain and Northern Ireland 2/, 3/ and the United States of America 2/, 4/, 5/ in connection with the legal procedures related to the attacks carried out against Pan American flight 103 and Union de transports aérens flight 772;

Determined to eliminate international terrorism,

1.   Condemns the destruction of Pan American flight 103 and Union de tranports aérens flight 772 and the resultant loss of hundreds of lives;

2.   Strongly deplores the fact that the Libyan Government has not yet responded effectively to the above requests to cooperate fully in establishing responsibility for the terrorist acts referred to above against Pan American flight 103 and Union de tranports aérens flight 772;

3.   Urges the Libyan Government immediately to provide a full and effective response to those requests so as to contribute to the elimination of international terrorism;

4.   Requests the Secretary-General to seek the cooperation of the Libyan Government to provide a full and effective response to those requests;

5.   Urges all States individually and collectively to encourage the Libyan Government to respond fully and effectively to those requests;

6.   Decides to remain seized of the matter.

1/   S/23306.

2/   S/23309.

3/   S/23307.

4/   S/23308.

5/   S/23317.

2. Security Council Resolution 748 (1992), March 31, 1992

**UNITED
NATIONS**

Security Council

Distr.
GENERAL

S/RES/748 (1992)
31 March 1992

RESOLUTION 748 (1992)

<u>Adopted by the Security Council at its 3063rd meeting,
on 31 March 1992</u>

<u>The Security Council</u>,

<u>Reaffirming</u> its resolution 731 (1992) of 21 January 1992,

<u>Noting</u> the reports of the Secretary-General, 1/ 2/

<u>Deeply concerned</u> that the Libyan Government has still not provided a full and effective response to the requests in its resolution 731 (1992) of 21 January 1992,

<u>Convinced</u> that the suppression of acts of international terrorism, including those in which States are directly or indirectly involved, is essential for the maintenance of international peace and security,

<u>Recalling</u> that, in the statement issued on 31 January 1992 on the casion of the meeting of the Security Council at the level of heads of State ...d Government, 3/ the members of the Council expressed their deep concern over acts of international terrorism, and emphasized the need for the international community to deal effectively with all such acts,

<u>Reaffirming</u> that, in accordance with the principle in Article 2, paragraph 4, of the Charter of the United Nations, every State has the duty to refrain from organizing, instigating, assisting or participating in terrorist acts in another State or acquiescing in organized activities within its territory directed towards the commission of such acts, when such acts involve a threat or use of force,

---

1/   S/23574.

2/   S/23672.

3/   S/23500.

92-14910   4192Z (E)   310392   *310392*   /...

Determining, in this context, that the failure by the Libyan Government to demonstrate by concrete actions its renunciation of terrorism and in particular its continued failure to respond fully and effectively to the requests in resolution 731 (1992) constitute a threat to international peace and security,

Determined to eliminate international terrorism,

Recalling the right of States, under Article 50 of the Charter, to consult the Security Council where they find themselves confronted with special economic problems arising from the carrying out of preventive or enforcement measures,

Acting under Chapter VII of the Charter,

1.   Decides that the Libyan Government must now comply without any further delay with paragraph 3 of resolution 731 (1992) regarding the requests contained in documents S/23306, S/23308 and S/23309;

2.   Decides also that the Libyan Government must commit itself definitively to cease all forms of terrorist action and all assistance to terrorist groups and that it must promptly, by concrete actions, demonstrate its renunciation of terrorism;

3.   Decides that, on 15 April 1992 all States shall adopt the measures set out below, which shall apply until the Security Council decides that the Libyan Government has complied with paragraphs 1 and 2 above;

4.   Decides also that all States shall:

(a) Deny permission to any aircraft to take off from, land in or overfly their territory if it is destined to land in or has taken off from the territory of Libya, unless the particular flight has been approved on grounds of significant humanitarian need by the Committee established by paragraph 9 below;

(b) Prohibit, by their nationals or from their territory, the supply of any aircraft or aircraft components to Libya, the provision of engineering and maintenance servicing of Libyan aircraft or aircraft components, the certification of airworthiness for Libyan aircraft, the payment of new claims against existing insurance contracts and the provision of new direct insurance for Libyan aircraft;

5.   Decides further that all States shall:

(a) Prohibit any provision to Libya by their nationals or from their territory of arms and related material of all types, including the sale or transfer of weapons and ammunition, military vehicles and equipment, paramilitary police equipment and spare parts for the aforementioned, as well as the provision of any types of equipment, supplies and grants of licensing arrangements, for the manufacture or maintenance of the aforementioned;

/... .

S/RES/748 (1992)
Page 3

(b) Prohibit any provision to Libya by their nationals or from their territory of technical advice, assistance or training related to the provision, manufacture, maintenance, or use of the items in (a) above;

(c) Withdraw any of their officials or agents present in Libya to advise the Libyan authorities on military matters;

6. Decides that all States shall:

(a) Significantly reduce the number and the level of the staff at Libyan diplomatic missions and consular posts and restrict or control the movement within their territory of all such staff who remain; in the case of Libyan missions to international organizations, the host State may, as it deems necessary, consult the organization concerned on the measures required to implement this subparagraph;

(b) Prevent the operation of all Libyan Arab Airlines offices;

(c) Take all appropriate steps to deny entry to or expel Libyan nationals who have been denied entry to or expelled from other States because of their involvement in terrorist activities;

7. Calls upon all States, including States not members of the United Nations, and all international organizations, to act strictly in accordance with the provisions of the present resolution, notwithstanding the existence of any rights or obligations conferred or imposed by any international agreement or any contract entered into or any licence or permit granted prior to 15 April 1992;

8. Requests all States to report to the Secretary-General by 15 May 1992 on the measures they have instituted for meeting the obligations set out in paragraphs 3 to 7 above;

9. Decides to establish, in accordance with rule 28 of its provisional rules of procedure, a Committee of the Security Council consisting of all the members of the Council, to undertake the following tasks and to report on its work to the Council with its observations and recommendations:

(a) To examine the reports submitted pursuant to paragraph 8 above;

(b) To seek from all States further information regarding the action taken by them concerning the effective implementation of the measures imposed by paragraphs 3 to 7 above;

(c) To consider any information brought to its attention by States concerning violations of the measures imposed by paragraphs 3 to 7 above and, in that context, to make recommendations to the Council on ways to increase their effectiveness;

/...

S/RES/748 (1992)
Page 4

    (d) To recommend appropriate measures in response to violations of the measures imposed by paragraphs 3 to 7 above and provide information on a regular basis to the Secretary-General for general distribution to Member States;

    (e) To consider and to decide upon expeditiously any application by States for the approval of flights on grounds of significant humanitarian need in accordance with paragraph 4 above;

    (f) To give special attention to any communications in accordance with Article 50 of the Charter from any neighbouring or other State with special economic problems that might arise from the carrying out of the measures imposed by paragraphs 3 to 7 above;

    10. Calls upon all States to cooperate fully with the Committee in the fulfilment of its task, including supplying such information as may be sought by the Committee in pursuance of the present resolution;

    11. Requests the Secretary-General to provide all necessary assistance to the Committee and to make the necessary arrangements in the Secretariat for this purpose;

    12. Invites the Secretary-General to continue his role as set out in paragraph 4 of resolution 731 (1992);

    13. Decides that the Security Council shall, every 120 days or sooner should the situation so require, review the measures imposed by paragraphs 3 to 7 above in the light of the compliance by the Libyan Government with paragraphs 1 and 2 above taking into account, as appropriate, any reports provided by the Secretary-General on his role as set out in paragraph 4 of resolution 731 (1992);

    14. Decides to remain seized of the matter.

-----

3. Security Council Resolution 883 (1993), November 11, 1993

UNITED
NATIONS

S

Security Council

Distr.
GENERAL

S/RES/883 (1993)
11 November 1993

RESOLUTION 883 (1993)

Adopted by the Security Council at its 3312th meeting,
on 11 November 1993

The Security Council,

Reaffirming its resolutions 731 (1992) of 21 January 1992 and 748 (1992) of 31 March 1992,

Deeply concerned that after more than twenty months the Libyan Government has not fully complied with these resolutions,

Determined to eliminate international terrorism,

Convinced that those responsible for acts of international terrorism must be brought to justice,

Convinced also that the suppression of acts of international terrorism, including those in which States are directly or indirectly involved, is essential for the maintenance of international peace and security,

Determining, in this context, that the continued failure by the Libyan Government to demonstrate by concrete actions its renunciation of terrorism, and in particular its continued failure to respond fully and effectively to the requests and decisions in resolutions 731 (1992) and 748 (1992), constitute a threat to international peace and security,

Taking note of the letters to the Secretary-General dated 29 September and 1 October 1993 from the Secretary of the General People's Committee for Foreign Liaison and International Cooperation of Libya (S/26523) and his speech in the General Debate at the forty-eighth session of the General Assembly (A/48/PV.20) in which Libya stated its intention to encourage those charged with the bombing of Pan Am 103 to appear for trial in Scotland and its willingness to cooperate with the competent French authorities in the case of the bombing of UTA 772,

Expressing its gratitude to the Secretary-General for the efforts he has made pursuant to paragraph 4 of resolution 731 (1992),

Recalling the right of States, under Article 50 of the Charter, to consult the Security Council where they find themselves confronted with special economic problems arising from the carrying out of preventive or enforcement measures,

93-62678 (E)

/...

S/RES/883 (1993)
Page 2

Acting under Chapter VII of the Charter,

1.   Demands once again that the Libyan Government comply without any further delay with resolutions 731 (1992) and 748 (1992);

2.   Decides, in order to secure compliance by the Libyan Government with the decisions of the Council, to take the following measures, which shall come into force at 00.01 EST on 1 December 1993 unless the Secretary-General has reported to the Council in the terms set out in paragraph 16 below;

3.   Decides that all States in which there are funds or other financial resources (including funds derived or generated from property) owned or controlled, directly or indirectly, by:

(a) the Government or public authorities of Libya, or

(b) any Libyan undertaking,

shall freeze such funds and financial resources and ensure that neither they nor any other funds and financial resources are made available, by their nationals or by any persons within their territory, directly or indirectly, to or for the benefit of the Government or public authorities of Libya or any Libyan undertaking, which for the purposes of this paragraph, means any commercial, industrial or public utility undertaking which is owned or controlled, directly or indirectly, by

(i) the Government or public authorities of Libya,

(ii) any entity, wherever located or organized, owned or controlled by (i), or

(iii) any person identified by States as acting on behalf of (i) or (ii) for the purposes of this resolution;

4.   Further decides that the measures imposed by paragraph 3 above do not apply to funds or other financial resources derived from the sale or supply of any petroleum or petroleum products, including natural gas and natural gas products, or agricultural products or commodities, originating in Libya and exported therefrom after the time specified in paragraph 2 above, provided that any such funds are paid into separate bank accounts exclusively for these funds;

5.   Decides that all States shall prohibit any provision to Libya by their nationals or from their territory of the items listed in the annex to this resolution, as well as the provision of any types of equipment, supplies and grants of licensing arrangements for the manufacture or maintenance of such items;

6.   Further decides that, in order to make fully effective the provisions of resolution 748 (1992), all States shall:

(a) require the immediate and complete closure of all Libyan Arab Airlines offices within their territories;

/...

S/RES/883 (1993)
Page 3

(b) prohibit any commercial transactions with Libyan Arab Airlines by their nationals or from their territory, including the honouring or endorsement of any tickets or other documents issued by that airline;

(c) prohibit, by their nationals or from their territory, the entering into or renewal of arrangements for:

(i) the making available, for operation within Libya, of any aircraft or aircraft components, or

(ii) the provision of engineering or maintenance servicing of any aircraft or aircraft components within Libya;

(d) prohibit, by their nationals or from their territory, the supply of any materials destined for the construction, improvement or maintenance of Libyan civilian or military airfields and associated facilities and equipment, or of any engineering or other services or components destined for the maintenance of any Libyan civil or military airfields or associated facilities and equipment, except emergency equipment and equipment and services directly related to civilian air traffic control;

(e) prohibit, by their nationals or from their territory, any provision of advice, assistance, or training to Libyan pilots, flight engineers, or aircraft and ground maintenance personnel associated with the operation of aircraft and airfields within Libya;

(f) prohibit, by their nationals or from their territory, any renewal of any direct insurance for Libyan aircraft;

7. <u>Confirms</u> that the decision taken in resolution 748 (1992) that all States shall significantly reduce the level of the staff at Libyan diplomatic missions and consular posts includes all missions and posts established since that decision or after the coming into force of this resolution;

8. <u>Decides</u> that all States, and the Government of Libya, shall take the necessary measures to ensure that no claim shall lie at the instance of the Government or public authorities of Libya, or of any Libyan national, or of any Libyan undertaking as defined in paragraph 3 of this resolution, or of any person claiming through or for the benefit of any such person or undertaking, in connection with any contract or other transaction or commercial operation where its performance was affected by reason of the measures imposed by or pursuant to this resolution or related resolutions;

9. <u>Instructs</u> the Committee established by resolution 748 (1992) to draw up expeditiously guidelines for the implementation of paragraphs 3 to 7 of this resolution, and to amend and supplement, as appropriate, the guidelines for the implementation of resolution 748 (1992), especially its paragraph 5 (a);

10. <u>Entrusts</u> the Committee established by resolution 748 (1992) with the task of examining possible requests for assistance under the provisions of Article 50 of the Charter of the United Nations and making recommendations to the President of the Security Council for appropriate action;

/...

11. Affirms that nothing in this resolution affects Libya's duty scrupulously to adhere to all of its obligations concerning servicing and repayment of its foreign debt;

12. Calls upon all States, including States not Members of the United Nations, and all international organizations, to act strictly in accordance with the provisions of the present resolution, notwithstanding the existence of any rights or obligations conferred or imposed by any international agreement or any contract entered into or any licence or permit granted prior to the effective time of this resolution;

13. Requests all States to report to the Secretary-General by 15 January 1994 on the measures they have instituted for meeting the obligations set out in paragraphs 3 to 7 above;

14. Invites the Secretary-General to continue his role as set out in paragraph 4 of resolution 731 (1992);

15. Calls again upon all Member States individually and collectively to encourage the Libyan Government to respond fully and effectively to the requests and decisions in resolutions 731 (1992) and 748 (1992);

16. Expresses its readiness to review the measures set forth above and in resolution 748 (1992) with a view to suspending them immediately if the Secretary-General reports to the Council that the Libyan Government has ensured the appearance of those charged with the bombing of Pan Am 103 for trial before the appropriate United Kingdom or United States court and has satisfied the French judicial authorities with respect to the bombing of UTA 772, and with a view to lifting them immediately when Libya complies fully with the requests and decisions in resolutions 731 (1992) and 748 (1992); and requests the Secretary-General, within 90 days of such suspension, to report to the Council on Libya's compliance with the remaining provisions of its resolutions 731 (1992) and 748 (1992) and, in the case of non-compliance, expresses its resolve to terminate immediately the suspension of these measures;

17. Decides to remain seized of the matter.

/...

S/RES/883 (1993)
Page 5

Annex

The following are the items referred to in paragraph 5 of this resolution:

I. Pumps of medium or large capacity whose capacity is equal to or larger
    than 350 cubic metres per hour and drivers (gas turbines and electric
    motors) designed for use in the transportation of crude oil and natural
    gas

II. Equipment designed for use in crude oil export terminals:

    -   Loading buoys or single point moorings (spm)

    -   Flexible hoses for connection between underwater manifolds (plem) and
        single point mooring and floating loading hoses of large sizes (from
        12" to 16")

    -   Anchor chains

III. Equipment not specially designed for use in crude oil export terminals but
     which because of their large capacity can be used for this purpose:

    -   Loading pumps of large capacity (4,000 m3/h) and small head (10 bars)

    -   Boosting pumps within the same range of flow rates

    -   Inline pipe line inspection tools and cleaning devices (i.e. pigging
        tools) (16" and above)

    -   Metering equipment of large capacity (1,000 m3/h and above)

IV. Refinery equipment:

    -   Boilers meeting American Society of Mechanical Engineers 1 standards

    -   Furnaces meeting American Society of Mechanical Engineers 8 standards

    -   Fractionation columns meeting American Society of Mechanical Engineers
        8 standards

    -   Pumps meeting American Petroleum Institute 610 standards

    -   Catalytic reactors meeting American Society of Mechanical Engineers 8
        standards

    -   Prepared catalysts, including the following:

            Catalysts containing platinum
            Catalysts containing molybdenum

V. Spare parts destined for the items in I to IV above.

-----

4. Security Council Resolution 1192 (1998), August 27, 1998

UNITED NATIONS

S

Security Council

Distr.
GENERAL

S/RES/1192 (1998)
27 August 1998

RESOLUTION 1192 (1998)

Adopted by the Security Council at its 3920th meeting,
on 27 August 1998

The Security Council,

Recalling its resolutions 731 (1992) of 21 January 1992, 748 (1992) of 31 March 1992 and 883 (1993) of 11 November 1993,

Noting the report of the independent experts appointed by the Secretary-General (S/1997/991),

Having regard to the contents of the letter dated 24 August 1998 from the Acting Permanent Representatives of the United Kingdom of Great Britain and Northern Ireland and of the United States of America to the Secretary-General (S/1998/795),

Noting also, in light of the above resolutions, the communications of the Organization of African Unity, the League of Arab States, the Non-Aligned Movement and the Islamic Conference (S/1994/373, S/1995/834, S/1997/35, S/1997/273, S/1997/406, S/1997/497, S/1997/529) as referred to in the letter of 24 August 1998,

Acting under Chapter VII of the Charter of the United Nations,

1. Demands once again that the Libyan Government immediately comply with the above-mentioned resolutions;

2. Welcomes the initiative for the trial of the two persons charged with the bombing of Pan Am flight 103 ("the two accused") before a Scottish court sitting in the Netherlands, as contained in the letter dated 24 August 1998 from the Acting Permanent Representatives of the United Kingdom of Great Britain and Northern Ireland and of the United States of America ("the initiative") and its attachments, and the willingness of the Government of the Netherlands to cooperate in the implementation of the initiative;

3. Calls upon the Government of the Netherlands and the Government of the United Kingdom to take such steps as are necessary to implement the initiative,

/...

S/RES/1192 (1998)
Page 2

including the conclusion of arrangements with a view to enabling the court described in paragraph 2 to exercise jurisdiction in the terms of the intended Agreement between the two Governments, attached to the said letter of 24 August 1998;

4. Decides that all States shall cooperate to this end, and in particular that the Libyan Government shall ensure the appearance in the Netherlands of the two accused for the purpose of trial by the court described in paragraph 2, and that the Libyan Government shall ensure that any evidence or witnesses in Libya are, upon the request of the court, promptly made available at the court in the Netherlands for the purpose of the trial;

5 Requests the Secretary-General, after consultation with the Government of the Netherlands, to assist the Libyan Government with the physical arrangements for the safe transfer of the two accused from Libya direct to the Netherlands;

6. Invites the Secretary-General to nominate international observers to attend the trial;

7. Decides further that, on the arrival of the two accused in the Netherlands, the Government of the Netherlands shall detain the two accused pending their transfer for the purpose of trial before the court described in paragraph 2;

8. Reaffirms that the measures set forth in its resolutions 748 (1992) and 883 (1993) remain in effect and binding on all Member States, and in this context reaffirms the provisions of paragraph 16 of resolution 883 (1993), and decides that the aforementioned measures shall be suspended immediately if the Secretary-General reports to the Council that the two accused have arrived in the Netherlands for the purpose of trial before the court described in paragraph 2 or have appeared for trial before an appropriate court in the United Kingdom or the United States, and that the Libyan Government has satisfied the French judicial authorities with regard to the bombing of UTA 772;

9. Expresses its intention to consider additional measures if the two accused have not arrived or appeared for trial promptly in accordance with paragraph 8;

10. Decides to remain seized of the matter.

-----

5. Letter to Bill Richardson, United States Permanent Representative to the United Nations, from Members of the United States House and Senate, May 19, 1997

May 19, 1997

The Honorable Bill Richardson
Permanent Representative to the United Nations
799 United Nations Plaza
New York, NY 10017

Dear Bill:

We are writing to inform you of our strong interest in the maintenance of, and strengthening of, United Nations sanctions against Libya.

As you know, the United Nations Security Council imposed, and regularly reviews, sanctions against Libya for the terrorist attacks on Pan Am Flight 103 and UTA Flight 772. Four hundred forty-one citizens from many countries, including 196 Americans were killed on these flights, and we strongly believe that we must make every effort to bring the perpetrators to justice.

We support stronger United Nations sanctions against Libya in that regard. The mild economic sanctions currently in place have clearly failed to bring to trial the two Libyans indicted for the Pan Am bombing, and Libya continues to provide them safe harbor. That being the case, there is no reason to believe that the current sanctions will be sufficient to persuade the Government of Libya to turn them over for trial in the future.

Furthermore, we are concerned that the U.N. sanctions against Libya are often broken with no repercussions for, and no public pressure brought to bear on, those responsible.

We believe that an international oil embargo is the only sanction likely to bring about Libyan compliance with Security Council Resolutions and we would encourage the United States to introduce such a resolution in the Security Council and to urge the members of the Security Council to support such a resolution, which is of utmost importance to the United States.

The families of the victims have waited more than eight years for justice—they should not have to wait any longer.

Respectfully,

Spencer Abraham	Byron L. Dorgan	Dirk Kempthorne	Daniel Patrick Moynihan
John Ashcroft	Richard J. Durbin	Edward M. Kennedy	Don Nickles
Joseph R. Biden, Jr.	Lauch Faircloth	John F. Kerry	Jack Reed
Christopher S. Bond	Russell D. Feingold	Herb Kohl	Harry Reid
Barbara Boxer	Dianne Feinstein	Mary L. Landrieu	Charles S. Robb
Dale Bumpers	Wendell H. Ford	Frank R. Lautenberg	Rick Santorum
Robert C. Byrd	John Glenn	Patrick J. Leahy	Paul S. Sarbanes
John F. Chafee	Phil Gramm	Carl Levin	Bob Smith
Dan Coats	Charles E. Grassley	Joseph I. Lieberman	Arlen Specter
Thad Cochran	Orrin G. Hatch	Trent Lott	Robert G. Torricelli
Kent Conrad	Jesse Helms	Connie Mack	John W. Warner
Alfonse M. D'Amato	Ernest F. Hollings	John McCain	Paul Wellstone
Mike DeWine	Kay Bailey Hutchison	Barbara A. Mikulski	
Christopher J. Dodd	James M. Jeffords	Carol Moseley-Braun	

6. Letter from Libyan Ambassador Abuzed Dorda to United States Senator Edward F. Kennedy, May 28, 1997

No.:

28 May 1997

The Honorable Senator Edward F. Kennedy
United States Congress
Washington D.C. 20515

Dear Senator Kennedy,

Mr. Bill Richardson, the United States Ambassador to the United Nations has announced that he has received a letter signed by 53 members of the U.S. Senate, led by you, demanding that he finds means to force Libya to achieve justice.

I believe that it is only fair that you hear directly from us of what would be useful in this regard, since it has become very obvious, that neither you nor the American public opinion have become aware of the details of the steps that Libya has been taking in order to speed-up the investigation of the two suspects as well as their trial.

We have exerted every effort possible in order to promptly uncover the real perpetrators of this repugnant crime. But, regrettably we found nobody who was willing to listen to us. And this confirms to us that the U.S. Administration's real interest is not finding the real perpetrators and punishing them, but using this incident, for well-known political ends against the regime in Libya.

Because, I feel that you have taken a personal interest in this incident, as well as in its victims and their families, my desire to write to you became stronger, to bring to your attention all the initiatives that we have put forward, and to assure you of my country's total readiness to immediately engage in the process of investigations and trial. I am personally ready to enter into negotiations over the procedural details in this question. I believe that as you have accepted the rationale and appreciated the importance of transferring the venue of the trial of the suspect in the Oklahoma City bombing, you would appreciate and understand the reasons for our demands that an agreement should be reached to hold the trial of the two Libyan suspects in a third country, where the necessary conditions for a fair and just trial can be guaranteed.

The economic boycott will not solve the problem, it would only make the waiting of the families of the victims longer than they have already endured. And, I can say in this regard, that they would be waiting for the rest of their lives, to no avail. For if sanctions, embargoes and other related measures were to achieve any results, they would have done so with Cuba, which is very close to your shores.

Economic boycotts are American measures. And are basically damaging to the U.S. economy. The U.S. is the prime loser, since there is always someone else who would replace the U.S. in satisfying the needs of Libya and countries other than Libya. Sooner or later the Americans would come to realize this.

Let us hope as we look to the future with optimism and confidence that constructive dialogue and cooperation would prevail in our relations, not rupture and boycotts. That cooperation will flourish in all economic fields; oil and gas, industry and trade, building and construction, health and education, which would benefit our two countries and peoples, instead of rupture and boycotts that will only benefit others, as is well-known, are many.

For all these reasons, I am enclosing herewith a summary of all the initiatives that we have advanced.

As we look forward to receiving your response, we wish to reiterate that we stand ready to start negotiations over the appropriate venue of the trial and discuss its arrangements, including the surrender of the two suspects to a third party or to a U.N. authority that is agreed upon, as soon as we receive your government's acceptance or that of your Ambassador to the United Nations.

I would be grateful if you would make this letter available to your other colleagues, the members of the U.S. Senate who joined in signing the letter I referred to above.

Respectfully yours,

ABUZED OMAR DORDA
Ambassador Extraordinary and Plenipotentiary
Permanent Representative of the Libyan Arab
Jamahiriya to the United Nations

7. Draft letter from South African president Nelson Mandela to Muammar Qadhafi, Undated but Circa January 1999

Draft Letter for President Mandela
(approved by the President)

My Dear Brother Leader

It is our great honour to convey to you our warmest fraternal greetings and to extend our good wishes to yourself, your family and the people of Libya during this holy month of Ramadan. You are in this time constantly in our thoughts as a fraternal people, just as we think of the entire people of the Maghreb and the Middle-East. It is our fond and sincere wish that lasting peace shall at last be found for our brothers and sisters who in so many cases suffered so long and so much, not only in those regions but all over our continent and in the world. We pray together with you, My Brother Leader, that this last year before we enter into the new century may see us mobilising the efforts of leaders across the world to work for peaceful and just settlements to the various conflicts which are still plaguing the lives of too many of our people across the globe.

We are very mindful and appreciative, My Brother Leader, of your own concern for assisting in bringing peace, stability and progress to our continent. Your various meetings with other leaders from the continent to address some of the major conflicts, bear testimony to that concern. It has been our privilege to interact with you on some of those issues and we must take this opportunity of again thanking you for your understanding and cooperation. We are very grateful for your understanding of South Africa's position borne out of our own experience that inclusive negotiations between erstwhile enemies were the only way of leading our country out of long and destructive conflict. We know, My Brother Leader, that with regards to, for example, the Democratic Republic of the Congo, you share our view that a process towards an inclusive political settlement is what is ultimately needed in that situation.

My Brother Leader, we write to you on this occasion particularly to raise once more the matter about which we have been exchanging ideas in our personal meetings, telephonic discussions and through our personal envoys; we refer to the matter of Lockerbie.

Since our last discussion, Brother Leader, and following your kind meeting with our personal envoy, Professor Jakes Gerwel, we consulted with the Secretary-General of the United Nations and had the opportunity of speaking to His Royal Highness, Crown Prince Abdullah bin Abdulaziz Al-Saud, as well as His Royal Highness Prince Bandar bin Sultan, who together with Professor Gerwel represented the Crown Prince and myself in the efforts to resolve the Lockerbie matter.

My Dear Brother Leader, it is our considered view that the time has come for us to finally move this matter towards a resolution. The Crown Prince and ourselves have brought our energies to bear on this matter in an attempt to have the United Kingdom and the United States agree after a decade to have the trial of the suspects held in a neutral country. The envoys of the Crown Prince and ourselves have represented your viewpoints regarding aspects of the eventual agreement between the governments of the United Kingdom and the Netherlands to those governments and to the Secretary-General of the UN. The Crown Prince and myself, personally and through our envoys, have implored the Secretary-General to involve himself in the clarification of those matters in the agreement which might still have stood in the way of a resolution of this long-standing dispute.

It is against that background, My Brother Leader, that I, together with His Royal Highness the Crown Prince, now wish to appeal to you to accept the Secretary-General's proposals put to yourself, and subsequently explained to the Crown Prince and myself, and to concretely progress by having the suspects delivered to the Netherlands in terms of the agreement. The Crown Prince and I, on behalf of the peoples and governments of our respective countries, can assure you, My Brother Leader, that we shall vigilantly watch over the rest of the process to ensure that the spirit and letter of the agreement are abided with. Our personal envoys with whom you have developed personal relationships, My Brother Leader, shall be at your disposal to ensure our continued and consistent personal involvement.

The time, My Brother Leader, has arrived for our continent to seek to liberate itself from all the constraints on our development. The decade-long restrictions on Libya and its people have not only constrained our friendly brothers and sisters in Libya but have represented a barrier to the development of that region and our common continent in which you, Brother Leader, have such an important role to play. We need now to progress also with regards to a resolution of the Lockerbie matter, and the proposals of the Secretary-General provide a basis for such progress, we believe.

We forward this letter to you as speedily as is possible, but shall strive to have our personal envoy Professor Jakes Gerwel, hopefully together with His Royal Highness Prince Bandar, deliver this letter and that from His Royal Highness the Crown Prince to you personally. We thank you, Brother Leader, for once more receiving them on our behalves.

Please remain assured, My Brother Leader, of our highest consideration.

8. Letter from Prince Abdullah of Saudi Arabia to Muammar Qadhafi, Undated but Circa January 1999

May peace and the blessings and mercy of God be upon you.

At the beginning of the holy month of Ramadan, I have the pleasure to convey to you every good wish and my heartfelt hope that the Almighty will bless this month for all of us in the Arab Islamic nation.

You are well aware of the Kingdom of Saudi Arabia's concern that a solution be found to the issue of the sanctions posed on the Libyan Arab Jamahiriya that will both satisfy you and protect the interests of the Government and people of your country, while at the same time leading to the goal to which we all aspire, namely, the irreversible lifting of those sanctions. Saudi Arabia has therefore gone to great lengths, with your full knowledge, in its mediation efforts with the Governments of the United States of America and the United Kingdom. These efforts have been coordinated with the sustained endeavors made by our friend His Excellency President Nelson Mandela and the timely follow-up of Mr. Kofi Annan, Secretary-General of the United Nations.

After intensive discussions with His Excellency President Mandela and Mr. Annan at the recent Gulf Cooperation Council summit held in Abu Dhabi, and pursuant to the discussions held with officials of the United Kingdom and the United States, we wish to advise you to accept the proposals made by the Secretary-General, which we agree represent the ideal solution to the issue.

Saudi Arabia will continue its indefatigable support for the position of the Libyan Arab Jamahiriya and will make every possible effort to ensure that a just solution is found that is satisfactory to yourself above all, and which will lead to the desired results. We are, furthermore, confident that the Secretary-General will continue to use all his good offices and make every effort to obtain the best possible results, which we hope to see as soon as possible.

May peace and the blessing of god be upon you.

9. Letter from Muammar Qadhafi to South African President Nelson Mandela, February 9, 1999 (in Arabic with English Translation)

بسم الله الرحمن الرحيم

الجماهيرية العربية الليبية
الشعبية الاشتراكية العظمى

أخي العزيز الرئيس نيلسون مانديلا البطل الافريقي التاريخي

بعد السلام .

نتيجة لمجهوداتكم الشكورة ، والأخوة قادة المملكة العربية السعودية
وتتويجا للرحلات المكوكية المضنية للمبعوثين السّاميين لكم الأمير بندر والبروفيسور
جاكس ، ودور السيد كوفي عنان ومساعديه ، تم التوصل الى أرضية صلح أن
تكون أرضية تفاهم ، خالية من المتاريس التى كانت قوية بتسوية المسائل التي
كانت محل بحث بما في ذلك رفع العقوبات ومكان المحاكمة ومحل تنفيذ
الحكم النهائي متى صدر بالادانة وبدو ان الأطراف المعنية بجهودكم
المتواصلة أدركت حسن النية لدى كل منها والصدق في حل هذا المشكل
والفضل يعود لكم في ذلك والى اخوتي قادة المملكة العربية السعودية . ولم
يعد الا صياغة الحل في شكله القانوني النهائي والملزم لكل الأطراف وعدم
الاعتماد على التعهدات الشفهية أو الثنائية ، لأن : القضية أخي الرئيس
العزيز تم اخضاعها لقرارات من مجلس الأمن ، وعليه لابد أن تحل بنفس
الأسلوب .

وتفضلوا أخي الرئيس العزيز بقبول فائق الاحترام ج؛

التقيد : معمر القذافي

التاريخ : 23 شـــــــــوال
الموافق : 9 فبراير 1999 افرنجي

[*English translation:*]

Great Socialist People's
Libyan Arab Jamahiriya

President Nelson Mandela,
historic African hero

Greetings,

As a result of the praiseworthy efforts of yourself and the leaders of Saudi Arabia, and to crown the exhausting shuttle journeys made to you by the high representatives Prince Bandar and Professor Jacks and the role played by Mr. Kofi Anan and his aides, an obstacle-free basis of understanding has been arrived at for settlement of the matters which were under discussion, including the lifting of sanctions, the place of trial, and the place for implementation of the final judgment if found guilty. It seems that, through your unceasing efforts, the parties concerned have shown goodwill and sincerity in resolving this problem, and the credit goes to you and to my colleagues the leaders of Saudi Arabia. There remains only to formulate the solution in its final legal form binding on all parties, and not to rely upon verbal or bilateral undertakings, because, my dear President, the case has been made subject to Security Council resolutions and accordingly must be resolved in the same way.

With my greatest respects,

(signature)
Colonel Muammar Al-Qaddhafi

23 Shawwal/9 February 1999

10. Letter from Kofi A. Annnan, Secretary-General of the United Nations, to Muammar Qadhafi, dated February 17, 1999, Including Attachment.

THE SECRETARY-GENERAL

17 February 1999

Excellency,

I have been greatly encouraged by the reports I have received on the outcome of your recent meetings with the envoys despatched by the leaders of Saudi Arabia and South Africa. In particular, I was very pleased to learn from President Mandela himself about Your Excellency's letter to him dated 9 February 1999 confirming the understanding reached on outstanding issues.

In pursuance of the understanding reached with the envoys, I attach a document setting forth the relevant details thereof. After reviewing this document, the Governments of the United Kingdom and the United States have confirmed to me that they share the understanding reflected therein. It is now my intention to report this understanding to the Security Council without delay to facilitate the immediate implementation of resolution 1192 (1998).

As Your Excellency is aware, the Security Council is due to undertake, on 26 February 1999, a review of the sanctions imposed on the Libyan Arab Jamahiriya. Hence, it would be most helpful if the practical arrangements already agreed upon between the Libyan legal team and my own Legal Counsel could be set in motion before that date.

His Excellency
Colonel Muammar Al-Qadhafi
Leader of the Revolution
Socialist People's Libyan Arab Jamahiriya
Tripoli   =

Excellency,

I am deeply conscious and appreciative of your own personal efforts in seeking solutions to the outstanding issues. It is heartening, indeed, that the efforts made jointly by all concerned, as well as the leaders of South Africa and Saudi Arabia, are now about to result in a satisfactory conclusion.

Please accept, Excellency, the assurances of my highest consideration.

Kofi A. Annan

[Here follows the attachment Annan mentions in paragraph 2 of his letter of 17 February 1999:]

Understanding on the Issues Outstanding from the Point of View of the Libyan Arab Jamahiriya

As provided for in Security Council resolution 1192 (1998) the two persons concerned will be transferred from Libya to the Netherlands and tried under Scottish law before a Scottish court sitting in the Netherlands.

If found guilty, after any necessary appeals process, they will serve their prison sentence in Scotland. If the two are not convicted, they will be free to return to Libya unimpeded.

There is no intention to interview them, or to allow them to be interviewed, about any issue not related to the trial. There will be no deviation from Scottish law which provides that the two persons have the right to refuse to see any police or intelligence officers. The two persons will not be used to undermine the Libyan regime.

The prisoners would be held in a distinct portion of a Scottish prison to provide maximum security. All necessary measures will be taken to ensure the safety and well-being of the two persons, if convicted. This facility will be given a special international designation, and special arrangements will be introduced to provide for a role for the United Nations in monitoring the treatment of the two persons concerned. These arrangements, which will be subject to discussions with the United Nations, will be regularly reviewed by the British Government to ensure that they worked effectively and satisfied the legitimate concerns of all parties.

The two prisoners would have unfettered access to legal and diplomatic representatives. An official Libyan presence in Scotland for that purpose will be allowed. Pursuant to the conditions of imprisonment set out in the relevant Scottish law, religious, health and dietary requirements of the two prisoners would be fully met. Visits by clerics and the supply of religious books would be arranged.

The two prisoners or their representatives will have the right to make representations to the authorities of the United Kingdom if they consider that some aspect of their place of imprisonment was contrary to humanitarian concerns. Any such representation would be very carefully considered by the United Kingdom authorities.

With reference to the measures set forth in Security Council resolutions 748 (1992) and 883 (1993), these measures shall be suspended immediately if the Secretary-General reports to the Council that the two persons concerned have arrived in the Netherlands for the purpose of trial before the Scottish court sitting in the Netherlands. These measures could only be reimposed by a new decision of the Council taken by an affirmative vote of nine Members of the Council, including the concurring votes of all the Permanent Members.

11. Letter from Libyan Foreign Minister Omar Muntasser to Kofi Annan, dated Feb. 19, 1999, in Response to Annan's letter to Colonel Qadhafi (in Arabic with English translation)

Great Socialist People's Libyan Arab Jamahiriya

The General People's Committee of Foreign Liaison and International Cooperation

The Secretary

لما جمرية الروية الرية الليبية الشعبية الاشتراكية العظمى

اللجنة الشعبية العامة

الاتصال الخارجى والتعاون الدولى

الأمين

صاحب السعادة / كوفى عنان
الأمين العام للأمم المتحدة
نيويورك

بعد التحية ،،

أود أن أشير إلى رسالتكم الموجهة للأخ القائد المؤرخة فى
17 فبراير 1999 إفرنجى ، وأتشرف بأن أشكركم على جهودكم
من أجل إيجاد حل لقضية لوكربى .

صاحب السعادة

لاشـك أنكـم تتذكـرون بإننـى فـى لقـائى معكم بمدينـة
سـرت بتاريخ 1998/12/5 إفرنجى ، أثنـاء الحديـث علـى
لنظـام الجماهيرى بليبيا ، أبلغتكـم بـأن الجماهيريـة تتكـون مـن
مؤتمـرات شعبية أساسية تقرر ولجـان شعبية تنفـذ، وأن تنفيـذ
لسياسـة الخارجيـة وفـق النظـام الجماهيـرى مـن المهـام
لمناطـة باللجنة الشعبية العامـة للاتصـال الخـارجى والتعاون
الدولى .

صاحب السعادة

إن مقابلة الأخ قـائد الثورة لمبعوثى رؤساء دول جنـوب
إفريقيا والسعودية تمت فقط لأنهما مبعوثـان من رؤسائهما اللذين
بهماعلاقة أخوية ونضالية خاصة بالأخ القائد .

صاحب السعادة

لقد إطلعنا على الرسالة التى أصابتنا بصدمة شديدة حيث أن بنقطتين اللتين أعتقدنا أننا قد تغلبنا عليهما ووجدنا لهما حلا لم تظهرا حسب الاتفاق النهائى الذى تم مع المبعوثين الامير (بندر بن سلطان) و (جاك غيروز) .

ولا : كان التفاهم أن يتم رفع العقوبات لأن التعليق لا يعتبر عمليا وفعا للعقوبات والنص على التعليق رغم التفاهم الذى تم يجعل من لعقوبات سيفا مسلطا على رقبة الشعب الليبى بالامكان إعادة فرضها فى أية لحظة ، والإشارة إلى أن العقوبات لايمكن إعادة فرضها فقط إلا بقرار جديد لمجلس الأمن بموافقة (9) أعضاء ، ما فى ذلك موافقة جميع الاعضاء الدائمين ، لا يأخذ فى الإعتبار قدرة الولايات المتحدة وبريطانيا داخل المجلس وخير مثال على ذلك الزج بقضية قانونية ، وهى قضية لوكربى فى مجلس الأمن وإعتماد قرارات جائرة 748 ، 883 ، 1192. نحن لا نركن لهذا طلاقا ، فامريكا لا يعوزها جمع اى عدد من الأصوات ترغيبا وترهيبا .

إن ليبيا لا تستجدى رفع العقوبات ، فهو مطلب قانونى وحق مشروع لها وليس منة من أحد ، وهو أمر تم الاتفاق عليه .

ثانيا : أما قضاء المشتبه فيهما العقوبة فى حالة الادانة ، فقد تمت الموافقة على اسكتلندا بناء على التفاهم في مسألة رفع العقوبــــات

على أن يسجنا في مكان يتبع الامم المتحدة وبه قنصلية ليبية تحت
حراسة القبعات الزرقاء ، وهو في الواقع داخل اسكتلندا.

نحن ، يا صاحب السعادة ، في إنتظار قرار ملزم نكل
لاطراف يثبت ما أتفق عليه بشكل نهائى قبل مغادرة المشتبه فيهما
لاراضى الليبية ، ونتمنى أن يكون في أقرب وقت .

وفى الختام ، صاحب السعادة ، نتطلع إلى تدخلكم
لشخصى لتسوية هاتين المسألتين حتى يتم طى ملف هذا الخلاف
نهائيا .

وتفضلوا ، صاحب السعادة ، بقبول فائسق التقدير
والاحترام

عمر مصطفى المنتصر
أمين اللجنة الشعبية العامة للاتصال
الخارجى والتعاون الدولى

حررت بتاريخ 4 ذى القعدة
الموافق 1999/2/19 إفرنجى
un18

[English translation:]

His Excellency Kofi Anan
Secretary General of the United Nations

I would like to draw your attention to your letter addressed to the Brother the Commander dated 17 February 1999 and I have the honor to thank you on your efforts to find a solution to the issue of Lockerbie.

Your Excellency,

There is no doubt that you remember that I had informed you, in our meeting at the city of Sirt on 5/12/1999, during our conversation concerning the Hamahiriya regime in Libya, that the Jamahiriya consists of principal popular assemblies which make the decisions, and popular committees which implement them, and that the implementation of the foreign policy, which is executed in accordance with the Jamahiriya regime, is one of the duties entrusted to the General Popular Committee for External Relations and International Cooperation.

Your Excellency,

The meeting of the Brother, the Commander of the revolution, with the representatives of the Heads of State of South Africa and Saudi Arabia was possible only because they had been sent by their presidents with whom the Brother the Commander has a special fraternal and struggle relationship.

Your Excellency,

We have read your letter which had a great shock on us, because the two issues, which we thought we have overcome them and we had a solution for them, those two issues have not been in accordance with the final agreement which had been concluded with the two representatives; Prince Bandar Sultan and Mr. Jacque Gurwell.

Firstly: the understanding was to lift the sanctions, because the suspension of the sanctions is not practically a lift of the sanctions. To mention the suspension of the sanctions despite the understanding reached, will make the sanctions a real threat to the Libyan people, because the could be re-imposed at any time, and to say that that sanctions could be re-imposed only with a new resolution of the Security Council and with the approval of 9 members, including the approval of all permanent members, does no take into account the power of the United States and Britain in the Council, and a very good example on that is the inclusion of a legal case, such as Lockerbie, in the Security Council and the adoption of the unjust resolutions 748, 883, and 1192. We do not depend upon this matter at all, because America is capable to mobilize any number of votes by applying the policy of the stick and the carrot.

Libya does not beg for the lifting of sanctions, because this is a legal request and a legitimate right and it is not a favor from anyone, and this matter had been agreed upon.

Secondly: as for the imprisonment of the suspects in case they are guilty, Scotland had been accepted in accordance with the understanding reached on the question of lifting the sanctions, on condition that they be incarcerated in any place belonging to the United Nations and which has a Libyan consulate, under the guard of the blue helmets, and it should be, indeed, inside Scotland.

Your Excellency,

We are awaiting the adoption of a resolution which must be binding on all parties and which will establish what had been agreed upon in a final form before the departure of the suspects from Libya, and we hope this would be as soon as possible.

In conclusion, we, Your Excellency, are looking forward for your personal intervention to settle those two questions, in order to put an end to this dispute once and for all.

Please accept, Your Excellency, our highest appreciation and respect.

(Signed) Omar Moustafa Al-Mountasser
Secretary of the General Popular Committee for
External Relations and International Cooperation
Date: 19/2/1992

12. Letter from Kofi Annan to Omar Muntasser, dated Feb. 25, 1999

THE SECRETARY-GENERAL

25 February 1999

Excellency,

I have the honour to refer to your letter of 19 February 1999 responding to mine of 17 February 1999.

Your letter addresses two specific issues, i.e. the lifting of sanctions and the place and conditions of imprisonment, should the accused be convicted. It also asks for my personal intervention to help settle these issues to the satisfaction of your Government and for a decision to be taken by me that will be binding on all parties.

With regard to the first issue, the last paragraph of the annex to my letter of 17 February 1999 recalls the relevant procedures set out in resolutions 883 (1993) and 1192 (1998). As you are aware, paragraph 16 of resolution 883 (1993) requests me to report to the Council on the compliance of the Libyan Arab Jamahiriya with the remaining provisions of the resolutions. Should my report conclude that the Libyan Arab Jamahiriya has complied in every possible way with these provisions, I would expect that the Council would adopt a favourable decision with respect to the lifting of the sanctions.

His Excellency
Mr. Omar Mustafa Muntasser
Secretary of the General People's
  Committee for Foreign Liaison
  and International Cooperation
  of the Socialist People's
  Libyan Arab Jamahiriya
Tripoli

Turning to the second issue, it continues to be my firmly held view that the arrangements described in the third, fourth and fifth paragraphs of the annex to my letter of 17 February 1999 would provide comprehensive and adequate guarantees for the well-being of the accused during their period of incarceration, should they be found guilty. As indicated in the annex, these arrangements would be subject to discussions with the United Nations. I stand ready personally to see to it that such discussions result in the best possible arrangements for United Nations monitoring.

With regard to your reference to a Libyan Consulate, I am informed that the British authorities are ready to give favourable consideration to this matter and to discuss it directly with the Libyan authorities.

The meetings held between the Libyan legal team and my Legal Counsel in October and November of 1998 served to clarify the legal issues to the satisfaction of all concerned. It is my assessment that we have now reached the point where a further postponement of the implementation of resolution 1192 (1998) could serve no useful purpose and could not be justified. It would be my expectation, therefore, that in light of the additional clarifications set out in this letter, the Libyan side will now be in a position to indicate a firm date for the transfer.

Please accept, Excellency, the assurances of my highest consideration.

Kofi A. Annan

13. Letter from Omar Muntasser to Kofi Annan, dated March 19, 1999 (in Arabic with English translation)

بسم الله الرحمن الرحيم

الجماهيرية العربية الليبية
الشعبية الاشتراكية العظمى

معالي الامّين العام للامم المتحدة
السيد / كوفى عنـــا ن

بعد التحية ،،

أود أن أعبر لمعاليكم عن شكر وتقدير الجماهيرية العظمى
لجهودكم الطيبة والحثيثة وكذلك للرئيس نلسون مانديلا رئيس
جمهورية جنوب افريقيا وخادم الحرمين الشريفين الملك فهـــد
بن عبد العزيز آل سعود ملك المملكة العربية السعودية وصاحب
السمو الملكى الامير عبد الله بن عبد العزيز لاجل التوصل الــى
حل عادل لقضية لوكربى ، والتى عانت الجماهيرية من أثرها بــلا
ذنب اقترفته لاكثر من عشر سنوات .

ان الجماهيرية توافق على مثول المتهمين أمام المحكمة فـــــى
(6 الطير / ابريل / 1999 ف) بناء على ما اتفق عليه فى النقاط
التالية : ــ

1 ــ تأتى محكمة اسكتلندية الى هولندا بغرض اجراء المحاكمـــة
للمتهمين وفق القانون الاسكتلندى فى اطار ما اتفق عليه
الفريق القانونى وبحضور مراقبين دوليين يعينهم الامــــين
العام للامم المتحدة وبالتشاور مع جمهورية جنوب افريقيـا
والمملكة العربية السعودية .

2 ــ قضاء المتهمين مدة العقوبة فى حالة الادانة فى اسكتلندا
تحت اشراف الامم المتحدة ورعاية القنصلية الليبية فـــى
اسكتلندا وحسب ما اتفق عليه مع الحكومة البريطانية مـــن
ترتيبات .

/ .. .

/ 2 /

3 — يتم تجميد العقوبات فورا على الجماهيرية حال وصول
المتهمين الى هولندا وترفع العقوبات نهائيا حال تقديم
الأمين العام تقريره بالتزام الجماهيرية بقرارات مجلس
الأمن خلال تسعين يوما .

كما يطيب لي التذكير مرة أخرى بالآتى :ـ

1 — ما سبق وأن أعلنته الجماهيرية مرارا من وقوفها ضد
الارهاب بكافة أشكاله وادانتها لكل الاعمال الارهابية ،
حيث أن الجماهيرية ضحية لمثل هذه الأعمال التى لا تقرها
الأديان السماوية ولا القوانين الدولية والانسانية .

2 — تتعهد الجماهيرية بالتعاون مع اجراءات التحقيق
والمحاكمة فى حدود التشريعات والقوانين السائدة بالجماهيرية
العربية الليبية الشعبية الاشتراكية العظمى .

3 — تكرر الجماهيرية ما سبق وأن أعلنته بشأن التعويضات
فى حالة ادانة المتهمين من قبل المحكمة وصدور قرار
نهائى بذلك من قبل المحكمة لذا فان الجماهيرية فى
اطار ما ذكر أعلاه ترى أن يصدر قرار من مجلس الأمن
بهذه الترتيبات والالتزامات الملزمة لكل الاطراف المعنية .

عمر المنتصر
امين اللجنة الشعبية العامة
للاتصال الخارجى والتعاون
الدولى

حررت بتاريخ : 2 ذى الحجة
المؤافق : 1999.3.19 افرنجى .

[English translation:]

19 March 1999

Mr. Kofi Annan,
Secretary-General of the United Nations,
New York

Dr. Mr. Annan,

I would like to express to you, Your Excellency, the Jamahiriya's thanks and appreciation for the sincere and good efforts of yourself as well as those of His Excellency President Mandela of South Africa, and of the Custodian of the Two Holy Mosques King Fahad bin Abdulaziz al Saud and His Royal Highness Crown Prince Abdullah bin Abudlaziz al Saud of the Kingdom of Saudi Arabia, to find a just solution to the Lockerbie issue, from which Libya has suffered for more than ten years.

The Jamahiriya agrees to ensure that the two suspects would be available for the Secretary General of the United Nations to take custody of them on or before 6 April 1999 for their appearance before the Court. This is based on the following agreed points:

1. A Scottish court shall be convened in the Netherlands for the purpose of trying the two suspects in accordance with Scottish law and based on the agreement reached between the legal experts of the United Nations and Libya, and with the presence of international observers appointed by the Secretary-General of the United Nations, and also in consultation with the Republic of South Africa and the Kingdom of Saudi Arabia.
2. The suspects if convicted will serve their prison sentence in Scotland under UN supervision and with assured access to a Libyan Consulate to be established in Scotland in accordance with the arrangements reached with the British Government.
3. The sanctions imposed on the Jamahiriya will be frozen immediately upon the arrival of the two suspects in the Netherlands. The sanctions will be lifted upon submission of the Secretary-General's Report to the Security Council within 90 days stating that the Jamahiriya has complied with the Security Council's resolutions.

Excellency, I would like to bring the following once again to your attention:

1. The Jamahiriya, as it has stated before on numerous occasions, opposes all forms of terrorism and condemns all acts of such heinous criminality. As you know the Jamahiriya itself is victim of such terrorist acts which no religious, human or international laws, could condone.
2. The Jamahiriya pledges co-operation within the framework of Libyan laws and legislation with the investigation, the procedures and the trial.
3. The Jamahiriya reiterates what it had previously declared regarding compensation in the event of the two suspects being found guilty by the court and a final verdict being reached.

In the light of the above, the Jamahiriya is of the view that the Security Council should pass a resolution with regard to this arrangement in a form binding on all concerned parties.

Omar Muntasser, Secretary of the General People's Committee for Foreign Liaison and International Co-operation.

14. U.N. Document S/1999/378, April 5, 1999: U.N. Secretary-General's Report of the Handover of the Libyan Defendants to the Scottish Court in the Netherlands

UNITED NATIONS

S

 Security Council

Distr.
GENERAL

S/1999/378
5 April 1999
ENGLISH
ORIGINAL: FRENCH

LETTER DATED 5 APRIL 1999 FROM THE SECRETARY-GENERAL ADDRESSED
TO THE PRESIDENT OF THE SECURITY COUNCIL

This letter constitutes the report to be submitted pursuant to paragraph 8 of Security Council resolution 1192 (1998).

On 27 August 1998, the Security Council adopted resolution 1192 (1998), in which it welcomed the initiative for the trial of the two persons charged with the bombing of Pan Am flight 103 before a Scottish court sitting in the Netherlands, as contained in the letter dated 24 August 1998 from the Acting Permanent Representatives of the United Kingdom of Great Britain and Northern Ireland and of the United States of America and its attachments, and the willingness of the Government of the Netherlands to cooperate in the implementation of the initiative.

In that resolution, the Security Council called upon the Government of the Netherlands and the Government of the United Kingdom to take such steps as were necessary, including the conclusion of arrangements with a view to enabling the court sitting in the Netherlands to exercise jurisdiction in respect of the trial of the two persons charged with the bombing of Pan Am flight 103. As has already been reported, that request has already been met. On 18 September 1998, the Government of the Netherlands and the Government of the United Kingdom signed an agreement concerning a trial in the Netherlands before a Scottish court, and subsequently they enacted the necessary legislation to give effect to the agreement. I should like to express my deep appreciation to both Governments for their willingness, in the interest of finding a constructive resolution to the matter at hand, to take this unprecedented step enabling a national court of one country to conduct a trial in another country.

By resolution 1192 (1998), the Council further requested the Secretary-General, after consultation with the Government of the Netherlands, to assist the Libyan Government with the physical arrangements for the safe transfer of the two accused from the Libyan Arab Jamahiriya direct to the Netherlands.

I am pleased to inform the Security Council that, as requested in the resolution, all the necessary assistance has been provided to the Libyan Government and that today, 5 April 1999, the two accused have safely arrived in the Netherlands on board a United Nations aircraft. During the flight the two accused were accompanied by my representative, Mr. Hans Corell, the Legal

S/1999/378
English
Page 2

Counsel, who has been in charge of the operation. After the aircraft landed at 9.45 a.m., New York time, at Valkenburg airport in the Netherlands, the two accused were detained by the Dutch authorities, as provided for in paragraph 7 of Security Council resolution 1192 (1998), pending their transfer for the purpose of trial before the Scottish court sitting in the Netherlands.

I am also pleased to report to the Security Council that I have been informed by the French authorities through a letter dated 13 October 1998 from the Permanent Representative of France to the United Nations that in regard to the requests in the letter from the French authorities dated 20 December 1991 (A/46/825-S/23306), in reporting to the Council under paragraph 8 of Security Council resolution 1192 (1998), I might indicate that the conditions set forth in resolution 1192 (1998) had been met, without prejudice to the other requests concerning the bombing of Pan Am flight 103.

Today's development would not have been possible without the demonstration of goodwill on the part of all the parties concerned and without their commitment to resolving all the issues related to the implementation of Security Council resolution 1192 (1998) in a satisfactory and mutually acceptable manner.

As has already been reported informally to the members of the Security Council, given the complex and sensitive nature of the arrangements foreseen in resolution 1192 (1998), issues of both a political and legal nature were raised by the Libyan Government regarding the implementation of the resolution. Those issues needed to be clarified to the satisfaction of all the parties concerned in order to achieve understanding on the implementation of the resolution.

Legal issues as well as practical arrangements related to the implementation of the resolution were discussed in October and November 1998 between the United Nations Legal Counsel, Mr. Hans Corell, and a Libyan legal team, headed by Mr. Kamel Hassan Maghur. They were resolved to the satisfaction of all those concerned, with the assistance of the Governments of France, the Netherlands, the United Kingdom and the United States. I should like to express my appreciation to the Libyan legal team and to the States concerned for the constructive manner in which they addressed the complex issues before them.

With a view to achieving progress in resolving some of the sensitive political issues of concern to the Libyan Government, on 5 December 1998, I travelled to the Libyan Arab Jamahiriya and had fruitful and constructive discussions with the Leader of the Revolution, Colonel Muammar Qaddafi, and senior Libyan officials. Following my visit, I sought the assistance of the Governments of South Africa and Saudi Arabia, with which I have been constantly in close touch to coordinate our joint efforts in search of a fair solution to the pending issues.

I should like, therefore, to express my appreciation to the Government of the Libyan Arab Jamahiriya and all the other parties concerned for their willingness to demonstrate sufficient flexibility in arriving at a mutually acceptable solution. I should like, in particular, to express gratitude to the Governments of Saudi Arabia and South Africa for their efforts and assistance.

/...

S/1999/378
English
Page 3

Paragraph 8 of Security Council resolution 1192 (1998) provides, inter alia, that if the Secretary-General reports to the Council that the two accused have arrived in the Netherlands for the purpose of trial before the Scottish court sitting in the Netherlands and that the Libyan Government has satisfied the French judicial authorities with regard to the bombing of UTA 772, the measures set forth in Security Council resolutions 748 (1992) and 883 (1993) shall be suspended immediately. As noted above, these requirements of the resolution have been met.

Paragraph 8 of resolution 1192 (1998) also reaffirms paragraph 16 of Security Council resolution 883 (1993), which provides that the Secretary-General is requested to report, within 90 days of the date of the suspension of the aforementioned measures, on compliance by the Libyan Arab Jamahiriya with the remaining provisions of Security Council resolutions 731 (1992) and 748 (1992) so that the measures might be lifted immediately if the Secretary-General reports that the Libyan Arab Jamahiriya has fully complied with those provisions.

Therefore, following the suspension of the measures referred to above, I shall proceed as expeditiously as possible with the preparation of this report. The Libyan Arab Jamahiriya has already provided extensive information and the necessary assurances on this matter, including to the Security Council.

Finally, let me also express the hope that the spirit of cooperation now established, will be maintained in future and that the start of the trial will mark the beginning of a process leading to the normalization of relations among all parties concerned for the benefit of the international community as a whole.

Accept, Sir, the assurances of my highest consideration.

(Signed)   Kofi A. ANNAN

-----

15. Letter from Hans Corell, United Nations Legal Advisor, to Kamel Hassan Maghur, Head of Libyan Legal Team, dated March 26, 1999, and Annexes:

$\frac{5}{622}$

UNITED NATIONS **NATIONS UNIES**

POSTAL ADDRESS-ADRESSE POSTALE: UNITED NATIONS, N.Y. 10017
TELEPHONE NO: (212)-963-1234; FAX NO. (212)-963-3155

26 March 1999

Your Excellency,

I have the honour to refer to the discussions that the two of us, assisted by the members of the Libyan Legal Team and the two staff members of my Office, had at the United Nations Headquarters in New York from 1 to 21 October and subsequently from 9 to 13 November regarding the implementation of Security Council resolution 1192 (1998) of 27 August 1998. In paragraph 5 of that resolution. the Council "requests the Secretary-General, after consultation with the Government of the Netherlands, to assist the Libyan Government with the physical arrangements for the safe transfer of the two accused from Libya direct to the Netherlands".

At the outset, I would like to express my deep appreciation to you personally and to the members of your Team for the professional and constructive atmosphere in which our discussions have been conducted. It has been a great pleasure to meet and work with you and other members of the Libyan Legal Team. I sincerely believe that our efforts have been an important and positive step towards the successful implementation of Security Council resolution 1192 (1998).

In the course of our deliberations the Libyan Legal Team sought clarifications regarding various aspects of the implementation of Security Council resolution 1192 (1998). This request was conveyed by me to the parties concerned, namely France, the Netherlands. the United Kingdom and the United States of America. In this regard I noted the fact that when that request for clarifications was conveyed to the parties concerned you agreed to proceed with that request as formulated on the basis of the understanding that it was without prejudice to the position of

Mr. Kamel Hassan Maghur
The Head of the Libyan Legal Team
c/o The Permanent Mission of the Socialist People's
Libyan Arab Jamahiriya to the United Nations

$$\frac{6}{622}$$

2

the Libyan legal Team on the matters reflected in the first section of the paper containing the request. The information provided by the parties concerned in response to the above request was conveyed by me to you and other members of the Libyan Legal Team. This led to some further requests for clarifications and to additional responses. Given the complex and sensitive nature of the matters at issue and in order to avoid any misunderstanding of what transpired from our discussions, as agreed, I provide herewith a detailed record of the clarifications given in response to the requests made by the Libyan Legal Team by the parties concerned regarding the implementation of Security Council resolution 1192 (1998).

On 5 October 1998 I forwarded, as agreed, to the competent authorities of France. the Netherlands, the United Kingdom and the United States a paper entitled "Request for clarification expressed by the Libyan legal team regarding the implementation of Security Council resolution 1192 (1998)", contained in Annex 1 to this letter, reflecting questions raised by the Libyan Legal Team at the start of our discussions with regard to the implementation of the aforementioned resolution.

At our meeting on 14 October 1998 I handed over to you a message stating that "I have been informed by the French authorities that the Secretary-General, in reporting under paragraph 8 of Security Council resolution 1192 (1998), 'pourrait indiquer que les conditions figurant dans le résolution 1192 ont été remplies. sans préjudice des autres demandes concernant l'attentat contre le vol 103 de la Panam'".

On 15 October 1998 I handed over to you copies of the responses provided by the United States the United Kingdom and the Netherlands, contained respectively in Annexes 2, 3 and 4 to this letter. I also informed you at that meeting that in his cover letter, dated 13 October 1998. the Legal Advisor of the Department of State noted that "the United States has only responded to those requests directed to the United States. However. the United States specifically joins in the additional responses provided by the United Kingdom."

At a meeting held on 16 October 1998, the Libyan Legal Team sought further clarifications regarding the implementation of Security Council resolution 1192 (1998) which were immediately orally conveyed to the competent authorities of the Netherlands, the United Kingdom and the United States.

$$\frac{7}{622}$$

3

On 19 October 1998 I provided you with copies of the supplementary written responses received from the United Kingdom and the United States, contained respectively in Annexes 5 and 6 to this letter. I also informed you about the additional clarifications provided by the competent Dutch authorities which had been conveyed to me orally on 19 October 1998 by a representative of the Dutch Permanent Mission to the United Nations. These clarifications, as recorded by me and my colleagues, are contained in Annex 7 to this letter.

As you know, on 27 October 1998 the Permanent Representative of the Libyan Arab Jamahiriya sent a letter to the President of the Security Council. In paragraph 6 of this letter, the Permanent Representative raised a number of questions related to the implementation of Security Council resolution 1192 (1998). On 30 October 1998 the Permanent Representative of the United Kingdom sent me a letter stating that he had been instructed to forward further clarifications concerning the points raised in paragraph 6 of the aforementioned letter. As these clarifications relate to the subject matter of our discussions, on 10 November I provided you with a copy of those clarifications, which are contained in Annex 8 to this letter.

When we resumed our discussions on 9 November 1998, you asked for additional clarifications on two points which are of particular concern to the Libyan Legal Team. The response that I conveyed to you at a meeting on 10 November 1998 after consultations with the competent authorities of the United Kingdom and the United States, is contained in Annex 9 to this letter.

The foregoing reflects what transpired during our discussions conducted with a view to facilitating the implementation of Security Council resolution 1192 (1998) and was stated in a draft of the present letter which I handed over to you at out meeting on 12 November 1998.

In the light of the additional information provided to me today by your Ambassador Dorda. I took note of the fact that the Libyan doctor on your team will need to be accompanied on the plane by a nurse and that. therefore. the Libyan team accompaning the two persons concerned will consist of seven people. Furthermore. according to the information, conveyed by Ambassador Dorda. the Libyan authorities cannot take any responsibility for the security of the plane. as the responsibility for the safety of the plane rests with the United Nations and the

$$\frac{8}{622}$$

4

country providing the plane. I take note of this information on the understanding that the competent Libyan authorities remain responsible for taking such security measures, as may be required, to ensure the safety of the plane in Libya.

Please, accept, Excellency, the assurances of my highest consideration.

Hans Corell
Under-Secretary-General
for Legal Affairs
The Legal Counsel

ANNEX 1. REQUEST FOR CLARIFICATION EXPRESSED BY
THE LIBYAN LEGAL TEAM REGARDING THE IMPLEMENTATION
OF SECURITY COUNCIL RESOLUTION 1192 (1998)

Three Matters of Main Concern

Would it be possible to ensure that despite the provisions of Article 29, paragraph 5 of the UK-Netherlands Agreement, the Agreement will not be amended to change its object and purpose of having a trial by a Scottish Court sitting in the Netherlands or to allow for the extradition of the two accused to the territory of either the United States or the United Kingdom?

Would it be possible to ensure that given the provisions of Article 16, paragraph 2 (b) of the UK-Netherlands Agreement, the accused will not be asked to consent to be transferred outside the Netherlands until the completion of the trial?

What are the legal grounds for the United Kingdom's insistence that, if the two accused are found guilty, the sentence will be served in Scotland and despite the provisions of Article 16, paragraph 2(b) of the UK-Netherlands Agreement, would it be possible to arrange for the accused, if convicted, to serve their term in the Netherlands, Libya, or any other third acceptable country instead of the United Kingdom?

Clarifications Sought from the Netherlands

Would it be possible for the lawyers of the accused to visit the location of the detention and the court facilities in the Netherlands where the trial will be held?

At which airport will the plane with the accused land in the Netherlands?

What procedures will be followed upon the arrival of the accused in the Netherlands, in particular, in the light of the fact that they expect to be accompanied on the plane by at least one lawyer and one family member each, as well as a doctor and possibly by an observe from a human right organization? Under what law will the accused by detained by the Dutch authorities? Will they be handcuffed upon their arrival?

Where will the accused by held in the Netherlands during the detention by the Dutch authorities and how will their safety by guaranteed? Will the accused by held in detention with other detainees or will they be in a separate detention facility?

What assurances could be obtained from the Dutch authorities that no authorities of a third country or other authorities, except for the Dutch authorities responsible for their detention, and members of the defence team, doctors and relatives, will have access to the accused during their detention by the Dutch authorities?

How long will the accused be detained by the Dutch authorities before they are transferred for purposes of the trial to the Scottish Court sitting in the Netherlands?

Will the Dutch authorities alert the media and allow it to be present at the airport?

Will the Dutch authorities undertake to issue multiple entry/exit visas to enable the members of the defence team of the accused to exit and re-enter the Netherlands as the need arises in their efforts to conduct and effective defence?

Will the Dutch authorities undertake to issue multiple entry/exit visas to a medical doctor accompanying the accused and to the family members of the accused who wish to attend the trial?

What protection will the lawyers of the accused and the documentation used by them enjoy in the Netherlands? Will their papers be protected from search and seizure? Will they enjoy the same protection as the Dutch lawyers have during court proceedings?

Will the Dutch authorities issue the necessary visas to all witnesses identified by the defence team?

Clarifications Sought from the United Kingdom

When, approximately, will the Scottish Court be ready for the trial in the Netherlands?

When will the UK announce the appointment of the three judges of the Scottish Court sitting in the Netherlands and, in the meantime, can the lawyers of the accused be provided with the list of eligible judges from which the members of the Court will be appointed?

Given the provisions of Article 1, paragraph (j) of the UK-Netherlands Agreement, what arrangements could be made to allow the foreign lawyers, who are members of the accused's legal defence team, to participate in the defence of the accused in the Scottish Court?

How frequently will relatives of the accused be allowed to visit them during the trial?

Will the British authorities within the framework of law provide the lawyers of the accused, including those who are not Scottish solicitors and advocates, with a reasonable opportunity to reproduce and/or examine the sealed materials when they are released?

Clarifications Sought from the UK and the USA

Will the UK and the USA ensure that any evidence or witnesses in their territory or under their control are, upon the request of the Scottish Court, made available at the Netherlands in accordance with their respective laws?

Will the UK and the USA undertake to issue visas to the lawyers of the accused so that they could have access to witnesses and documents in their territory or under their control identified by the Prosecution or the Defence if they are not available in the Netherlands?

Clarifications Sought from the UK, the USA and France

Since the French judicial authorities have stated their satisfaction with regard to the bombing of UTA 772 (S/1997/858), will the measures set forth in Security Council resolutions 748 (1992) and 883 (1993) be immediately suspended upon the arrival of the two accused int he Netherlands as provided for in paragraph 8 of Security Council resolution 1192 (1998)?

ANNEX 2. [RESPONSES TO] REQUEST FOR CLARIFICATION EXPRESSED BY THE LIBYAN LEGAL TERM REGARDING THE IMPLEMENTATION OF SECURITY COUNCIL RESOLUTION 1192 (1998) [BY THE UNITED KINGDOM, THE UNITED STATES, AND FRANCE]

Answers by the Government of the United Kingdom

Three Matters of Main Concern

Question One

The purpose of Article 29 (5) of the Netherlands-United Kingdom Agreement is only to enable amendments of a technical nature to be made. It cannot be used to amend the Agreement in any way to change its object and purpose, since to do so would amount to a breach of Resolution 1192. The text of the Agreement was communicated to the Secretary-General, and then to the Security Council, by the letter from the Acting Permanent Representatives of the United Kingdom and of the United States of 24 August 1998 (S/1998/795). This is referred to in the preamble to Resolution 1192, and in operative paragraph 2 which welcomes the initiative 'as contained in the letter dated 24 August 1998.' Operative paragraph 3 calls upon the Governments of the Netherlands and of the United Kingdom to take such steps as are necessary to implement the initiative, including the conclusion of arrangements with a view to enabling the court to exercise jurisdiction 'in the terms of the intended Agreement between the two Governments, attached to the said letter of 24 August 1998.' For the two Governments to make a change to the Agreement which would have a significant effect on the terms of the initiative would therefore be a breach of their obligations under the resolution. There is therefore no question of the Agreement being amended to enable the two accused to be extradited from the Netherlands to another country for the purposes of trial.

Question Two

The accused will not be asked by the United Kingdom to consent to being transferred outside the Netherlands before the end of the trial. Article 16(2) contains the essential provision that the accused shall not be transferred to the territory of the United Kingdom. This is a reflection of the assurances in paragraph 4 of the letter of 24 August 1998 that the two accused will have safe passage from Libya to the Netherlands for the purpose of the trial; that while they are in the Netherlands neither the United Kingdom nor the United States shall seek their transfer to any jurisdiction other than the Scottish court sitting in the Netherlands; and that, if acquitted, the two accused shall have safe passage back to Libya. The provision includes only two exceptions. The second provides for transfer to Scotland on conviction. The first was inserted to cover the possibility that the accused might, after taking advice from their counsel, prefer to be tried by a judge and jury. For this purpose they would have to go to Scotland. Sub-paragraph (2)(a) therefore provides for this possibility, but requires that three pre-conditions be met: the accused would have to give their written agreement; they would have to confirm their agreement in person to the High Court of Justiciary; and such confirmation must be done in the presence of any counsel instructed by them.

Question Three

The purpose of holding a Scottish trial in the Netherlands is to meet the concerns expressed that the publicity which the case has received in Scotland would adversely influence a Scottish jury so that the two accused might not have a fair trial in Scotland. Although the United Kingdom does not agree with that view, in the interest of seeing that justice is done it agreed that the trial could take place in the Netherlands. However, as was made clear in paragraphs 3 and 4 of the letter of 24 August 1998, apart from replacing the jury by a panel of three Scottish High Court judges, Scottish law and procedure would apply and, therefore, if the two accused were to be convicted they would serve their sentence in the United Kingdom, in practice in Scotland. The proposal to try the accused before a Scottish court in the Netherlands had been suggested by Libya and various international organisations on several occasions, but contrary to the statement of the Libyan Permanent Representative to the United Nations, in the General Debate on 29 September 1998, there has never been any general understanding nor suggestion that any sentence would be served other than in Scotland. Since the only purpose of moving the trial to the Netherlands is to avoid any suggestion that trial procedure would be unfair to the accused, there is no reason why the sentences should not be served in Scotland. When a person is convicted by a national court and sentenced to imprisonment, the sentence is served in the country concerned. Accordingly, if found guilty, the two accused will serve their sentences in Scotland.

Clarifications Sought from the United Kingdom

Question One

Premises for the Scottish Court are available, but some adaptation of these will be needed to make them suitable for the proceedings. The necessary preparations are being made. The completion of the work will depend upon when the two accused arrive in the Netherlands. Their first appearance will be before the Sheriff, and facilities for this will be available whenever the accused are extradited by the Dutch authorities. After first appearance, time is ordinarily allowed, usually of not less than three months, for the parties to prepare for trial. The trial court and ancillary facilities will be ready for the commencement of the trial.

Question Two

In terms of the Order in Council, the judges will be appointed by the Lord Justice Clerk after the accused have arrived in the Netherlands. He will select them from the then current list of Lords Commissioners of Justiciary and from those retired or temporary judges who are entitled to sit in the High Court of Justiciary. Apart from the Lord Justice General and Lord Justice Clerk, there are at present 25 Lords Commissioners of Justiciary. A list of their names will follow as soon as possible. Any judge who has had a previous connection with the Lockerbie case would not be considered eligible for selection.

Question Three

Under Scots law only persons having the right to practise before the Scottish Courts may act as solicitors or advocates in the case. Unless foreign lawyers who are members of the accused's legal defence team have a right of audience before the Sheriff court or the High Court of Justiciary, they will not be entitled to address either court or examine witnesses, but they may, if the solicitors and advocates of the accused and the accused themselves agree, assist the solicitors and advocates. The United Kingdom/Netherlands Agreement recognises that other persons (who may include foreign lawyers) may assist solicitors or advocates and they are given certain privileges under Article 15(3).

Question Four

As untried prisoners the accused will be subject to the Scottish Prison Service's prison rules which entitle untried prisoners to daily visits of at least 30 minutes duration during the week from Monday to Friday. If there are no visits between Monday and Friday untried prisoners are entitled to a visit on Saturday or Sunday, although visits are allowed on Saturday and Sunday on a discretionary basis. In practice it is Scottish Prison Service policy to encourage the maintenance of family ties and, where practicable, visits are extended beyond the minimum required by the prison rules. In the circumstances of the trial in the Netherlands, arrangements will be made to allow for daily access to the accused, by family members who wish to visit them during the course of proceedings.

Question Five

Documentary and label productions (ie documentary and physical exhibits) will be available for inspection by the Scottish legal representatives of the accused at the premises of the court, or in the United Kingdom in advance of the trial, in accordance with usual practice. Copies of documentary productions will be made available to these representatives of the accused in the ordinary way. While such facilities will be afforded to representatives who are entitled to practise before the Scottish courts—ie solicitors and advocates—they are entitled to afford access to copy documents to others assisting them for the purposes of preparing the defence of the case. The court authorities will allow access to original productions for inspection to persons, including foreign lawyers, who are authorised and accompanied by the solicitors or advocates of the accused.

Clarifications Sought from the United Kingdom and the United States

Question One

Under Scots law the defence may cite (summon) any witness in the United Kingdom without recourse to the Court, although the Court is entitled to excuse the attendance of any witnesses if it is satisfied that the witness cannot give relevant evidence. If a witness fails to appear, the defence may apply for a warrant for his arrest. The High Court of Justiciary will have the same power to order recovery or production of documents or other items within the United Kingdom as it has in any other case and may, on the application of the prosecutor or defence, issue a letter of request to other jurisdictions seeking assistance in the production of evidence, examination of witnesses or attendance of witnesses.

Question Two

Where the Scottish solicitors or advocates of the accused consider that the presence of a person is necessary for the proper investigation or conduct of the defence, the United Kingdom will consider that person's visa application sympathetically.

Clarifications Sought from the United Kingdom, the United States and France

In paragraph 8 of Resolution 1192 the Security Council decided that the measures set forth in Resolution 748 and 883 "shall be suspended immediately" if the Secretary-General reports to the Council that the two accused have arrived in the Netherlands for the purposes of trial before the Scottish court (or have appeared for trial before an appropriate court in the United Kingdom or United States) and that the Libyan Government has satisfied the French judicial authorities with regard to the bombing of UTA 772. It is for the French Government to say whether the Libyan Government has satisfied the French judicial authorities. If the Secretary-General then reports that both conditions have been met, sanctions will be suspended immediately.

ANNEX 3. U.S. RESPONSES TO REQUESTS FOR CLARIFICATION EXPRESSED BY THE LIBYAN TEAM REGARDING THE IMPLEMENTATION OF SECURITY COUNCIL RESOLUTION 1192 (1998)

Will the UK and USA ensure that any evidence or witnesses in their territory or under their control are, upon the request of the Scottish Court, made available at the Netherlands in accordance with their respective laws?

Answer: The United States will comply with all requests of the Scottish Court in a manner fully consistent with U.S. law. The relevant procedures are contained at 28 U.S.C. section 1781 *et seq.* and provide a mechanism for the receipt and execution of requests for judicial assistance from foreign tribunals.

Will the UK and USA undertake to issue visas to the lawyers of the accused so that they could have access to witnesses and documents in their territory or under their control identified by the Prosecution or the Defense if they are not available in the Netherlands?

Answer: Regarding access to the United States, counsel for the prosecution and defense will be permitted to enter the United States in accordance with U.S. law.

Regarding access to witnesses, U.S. law does not obligate witnesses to meet with counsel; with witness' consent, however, counsel may do so. As for documents, as noted above, the United States will comply with all requests of the Scottish Court in a manner fully consistent with U.S. law.

Since the French judicial authorities have stated their satisfaction with regard to the bombing of UTA 772 (S/1997/858), will the measures set forth in Security Council resolutions 748 (1992) and 883 (1993) be immediately suspended upon the arrival of the two accused in the Netherlands as provided for in paragraph 8 of Security Council resolution 1192 (1998)?

Answer: In paragraph 8 of Resolution 1192 the Security Council decided that the measures set forth in Resolution 748 and 883 "shall be suspended immediately" if the Secretary-General reports to the Council that the accused have arrived in the Netherlands for the purpose of trial before the Scottish court (or have appeared for trial before an appropriate court in the United Kingdom or United) and that the Libyan Government has satisfied the French judicial authorities with regard to the bombing of UTA 772. It is for the French Government to say whether the Libyan Government has satisfied the French judicial authorities. If the Secretary-General then reports that both conditions have been met, sanctions will be suspended immediately.

ANNEX 4. REQUEST FOR CLARIFICATION EXPRESSED BY
THE LIBYAN LEGAL TEAM REGARDING THE IMPLEMENTATION
OF SECURITY COUNCIL RESOLUTION 1192 (1998)

Preliminary remarks by the Netherlands

Before providing the clarifications sought from the Netherlands it might be helpful to explain the procedure which will be followed as from the moment of the arrival of the two accused in the Netherlands. Pursuant to operative point 7 of SC resolution 1192 (1998) the two accused will upon their arrival in the Netherlands be detained by the Netherlands authorities pending their transfer from the United Kingdom to the Netherlands for provisional arrest of the two accused for the purpose of extradition to the Scottish Court sitting in the Netherlands. Following their arrest the two accused will be detained in a Netherlands detention facility and be subjected to the extradition procedure in accordance with the Netherlands Extradition Act of 1967. Following the decision by the Netherlands authorities upon the extradition request the two accused will be surrendered by the Dutch authorities to the Scottish Court sitting in the Netherlands. At the moment of their surrender the involvement of the Dutch authorities with the accused ends.

Given the above it should be clear that the extradition procedure is a preliminary procedure for the trial. The two accused are not standing trial in the Dutch court. In this context the Dutch authorities will in legal terms regard the two accused as persons claimed for the purpose of extradition. This term will be used in the following answers.

Finally it is thought to be relevant to note that according to Netherlands law the persons claimed have the right of counsel in view of the extradition procedure. Detailed questions on their obligations and rights under Dutch law should be put to their counsels.

Would it be possible for lawyers of the accused to visit the location of the detention and the Court facilities in the Netherlands where the trial will be held?

Visits to the detention and the Court facilities in the Netherlands should be addressed to the competent Scottish authorities.

At which airport will the plane with the accused land in the Netherlands?

Given the fact that the safety of the transfer to and the arrival in the Netherlands of the persons claimed is essential, disclosure of information on the airport of arrival is not advisable until the Netherlands gets notice from the SG UN of the planned physical arrangements for the transfer of the persons claimed to the Netherlands.

What procedures will be followed upon arrival of the accused in the Netherlands, in particular in the light of the fact that they expect to be accompanied on the plane by at least one lawyer and one family member each, as well as a doctor and possibly by an observer from a human right organisation? Under what law will the accused be detained by the Dutch authorities?

As stated in the preliminary remarks the Netherlands authorities will arrest the persons claimed upon their arrival in the Netherlands on the basis of the request for provisional arrest for the purpose of extradition. Immediately after their arrest they will be transferred to a Netherlands detention facility, which is the normal procedure for every person claimed in the Netherlands. Their arrest and subsequent detention is governed by the Netherlands Extradition Action of

1967. Since the transfer after an arrest is a matter solely for the arresting officers and the transportation team, there does not exist a possibility for accompanying the persons claimed by other persons.

Will they be handcuffed upon their arrival?

In the Netherlands in cases of arrest for the purpose of extradition handcuffs are used. Thus the persons claimed will be handcuffed upon arrest.

Where will the accused be held in the Netherlands during the detention by the Dutch authorities?

As stated in the preliminary remarks the persons claimed will be transferred to a Netherlands detention facility. The exact location of that detention centre will not be disclosed, since it is not customary in the Netherlands to disclose this type of information beforehand. However, after the transportation of the persons claimed and their admittance in the detention centre, the lawyers who have presented themselves in accordance with Netherlands law as counsels for the persons claimed will be informed about the name and location of the detention centre.

How will their safety be guaranteed? Will the accused be held in detention with other detainees or will they be in a separate detention facility?

The Netherlands assumes the responsibility to ensure the safety of the persons claimed during their detention in the Netherlands detention facility.

The persons claimed will be detained accordingly. For safety reasons further details can not be disclosed beforehand.

What assurances could be obtained from the Dutch authorities that no authorities of a third country or other authorities, except the Dutch authorities responsible for their detention and members of the defence team, doctors and relatives will have access to the accused during their detention by the Dutch authorities?

Since the only purpose of the detention of the persons claimed under Dutch authority will be the extradition procedure, the rules applicable to all persons who are detained for the purpose of their extradition will apply. During the office hours of the detention centre, they will have the right to receive the lawyers who have presented themselves in accordance with Netherlands law as counsels for the persons claimed, without supervision. Other visitors can be received, under supervision, during the visitors hours of the detention centre. The responsibility for the health and the medical treatment of detainees rests with the medical service of the detention centre. Visits of private doctors are allowed for the sole purpose of consulting them, unless the persons claimed themselves wish to see them.

How long will the accused be detained by the Dutch authorities before they are transferred for the purpose of the trial to the Scottish court sitting in the Netherlands?

As stated in the preliminary remarks the persons claimed will be detained for the purpose of their extradition. Their detention by the Dutch authorities ends after completion of the extradition procedure when they are surrendered to the Scottish Court sitting in the Netherlands. The duration of the extradition procedure depends mainly on the positions they choose to take in that procedure.

Will the Dutch authorities alert the media and allow it to be present at the airport?

Due to rules concerning the right of privacy, which in the Netherlands also apply to persons under arrest, the Netherlands authorities do not invite the press to witness any arrest. In the present case it is presumed that as from their departure from Libya the time of arrival of the persons claimed will one way or another become public. In conformity with the freedom of press in the Netherlands, press/tv reporters, who show an interested will be allowed to be present at the airport at the time of the arrival of the accused under such conditions that are necessary to ensure the safe operation of the airport, the safe arrival of the persons claimed, their subsequent arrest as well as their orderly transfer to the detention facility.

Will the Dutch authorities undertake to issue multiple entry/ext visas to enable members of the defence team of the accused to exit and reenter the Netherlands as the need arises in their efforts to conduct an effective defence?

The Netherlands will be bound by Article 15 and the related Articles 20 (I) and 21 of the UK/Netherlands Agreement. The Netherlands will provide in accordance with these provisions the appropriate visas.

Will the Dutch authorities undertake to issue multiple entry/exit visas to a medical doctor accompanying the accused and to the family members of the accused who wish to attend the trial?

The Netherlands will take visa application by persons mentioned in the question in consideration and will decide on these at their earliest convenience.

What protection will the accused and the documentation used by them enjoy in the Netherlands? Will their papers be protected from search and seizure? Will they enjoy the same protection as the Dutch lawyers having during the court proceedings?

During their detention under Dutch authority the normal rules will apply to the persons claimed, which are that they can correspond freely with the lawyers who have presented themselves in accordance with Netherlands law as counsels for the persons claimed. This correspondence is privileged, and therefore protected from search and seizure.

During their detention under Scottish authority the Scottish rules apply, where the Netherlands will be bound by Article 15 of the UK/Netherlands Agreement.

Will the Dutch authorities issue the necessary visas to all witnesses identified by the defence team?

Neither the definition of witness in Article 1 (k) nor the specific provision on witnesses (Article 17) of the UK/Netherlands Agreement, provide for a distinction between witnesses for the prosecution or for the defence. the Netherlands will be bound by Article 17 (l) and the related Articles 20 (l) and 21. The Netherlands will provide in accordance with these provisions the appropriate visas.

ANNEX 5. REQUEST FOR CLARIFICATION EXPRESSED BY THE LIBYAN LEGAL TEAM REGARDING THE IMPLEMENTATION OF SECURITY COUNCIL RESOLUTION 1192 (1998): SUPPLEMENTARY ANSWERS BY THE GOVERNMENT OF THE UNITED KINGDOM

Three Matters of Main Concern

Question Two

There would be no question of the two accused being transferred to the United Kingdom without their consent, except for the purpose of serving a custodial sentence following conviction. The sole purpose of Article 16 (2) (a) is to protect the accused's rights. Although the United Kingdom has no doubt that trial in the Netherlands before three High Court judges will be entirely fair to the accused, we cannot take away from the accused the right, after taking their own legal advice, to opt for trial by jury, which would have to take place in Scotland.

Question Three

Those convicted by a court in Scotland serve their sentence in Scotland, or elsewhere in the United Kingdom, in accordance with domestic legislation (not custom).

Clarifications Sought from the United Kingdom

Question One

The Scottish court will be ready to receive the accused when the Netherlands authorities are ready to transfer them. The precise timetable will depend on when Libya is prepared to deliver the accused to the Netherlands.
Clarifications Sought from the United Kingdom and the United States

Question Two

Each application for entry clearance is treated on its individual merits. Applications from members of the defence team who are not British nationals would be considered promptly in the light of all available information, and we would hope for a positive outcome.

ANNEX 6. U.S. FURTHER RESPONSE TO REQUEST FOR CLARIFICATION EXPRESSED BY THE LIBYAN TEAM REGARDING THE IMPLEMENTATION OF SECURITY COUNCIL RESOLUTION 1192 (1998)

Will the UK and USA undertake to issue visas to the lawyers of the accused so that they could have access to witnesses and documents in their territory or under their control identified by the Prosecution or the Defense if they are not available in the Netherlands?

Answer: Regarding access to the United States, counsel for the prosecution and defense will be permitted to enter the United States in accordance with U.S. law.

Regarding access to witnesses, U.S. law does not obligate witnesses to meet with counsel; with witness' consent, however, counsel may do so. As for documents, as noted above, the United States will comply with all requests of the Scottish Court in a manner fully consistent with U.S. law.

Further Response of the United States: As noted above, counsel for the prosecution and defense will be permitted to enter the United States in accordance with U.S. law. The United States has been asked for further clarification whether visa applications by defense counsel will be reviewed favorably. The United States provides the following additional response.

The eligibility of any given person for admission to the United States is governed by U.S. immigration laws and can only be decided on a case-by-case basis. That being said, the United States is prepared to look favorably on visa applications on behalf of defense counsel of any nationality who wish to travel to the United States to interview witnesses or to seek evidence for the defense. Moreover, defense counsel from certain countries, e.g. the Netherlands or Scotland, could be eligible to travel to the United States without visas under the Visa waiver Pilot Program.

While eligibility for a visa or admission cannot be definitively determined until an actual application is made, if the specific identities of defense counsel are provided, the United States will determine promptly whether any of them would be likely to encounter difficulties in obtaining visas and/or admission.

ANNEX 7. [ADDITIONAL RESPONSE BY THE NETHERLANDS]

1. Clarifications provided by the Dutch authorities on 15 October 1998 in response to the questions raised by the Libyan legal team regarding the implementation of the relevant provisions of Security Council resolution 1192 (1998) are factual and based on the applicable Dutch law. They accurately reflect the procedures to be applied under the applicable Dutch law for the detention of the accused upon their arrival in the Netherlands and pending their transfer to the Scottish Court sitting in the Netherlands.

2. Notwithstanding that the Dutch authorities are of the view that some of the concerns expressed by the Libyan legal team regarding the conditions under which the two accused will be detained by the Dutch authorities are exaggerated, they can provide the following additional clarifications.

3. Pursuant to paragraph 7 of Security Council resolution 1192 (1998), the Dutch authorities are required to detain the two accused upon their arrival in the Netherlands and pending their transfer to the Scottish Court sitting in the Netherlands and this provision of the resolution will be duly implemented in accordance with the applicable Dutch law. Detention period will be as short as possible and will depend on the time required for the establishment of the Court. During that time the Dutch authorities will take all the necessary measures to ensure full protection and security of the two detainees.

4. As noted above, upon arrival of the two accused in the Netherlands they will have to be detained and hand-cuffed under the Dutch law. However, at the time of their arrival and subsequently during the whole period of their detention, every effort will be made to prevent their media exposure. The Dutch authorities will strictly observe this requirement. To that end, the accused will be received upon their arrival in a separate area. Contrary to what has been stated by the Libyan legal team, the Dutch authorities have not disclosed to the media a point of the arrival of the accused in the Netherlands. That point will continue to be kept confidential.

5. To ensure the safety and security of the accused the Dutch authorities cannot disclose at this stage the exact location of a detention facility. The Libyan legal team will be provided with that information at the airport immediately upon the arrival of the accused in the Netherlands. Although members of the legal team, relatives and doctors will not be allowed to accompany the two detainees when they are transferred to a detention facility, they will be allowed soon thereafter to visit them in accordance with the applicable Dutch law.

6. The Dutch authorities will give favourable consideration to visa applications submitted by members of the Libyan legal team, relatives of the accused and their doctors. Issuance of visas will be greatly facilitated if names of such persons could be provided in advance.

7. The Dutch authorities would like to emphasise that their willingness to provide clarifications should not be construed as their entering into negotiations with the Libyan side regarding the implementation of Security Council resolution 1192 (1998).

ANNEX 8. UNITED KINGDOM'S ADDITIONAL RESPONSE

(a) The letter from the Libyan Permanent Representative does not make clear why imprisonment in Scotland is an issue of concern. It does not follow that because the arrangements for the trial are exceptional, the arrangements for serving of sentence should also be exceptional. There is every reason why the due process of law should apply in the event of conviction by a Scottish court; that means imprisonment in Scotland.

If there are questions about the conditions of imprisonment in Scotland the United Kingdom will be happy to provide clarification. The report of the United Nations legal experts' visit to Scotland in December 1997 (S/1997/991) noted that "All aspects of the prison facilities, cells, rules and regulations meet the provisions of international law, in particular the European Convention on Human Rights" and that the facility at Barlinnie Prison where, if convicted, the two would be sent "meets the highest standards one may expect of a prison." The conditions of imprisonment are set out in the Prison and Young Offenders Institutions (Scotland) Rules 1994 (as amended). These rules make clear that, if convicted, the two accused can be assured that their religious, health and dietary requirements would be fully catered for. Visits by clerics would be arranged and religious books and items provided. There would be unfettered access to diplomatic and legal representatives and regular visits from family members. All prisoners may request visits by the independent Scottish Council for Civil Liberties, and have access to the Independent Complaints Commissioner and the court if they wish to bring any complaint against the prison. Access to prisoners by other persons is strictly circumscribed by prison rules.

The United Kingdom Government is also willing, in order to satisfy any concerns of the Libyan Government or the international community as to the future welfare of the two, if convicted, to agree to ongoing visits by international observers who would have automatic and unlimited right of access to the two. It is willing to discuss these arrangements with representatives of the United Nations and other interested international organisation.

(b) Resolution 1192 (1998) makes clear that sanctions against Libya will be suspended immediately if the two accused arrive in the Netherlands for the purpose of trial, in accordance with the resolution. This resolution does not specify the conditions for the lifting of sanctions, as they are contained in the previous resolutions which it reaffirms. Resolution 883 (1993) states that within 90 days of suspension, the Secretary-General should report to the Security Council on Libya's compliance with the decisions of resolutions 731 (1992) and 748 (1992) relating to both the Lockerbie and UTA bombings, including the requirement that Libya should continue to cooperate with legal proceedings and pay appropriate compensation, and that it should demonstrate its renunciation of terrorism.

(c) The facility which has generously been made available by the Government of the Netherlands for the purpose of a trial is a purely Dutch facility, and has been so since 1996. No other party has any automatic right of access and, contrary to some reports, it does not have an airfield. Camp Zeist currently contains an air museum, a hospital and a school. It was chosen as providing the best space, security and infrastructure for conversion to a trial site. There is absolutely no question of the Kingdom or the United States of America using the facility as staging point for the forceful transfer of the accused to their territory. To do so would be a clear breach of binding obligations under resolution 1192 (1998). The objective of the United Kingdom and United States is a free and fair trial, witnessed by international observers. The facility at Zeist is entirely suitable for this purpose. This can, of course, be confirmed with the Dutch Government.

ANNEX 9. NETHERLANDS' ADDITIONAL RESPONSE

1. As has previously been made clear, any Libyan witnesses will be immune from arrest while in the Netherlands in relation to any offences, including the bombing of Pan Am 103, committed prior to their arrival in the Netherlands for the purpose of the trial. Like any other witnesses, unless they are arrested in connection with an offence while they are in the Netherlands, they will be free to leave the Netherlands at the end of the trial, or, if the Court so agrees, on completion of their testimony.

2. The families and lawyers of the accused will not be confined to the premises for the duration of the trial, and will have the right to enter the premises at all reasonable times, in particular when the Court is sitting, and to leave the premises at any time. They are entitled to reside outside the premises.

16. Text of United States' and United Kingdom's Requirements for Libya to Meet Re: U.N. Security Council Resolution 748 of 1992, as Presented in First Tri-Lateral U.S.-U.K.-Libya Meeting Hosted by Secretary General Kofi A. Annan on May 6, 1999

Results of U.S., U.K. and Libya Meeting with the U.N. Secretary General on 6 May 1999

(I.a.) *TERRORISM*

Requirement: "Libya (must) commit itself concretely and definitively to cease all forms of terrorist action and all assistance to terrorist groups. Libya must promptly, by concrete actions, prove its renunciation of terrorism." This requirement is contained in the joint U.S./UK/French demand and was incorporated directly into UNSCR 748 as a demand of the Council.

Meeting the Requirement: Libya should:

(a) Commit definitively to cease all forms of terrorist action and terminate all assistance to terrorist groups. This commitment should be made directly by Col. Qadhaffi;

(b) End all support for the Abu Nidal Organization, Fatah-The Intifada, the PFLP-GC, the Abu Sayyaf Group and the Kurdistan Workers' Party (PKK);

(c) Provide counter-terrorism information of interest to the United States, such as information of Egyptian and Algerian Extremist Groups, Lebanese and Gulf Hizballah Groups, Iran and Sudan; and

(d) Take clear steps to become party to the International Counter-Terrorism Conventions.

(I.b.) *ACCEPT RESPONSIBILITY*

Requirement: "Accept responsibility for the actions of Libyan officials." This is contained in the U.S./U.K. demand.

Meeting the Requirement: Libya should provide, in writing, a clear statement that Libya accepts responsibility for the actions of its officials.

(I.c.) *COOPERATIVE WITH THE INVESTIGATION*

Requirement: "Disclose all it knows of this crime, including the names of all those responsible, and allow full access to all witnesses, documents and other material evidence, including all the remaining timers." This is part of the joint U.S./U.K. demand. In addition, UNSCR 1192 provides that "The Libyan Government shall ensure that any evidence or witnesses in Libya are, upon the request of the court, promptly made available at the court in the Netherlands for the purposes of the trial."

Meeting the Requirement: It is exceedingly unlikely that this requirement can be satisfied in advance of the trial, because it contemplates Libyan cooperation with requests made by the Scottish court—requests which will likely occur during the trial and, necessarily, long after the SYG issues his 90-day report. It may be possible to make a determination on this issue prior to conclusion of the trial, depending on Libya's response to requests made through the court by the Scottish prosecutors, and on the pace and course of the trial itself. Recalling Libya's failure to cooperate with investigations in the past—as noted in UNSCR 731, OP2—the United States expects Libya to meet a high standard in this regard and reserves the right to make its own assessment in this matter.

(I.d) COMPENSATION

Requirement: "Pay appropriate compensation." This is a joint U.S./U.K. demand set forth in S/23308.

Meeting the Requirement: Libya should pay appropriate compensation. The United States encourages Libya to meet with legal counsel for the Pan Am 103 families to discuss settlement.

17. Text of United Kingdom's Requests for Libya's Cooperation with Scottish Judicial Authorities, May 6, 1999

Libyan Co-Operation with the Scottish Judicial Authorities

1. In 27 November 1991 the United Kingdom and United States Governments made a joint declaration with regard to the Lockerbie disaster and the issue of warrants for the arrest of Abdelbaset Ali Mohmed Al Megrahi and Al Amin Khalifa Fhimah that the Government of Libya must, inter alia,

> "Disclose all it knows of this crime, including the names of all those responsible, and allow full access to all witnesses, documents and other material evidence, including all the remaining timers."

2. The declaration was circulated at the United Nations on 31 December 1991 as part of Security Council Documents S/23307 and S/23308.

3. On 21 January 1992 the Security council of the United Nations adopted Resolution No. 731 (1992), in paragraph 3 of which it urged the Libyan Government immediately to provide a full and effective response to requests, including, inter alia, the above joint declaration "to cooperate fully in establishing responsibility for the terrorists acts referred to above against Pan American flight 103 and Union de transports aerens flight 772" (ibid, paragraph 2)

4. On 31 March 1992 the Security Council of the United Nations adopted Resolution No. 748 (1992), in which, acting under Chapter VII of the Charter of the United Nations, it decided that, inter alia, the Libyan Government must "now comply without further delay with paragraph 3 of resolution 731 (1992) regarding the requests contained in documents S/23308 and S/23309."

5. On 11 November 1993 the Security Council, again acting under Chapter VII of the Charter of the United Nations, adopted Resolution No. 833 (1993) in which it demanded once again that the Libyan Government comply without any further delay resolutions 731 (1992) and 748 (1992).

6. On 27 August 1998 the Security Council, again acting under Chapter VII of the Charter of the United Nations, adopted Resolution No. 1192 (198) in which, inter alia, in paragraph 1, it demanded once again that the Libyan Government immediately comply with the foregoing resolutions, in paragraph 2 it welcomed the initiative for the trial of the two accused before a Scottish court sitting in the Netherlands and, in paragraph 4, it decided

> "that all States shall cooperate to this end, and in particular that the Libyan Government shall ensure the appearance in the Netherlands of the two accused for the purpose of trial by the court described in paragraph 2, and that the Libyan Government shall ensure that any evidence of witnesses in Libya are, upon the request of the court, promptly made available at the court in the Netherlands for the purpose of the trial."

7. Libya thus requires to co-operate with the Scottish judicial authorities in

the following ways: On receipt of a Letter of Request issued by the competent prosecuting authority in Scotland, i.e. the Lord Advocate or by the competent judicial authority, i.e. the High Court of Justiciary, the Libyan Government will ensure promptly and in accordance with any timescale described in the Letter of Request, or, in the case of any request where there is no indication of a specific timescale, within fourteen days of receipt of the Letter of Request, that

(a) any documentary or other real evidence requested is made available to the relevant Scottish authorities, whether in Scotland, the Netherlands or Libya, as described in the Letter of Request.

(b) arrangements are made for any interviews which may be requested with individuals and that such arrangements are communicated to the relevant Scottish authorities.

(c) any enquiries which the Libyan authorities may be required to carry out, are carried out and the results communicated to the relevant Scottish authorities.

(d) any witness whose attendance may be required at the court in the Netherlands for the purpose of the trial is duly cited and appropriate arrangements are made for their attendance at the premises of the Scottish Court in the Netherlands, subject to payment or reimbursement of travelling and subsistence expenses of the witness by the party to the proceedings who has requested the attendance of the witness.

8. Any evidence provided in response to a Letter of Request will not, without the consent of the appropriate authority in Libya, be used for any purpose other than the Lockerbie criminal investigation and criminal proceedings arising out of it.

9. Any witness entering the Netherlands and attending at the premises of the Scottish Court in the Netherlands for the purpose of the trial shall not be prosecuted, detained or subjected to any other restriction of his or her personal liberty, by the authorities of the Netherlands or the Scottish authorities in respect of acts or convictions prior to his or her entry into the territory of the Netherlands, but that immunity shall cease on the departure of the witness from the territory of the Netherlands, or following the elapse of 15 days from the date when his or her presence at the trial is no longer required and during which he or she has had the opportunity to leave the Netherlands and has not done so for, having left it, has returned, unless such return is for the purposes of the trial. Furthermore, such a witness shall not be subjected by the authorities of the Netherlands to any measure which may affect the free and independent exercise of his or her functions.

CROWN OFFICE
Edinburgh
6 May 1999

18. U.N. Document S/2003/818

United Nations   S/2003/818

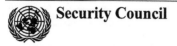 **Security Council**

Distr.: General
15 August 2003
English
Original: Arabic and English

**Letter dated 15 August 2003 from the Chargé d'affaires a.i.
of the Permanent Mission of the Libyan Arab Jamahiriya
to the United Nations addressed to the President of the
Security Council**

I am pleased to inform you that the remaining issues relating to the fulfilment of all Security Council resolutions resulting from the Lockerbie incident have been resolved. I am also pleased to inform you that my country is confident that the representatives of the United Kingdom and the United States of America will be confirming this development to you and to members of the Council as well.

The Libyan Arab Jamahiriya has sought to cooperate in good faith throughout the past years to bring about a solution to this matter.

In that context and out of respect for international law and pursuant to the Security Council resolutions, Libya as a sovereign State:

• Has facilitated the bringing to justice of the two suspects charged with the bombing of Pan Am 103 and accepts responsibility for the actions of its officials.

• Has cooperated with the Scottish investigating authorities before and during the trial and pledges to cooperate in good faith with any further requests for information in connection with the Pan Am 103 investigation. Such cooperation would be extended in good faith through the usual channels.

• Has arranged for the payment of appropriate compensation. To that end, a special fund has been established and instructions have already been issued to transmit the necessary sums to an agreed escrow account within a matter of days.

The Libyan Arab Jamahiriya, which during the last two decades has, on numerous occasions, condemned all acts of terrorism in its correspondence to the General Assembly and to the Security Council, reaffirms its commitment to that policy. The following are examples of that policy. The Libyan Arab Jamahiriya confirms its support for Security Council resolutions 1373 (2001) which stipulates, according to Chapter VII of the Charter of the United Nations, that all States are to "refrain from providing any form of support, active or passive, to entities or persons involved in terrorist acts"; that they are to "take the necessary steps to prevent the commission of terrorist acts, including taking action and sharing information to provide early warning to other States"; that they are to "deny safe haven to any person who finances, plans, supports, or commits terrorist acts"; that they are to

03-46760 (E)   160803
0346760

"ensure that any person who participates in the financing, planning, preparation or perpetration of terrorist acts or in supporting terrorist acts is brought to justice"; and that they are to "afford one another the greatest measure of assistance in connection with criminal investigations or proceedings relating to the financing or support of terrorist acts, including assistance in obtaining evidence in their possession, deemed necessary for legal proceedings".

In that connection, the Libyan Arab Jamahiriya is committed to be cooperative in the international fight against terrorism. It is also committed to cooperate with efforts to bring to justice those who are suspects.

In addition, the Libyan Arab Jamahiriya renews its support for the Declaration on Measures to Eliminate International Terrorism as well as its support for such General Assembly resolutions as resolution 55/158, in which the Assembly "strongly condemns all acts, methods and practices of terrorism as criminal and unjustifiable, wherever and by whomsoever committed".

The Libyan Arab Jamahiriya continues to endorse the Declaration on Measures to Eliminate International Terrorism, which is contained in the annex to General Assembly resolution 49/60. That Declaration stipulates that all States shall "refrain from organizing, instigating, assisting or participating in terrorist acts in territories of other States, or from acquiescing in or encouraging terrorist activities within their territories directed towards the commission of such acts". It also stipulates that "those responsible for acts of international terrorism must be brought to justice".

In line with this forceful denunciation of terrorism in all its forms, the Libyan Arab Jamahiriya has signed regional conventions and bilateral agreements as well as the twelve international conventions to fight terrorism. It recently reported those steps to the Security Council and pledged to refrain from becoming involved in any acts of terrorism. In particular, the Libyan Arab Jamahiriya pledged "not to engage in, attempt, or participate in any way whatever in the organization, financing or commission of terrorist acts or to incite the commission of terrorist acts or support them directly or indirectly; and to prevent its territory from being used for the planning, organization or perpetration of terrorist offences by, inter alia, preventing the illicit entry, sheltering or sojourn of terrorist elements or by receiving, sheltering, training, arming or financing them or by providing them with facilities" (see S/2001/1323). Libya's report to the Security Council also detailed the specific steps that were taken to implement those pledges.

Suffice it to say that the Libyan Arab Jamahiriya has pledged itself not only to cooperate in the international fight against terrorism but also to take practical measures to ensure that such cooperation is effective.

The Libyan Arab Jamahiriya appreciates the efforts made and the parts played by the Member States of the United Nations, by the Secretary-General and by other entities in bringing about the resolution of this long-standing matter. In expressing such appreciation, the Libyan Arab Jamahiriya affirms that it will have fulfilled all Security Council requirements relevant to the Lockerbie incident upon transfer of the necessary sums to the agreed escrow account. It trusts that the Council will agree. Therefore, in accordance with paragraph 16 of Council resolution 883 (1993) and paragraph 8 of resolution 1192 (1998), the Libyan Arab Jamahiriya requests that in that event the Council immediately lift the measures set forth in its resolutions 748 (1992) and 883 (1993).

I should be grateful if you would have the present letter circulated as a document of the Security Council.

(*Signed*) Ahmed A. **Own**
Ambassador
Chargé d'affaires a.i.

19. U.N. Document S/2003/819

United Nations   S/2003/819

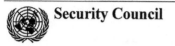 **Security Council**

Distr.: General
15 August 2003
English
Original: Arabic and English

Letter dated 15 August 2003 from the Permanent Representatives of the United Kingdom of Great Britain and Northern Ireland and the United States of America to the United Nations addressed to the President of the Security Council

In view of the letter dated 15 August 2003 addressed to you by the Libyan Arab Jamahiriya related to the bombing of Pan Am 103 (S/2003/818) and in the light of the actions and commitments that form the background to the letter, the Governments of the United Kingdom and the United States of America are prepared to allow the lifting of the measures set forth by the Council in its resolutions 748 (1992) and 883 (1993) once the necessary sums referred to in the Libyan letter have been transferred to the agreed escrow account.

In its letter, the Libyan Arab Jamahiriya has pledged before the Council to cooperate in the international fight against terrorism and to cooperate with any further requests for information in connection with the Pan Am 103 investigation. We expect Libya to adhere scrupulously to those commitments.

We should be grateful if you would have the present letter circulated as a document of the Security Council.

(*Signed*) Emyr **Jones Parry**
Permanent Representative
United Kingdom Mission to the
United Nations

(*Signed*) John D. **Negroponte**
Permanent Representative
United States Mission to the
United Nations

20. U.N. Document S/RES/1506 (2003)

United Nations   S/RES/1506 (2003)

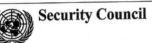 **Security Council**

Distr.: General
12 September 2003

Resolution 1506 (2003)

Adopted by the Security Council at its 4820th meeting (Part II), on 12 September 2003

The Security Council,

Recalling its resolutions 731 (1992) of 21 January 1992, 748 (1992) of 31 March 1992, 883 (1993) of 11 November 1993 and 1192 (1998) of 27 August 1998, relating to the destruction of Pan Am flight 103 over Lockerbie, Scotland, and the destruction of Union de transports aeriens flight 772 over Niger,

Recalling the statement by its President on 8 April 1999 (S/PRST/1999/10),

Welcoming the letter to the President of the Council dated 15 August 2003 from the Chargé d'affaires a.i. of the Permanent Mission of the Libyan Arab Jamahiriya, recounting steps the Libyan Government has taken to comply with the above-mentioned resolutions, particularly concerning acceptance of responsibility for the actions of Libyan officials, payment of appropriate compensation, renunciation of terrorism, and a commitment to cooperating with any further requests for information in connection with the investigation (S/2003/818),

Also welcoming the letter to the President of the Council dated 15 August 2003 from the Permanent Representatives of the United Kingdom and the United States of America (S/2003/819),

Acting under Chapter VII of the Charter of the United Nations,

1.   *Decides* to lift, with immediate effect, the measures set forth in paragraphs 4, 5 and 6 of its resolution 748 (1992) and paragraphs 3, 4, 5, 6 and 7 of its resolution 883 (1993);

2.   *Decides further* to dissolve the Committee established by paragraph 9 of resolution 748 (1992);

3.   *Decides also* that it has concluded its consideration of the item entitled "Letters dated 20 and 23 December 1991 from France, the United Kingdom of Great Britain and Northern Ireland and the United States of America" and hereby *removes* this item from the list of matters of which the Council is seized.

03-49881 (E)

Notes

Chapter 1

1. In 1990, after Iraq's occupation of Kuwait, the United States needed to neutralize Iran and sought the participation of Syria in the alliance formed to liberate Kuwait. President Bush sent the Iranian leaders a letter informing them that his efforts were not directed at their country and personally met Syrian President Hafez Assad in Geneva to put the final touches on an unlikely alliance for the Desert Storm operation.

2. *The New York Times*, April 1, 1992.

3. Counts of accusation as stated in a letter from the United States to the United Nations A/46/831,s/23317, December 23, 1991.

4. United Nations document A/46/826, s/23307, December 31, 1991.

5. United Nations document A/46/825, s/23306, December 20, 1991.

6. United Nations document S/23221, November 16, 1991.

7. United Nations document A/46/660, s/23226, November 20, 1991.

8. United Nations document A/46/845, s/23417, January 13, 1992.

9. United Nations document A/46/841, s/23396, January 9, 1992.

10. Kofi Annan. A report to the General Assembly titled "Renewal of the United Nations: A Programme of Reform"(United Nations Document A/51/950).

11. The text of UNSC Resolution 731 (1992) may be found in the Appendix.

12. The Security Council recommends to the General Assembly to elect a Secretary General for one term of five years. That means permanent members of the council, such as the United States and the UK, have veto powers.

13. Boutros Boutros-Ghali. *Unvanquished*. Random House, New York, 1999, p 303.

14. UN document s/23574, February 11, 1992.

15. Boutros Boutros-Ghali. *Unvanquished*. Random House, New York, 1999, 24–25.

Chapter 2

1. Boutros Boutros-Ghali. *Unvanquished*. Random House, New York, 1999, 188.

2. UN document s/23672, March 3,

1992. All quotes in the paragraph that follows are drawn from this same report.

3. *Asharq Al-Awsat* (newspaper). London, March 19, 1992.

4. *Le Figaro*. March 27, 1992.

5. It is said that Qadhafi himself writes these commentaries.

6. The voting went as follows: In support: United States, United Kingdom, France, Russia, Ecuador, Austria, Belgium, Venezuela, Japan and Hungary. Against: none. Abstention: China, Morocco, Cape Verde, India and Zimbabwe.

7. United Nations document S/23796, April 9, 1992.

8. Boutros Boutros-Ghali. *Unvanquished*. Random House, New York, 1999, 190.

9. Omar Al-Muntasser. Interview with *Asharq Al-Awsat* (newspaper). London. June 27, 1993.

10. Boutros Boutros-Ghali. Unvanquished. Random House, New York 1999, p. 200.

11. UN document S/26500, September 28, 1993.

12. A "nonpaper" is a paper with no headings officially linking it to a particular country or individual. A nonpaper presents talking points without representing them as the official position of any country.

13. Full text of UNSCR 883 (1993) may be found in the Appendix.

14. The voting result was: In favor: Brazil, Cape Verde, France, Hungary, Japan, New Zealand, Russian Federation, Spain, United Kingdom of Great Britain and Northern Ireland, United States of America, Venezuela. Against: None. Abstaining: China, Djibouti, Morocco, Pakistan.

Chapter 3

1. Boutros Boutros-Ghali. *Unvanquished*. Random House, New York, 1999, 188.

2. UN document s/23672, March 3, 1992. All quotes in the paragraph that follows are drawn from this same report.

3. *Asharq Al-Awsat* (newspaper). London, March 19, 1992.

4. *Le Figaro*. March 27, 1992.

5. It is said that Qadhafi himself writes these commentaries.

6. The voting went as follows: In support: United States, United Kingdom,

France, Russia, Ecuador, Austria, Belgium, Venezuela, Japan and Hungary. Against: none. Abstention: China, Morocco, Cape Verde, India and Zimbabwe.

7. United Nations document S/23796, April 9, 1992.

8. Boutros Boutros-Ghali. *Unvanquished*. Random House, New York, 1999, 190.

9. Omar Al-Muntasser. Interview with *Asharq Al-Awsat* (newspaper). London. June 27, 1993.

10. Boutros Boutros-Ghali. Unvanquished. Random House, New York 1999, p. 200.

11. UN document S/26500, September 28, 1993.

12. A "nonpaper" is a paper with no headings officially linking it to a particular country or individual. A nonpaper presents talking points without representing them as the official position of any country.

13. Full text of UNSCR 883 (1993) may be found in the Appendix.

14. The voting result was: In favor: Brazil, Cape Verde, France, Hungary, Japan, New Zealand, Russian Federation, Spain, United Kingdom of Great Britain and Northern Ireland, United States of America, Venezuela. Against: None. Abstaining: China, Djibouti, Morocco, Pakistan

Chapter 4

1. Fouad Matar. *Egypt's Political Earthquakes*. The First Arab and International Publisher and the Arab Institution for Studies and Publications. Beirut. April 1999, 111.

2. *Libyan American Relations 1940–1992*. Essayed Awad Osman. Published by the Centre for Arab Civilization, Cairo, 1994.

3. Qadhafi speech, March 2, 1999.

4. Henry Kissinger. *Years of Upheaval*. Weidenfeld and Nicolson and Michael Joseph, London, 1982, 859.

5. Henry Kissinger. *Years of Upheaval*. Weidenfield and Nicolson and Michael Joseph, London, 1982, 860.

Chapter 5

1. In May 1971, Soviet President Niko-

lai Bodgorni visited Egypt less than six months after the death of President Nasser. For internal conflict reasons (connected to the presence of some opposed to the presidency of Sadat), the Egyptian president signed a "friendship treaty" with Bodgorni. Qadhafi, then part of a union effort with Egypt and Sudan as well as Syria, opposed the treaty based on a view equating it with the treaty between Great Britain and royal Egypt. He saw the treaty with the Soviet Union as a direct threat to the Libyan revolution. He thought that colonial powers start relations with other states in a very smooth way with expressions of equal partnership before jumping, at the first possible opportunity, to explore the needs of the smaller states, taking away much of their sovereignty. Sadat knew of these fears Qadhafi had, leading him to keep the idea of the treaty a secret from his partner in that union.

2. Mohammed Heikal. *Autumn of Fury: The Assassination of Sadat*. Random House, New York, 1983, 94.

3. Zbigniew Brzezinski. *Power and Principle: Memoirs of the National Security Adviser 1977–1981*. Farrar, Strauss, and Giroux, New York, 1983, 93.

4. Alexander Haig. *Caveat: Realism, Reagan, and Foreign Policy*. Macmillan, New York, 1984, 77.

5. Alexander Haig. Ibid, 109.

6. Ali Treiki. *At-Tadamon* (weekly magazine), London, no. 159, April 26, 1986, 17.

7. George Shultz. *Turmoil and Triumph: My Years as Secretary of State*. Charles Scribner's Sons, New York, 1993, 680.

8. Shultz. Ibid.

9. George Shultz. *Turmoil and Triump: My Years as Secretary of State*. Charles Scribner's Sons, New York, 1993, 680.

10. Shultz. Ibid.

11. Chadian president Hussein Hibri was an ally of France before turning to the United States for full support. France was angered by that move and turned to Libya to assist in Hibri's downfall, bringing Idriss Debi to the presidency and working through the International Court of Justice to solve the problem of the Ouzo strip, giving sovereignty over it to Chad. Libya accepted that 1994 ruling, and relations with the new regime in Chad grew to a very strong alliance.

12. Those groups were moved to Chad from Sudan after the fall of the Nimeiri regime in Sudan in 1989. When Debi took over, they were expelled from Chad.

13. The targets of that attack included Qadhafi's home, which resulted in the killing of his adopted daughter, and his tent home as well as many official buildings housing military and intelligence offices. There was considerable damage, including deaths and injuries, throughout Tripoli and environs.

14. Article 51 states: "Nothing in the present Charter shall impair the inherent right of individual or collective self-defense if an armed attack occurs against a Member of the UN, until the Security Council has taken measures necessary to maintain international peace and security. Measures taken by members in the exercise of this right of self-defense shall be immediately reported to the Security Council and shall not in any way affect the authority and responsibility of the Security Council under the present Charter to take, at any time, such action as it deems necessary in order to maintain or restore international peace and security."

15. Margaret Thatcher. *The Downing Street Years*. Harper Collins, 1993, 443.

16. Fouad Matar. *Attadamon* (magazine). London, April 19, 1986.

Chapter 6

1. George Bush and Brent Scowcroft. *A World Transformed*. Vintage, New York, 1999, 364.

2. Ibid., 370.

3. Mikhail Gorbachev. *On My Country and the World*. Columbia University Press, New York, 1999, 211.

4. *Patterns of Global Terrorism: 1998. Overview of State-Sponsored Terrorism*. A report by the State Department of the United States.

5. Boutros Boutros-Ghali. *Unvanquished*. Random House, New York, 1999, 206.

6. United Nations Document S/1995/973, November 20, 1995.

7. United Nations document S/23828, April 21, 1992.

8. UN document S/1997/858, November 6, 1997.

Chapter 7

1. "In the case of Members of the

United Nations not represented in the Permanent Court of Arbitration, candidates shall be nominated by national groups appointed for this purpose by their governments under the same conditions as those prescribed for members of the Permanent Court of Arbitration by Article 44 of the Convention of The Hague of 1907 for the pacific settlement of international disputes." Article 4, para. 2 of the *Statute of the International Court of Justice.*

2. UN document S/1998/239, March 16, 1998. Full text may be found in the Appendix.

3. UN document S/1998/263, March 24, 1998. Full text may be found in the Appendix.

4. UN document S/1998/83, January 28, 1998.

5. UN document S/1998/192, March 4, 1998.

6. UN document S/1998/199, March 1998.

7. A briefing by Martin Indyk, Assistant Secretary of State for Near-Eastern Affairs, at the State Department, Washington, D.C., March 19, 1998.

Chapter 8

1. Originally, this act was introduced by Senator Alfonse D'Amato as a reaction to European refusal of U.S. sanctions against Iran. Senator Kennedy, to D'Amato's liking, interfered and requested that the congressional legislation include Libya as well. He succeeded.

2. UN document S/1997/529, July 9, 1997.

3. *Asharq Al-Awsat* (newspaper). London, September 23, 1997, 4.

4. UN document S/1997/497, June 27, 1997.

5. UN document S/1998/549, June 22, 1998.

Chapter 9

1. Reuters news agency, March 20, 1998.

Chapter 10

1. "Doctrine of the International Com-

munity." Speech by Prime Minister Tony Blair to the Economic Club of Chicago, Hilton Hotel, Chicago, April 22, 1999.

2. UN document S/1997/845, October 31, 1997.

3. The 10 nonpermanent members of the Security Council are elected by special arrangement. Every year, five of the members are elected to represent their continents for two years. The Arab countries, belonging to two different geographical groups (Asia and Africa) take turns among themselves in that one Arab state would be a member at all times. So, for one two-year term the seat would be occupied by an African-Arab country, to be followed by an Asian-Arab country the following term. In 1996, the arrangement should have brought Libya to represent the Arab-African states. But the United States forcefully opposed such membership by a country under sanctions and fought the process to the extent that Arabs were about to lose their seat for the first time. Libya accommodated the Arabs by exchanging turns with Egypt, meaning it will occupy the seat in the 2004–2005 term.

4. UN document S/1997/880, November 12, 1997.

5. UN document S/1997/844, November 4, 1997.

6. UN document S/1997/991, December 18, 1997.

7. UN document S/1998/201, March 6, 1998.

8. Full text of Dorda's letter to Senator Kennedy may be found in the Appendix.

9. Madeleine Albright, *Madam Secretary: A Memoir* (New York: Miramax, 2003), p. 330.

Chapter 11

1. UN document S/1998/5, January 6, 1998.

2. The members of the OAU committee were Zimbabwe, Cameroon, Ghana, Tunisia and Uganda. The members of the Non-Aligned committee were Burkina-Faso, Zimbabwem, the Laos Democratic Republic, Cuba, South Africa and Malaysia.

3. UN documents S/1998/596, S/1998/598, and S/1998/599.

4. UN document S/1998/597, July 1, 1998.

Chapter 12

1. Associated Press, London, July 22, 1998.

Chapter 13

1. Interview on NBC-TV "Today" Show with Katie Couric, Washington, D.C., August 21, 1998.
Ms. COURIC: But in a similar situation, we apparently know who's responsible for the explosion aboard Pan Am flight 103. Libya has refused to extradite those terrorists to either the United States or Great Britain. Why not a military message to Libya?
SECRETARY ALBRIGHT: That message had been sent already by President Reagan. We are now dealing with a very specifically intelligence-related attack. We know what was going on, and we think that this attack was legitimate in terms of what it did in response to attacks on Americans. I think we have taken a very strong response here unilaterally, and it's the right approach. As for the others, each particular situation is different, and we will continue to investigate the Khobar Towers.
2. UN document S/1998/795, August 24, 1998.
3. UN document S/1998/803, August 25, 1998.
4. White House press briefing, August 26, 1998. Briefer Barry Toiv.
5. State Department Press Briefing, August 26, 1998, Briefer James Foley.
6. UN document S/1998/808, August 26, 1998.
7. UN S/Res 1192 (1998).

Chapter 14

1. Muammar Qadhafi. الهروب الى الجحيم. معمر القذافي [Escape to Hell and Other Stories].
2. Ibid.
3. Asharq Al-Awsat, London, 4 Sept. 1998.
4. Reuters report, 6 August 1999.

Chapter 15

1. Letters included in UN documents

895, 902, 903 and 926, October 7, 1998.
2. See Appendix, document 15, annex 4.
3. See Appendix, document 15, annex 7.
4. See Appendix, document 15, annex 2.
5. See Appendix, document 15, annexes 3, 5, 6, 8 and 9.
6. Remarks by President Bill Clinton at the tenth anniversary of the Pan Am 103 disaster. Arlington National Cemetery, Arlington, Virginia. December 21, 1998.
7. See copy of letter in Appendix.
8. See copy of letter in Appendix.

Chapter 16

1. The text of this letter in its original Arabic may be found in the Appendix.
2. The full text of the letter dated February 17, 1999, from Annan to Qadhafi may be found in the Appendix.
3. The full text of the letter from Libya's foreign minister to the Secretary General, dated February 17, 1999, may be found in the Appendix (in Arabic with English translation).
4. The full text of this letter from the Secretary General to Libya's foreign minister, dated February 25, 1999, may be found in the Appendix.
5. Quotes from Qadhafi through the end of this chapter are drawn from reports by JANA, the official news agency of Libya.

Chapter 17

1. The full text of this letter, dated March 19, 1999, may be found in the Appendix (in Arabic and in English translation).
2. UN document S/1999/378, April 5, 1999. Full text may be found in Appendix.
3. UN document S/PRST/1999/10, April 8, 1999.
4. UN document S/1999/407, April 5, 1999.
5. The full text of this document may be found in the Appendix.
6. UN document S/1999/726, June 30, 1999.

Chapter 19

1. UN document S/2003/818.
2. UN document S/2003/819.

Bibliography

Al-Bawab, Suleiman Salim. *Why Libya? The Lockerbie Crisis.* Cairo: Almanara, 1993.

Albright, Madeleine. *Madame Secretary: A Memoir.* New York: Miramax, 2003.

Boutros-Ghali, Boutros. *Unvanquished.* New York: Random House, 1999.

Bradlee, Ben, Jr. *Guts and Glory.* New York: Donald I. Fine, 1988.

Brzezinski, Zbignew. *Power and Principle.* New York: Farrar Straus Giroux, 1983.

Bush, George. *A World Transformed.* New York: Vintage Books, 1998.

Centre for Arab Unity Studies. *The Arabs and Africa.* Beirut: Centre for Arab Unity Studies, 1994.

Clifford, Clark. *Counsel to the President.* New York: Anchor Books, 1991.

Croate, Roger A. *U.S. Policy and the Future of the United Nations.* New York: The Twentieth Century Fund Press, 1994.

Fahmy, Ismail. *Negotiating for Peace in the Middle East.* London: Croom Helm, 1983.

Flores, Charles. *Shadows of Lockerbie.* Valletta, Malta: Edam Publishing House, 1997.

Frum, David. *The Right Man.* New York: Random House, 2003.

Gorbachev, Mikhail. *On My Country and the World.* New York: Columbia University Press, 2000.

Haig, Alexander. *Caveat: Realism, Reagan and Foreign Policy.* New York: Macmillan, 1984.

Hamida, Ali Abdellatif. *The Society, State and Colonialism in Libya.* Beirut: Centre for Arab Unity Studies, 1995.

Heikal, Mohamed. *Autumn of Fury*. New York: Random House, 1983.

Hersh, Seymour, M. *The Price of Power*. New York: Summit Books, 1983.

Hoffman, Bruce. *Inside Terrorism*. New York: Columbia, 1998.

Kissinger, Henry. *Years of Renewal*. New York: Simon and Schuster, 1999.

_____. *Years of Upheaval*. London: Weidenfeld & Nicolson Ltd., 1982.

Kodard, Donald and Lister Colman. *In the Hand of the Octopus*. Malta: Edam Publishing House, 1996.

Matar, Fouad. *Egypt's Political Earthquakes*. Beirut: International Publisher/Arab Institution for Studies and Publications, 2000.

Osman, Essayed Awad. *Libyan-American Relations 1940–1992*. Cairo: Centre for Arab Civilization.

Powell, Colin. *My American Journey*. New York: Random House, 1995.

Quandt, William B. *Camp David*. Washington, D.C.: Brookings Institution, 1986.

Reagan, Ronald. *An American Life*. New York: Simon and Schuster, 1990.

Shultz, George. *Turmoil and Triumph: My Years as Secretary of State*. New York: Chas. Scribner & Sons, 1993.

Thatcher, Margaret. *The Downing Street Years*. New York: HarperCollins, 1993.

Woodward, Bob. *Bush at War*. New York: Simon & Schuster, 2002.

_____. *Veil*. New York: Simon and Schuster, 1987.

Index

321